Robinson, Duncan W.
Judge Robert McAlpin Williamson, Texas' three-legged Willie.

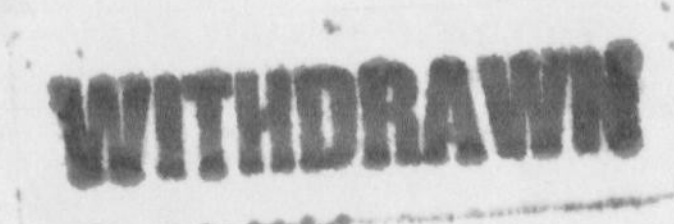

ROBERT McALPIN WILLIAMSON

Robert McAlpin Williamson

Judge Robert McAlpin Williamson

TEXAS' THREE-LEGGED WILLIE

By

DUNCAN W. ROBINSON

TEXAS STATE HISTORICAL ASSOCIATION

AUSTIN, TEXAS

1948

PRINTED IN UNITED STATES OF AMERICA
THE DU BOIS PRESS, ROCHESTER, N.Y.

To

JAMES D. WILLIAMSON

grandson of ROBERT MCALPIN WILLIAMSON, whose devotion to the memory of his grandfather has been responsible for the writing of this biography

Preface

This is the story of Robert McAlpin Williamson, widely known throughout Texas in colonial days as "Three-Legged Willie." That his biography has been so long delayed is strange, for Texans are famous for their tendency to extol their forefathers in terms so unrestrained that their superlatives overwhelm strangers living north of the sovereign state of Oklahoma. Yet despite such habitual enthusiasm, the deeds of Williamson have survived largely in oral legendry. As a result, a character arresting and colorful, and in many respects as accomplished as any that the biographers and historians have extolled, has been relatively forgotten.

In the eventful decades from 1830 to 1850, however, Williamson was recognized by his contemporaries in Texas as a man of consequence. For example, Colonel John S. Ford, who served with Williamson in the Texas National Congress, is authority for the assertion that Williamson "did more than any one man to nerve our people to strike for liberty."[1] This view is substantiated by an almost similar statement by Henderson Yoakum, one of the better early historians of Texas.[2]

Indeed, if Williamson's friend, William Barret Travis, by dying in the Alamo, created the revengeful zeal necessary for the actual fighting of the Texas Revolution, if Williamson's remote cousin, Sam Houston, was the man whose leadership at San Jacinto made the revolution a military success, and if the personal character of Williamson's one-time employer, Stephen F. Austin, supplied the stability which made the

[1]Colonel John S. Ford to Governor O. M. Roberts, March 20, 1897, quoted in Benjamin R. Sleeper, Three-Legged Willie and the Texas Revolution, a paper read before the Philosophers' Club, Waco, Texas, February 28, 1936. Typed copy in R. M. Williamson Folder, Biographical File, University of Texas Archives. Hereafter cited Sleeper, Three-Legged Willie.

[2]Sleeper, Three-Legged Willie.

revolution respectable in the eyes of solid people in the United States, then it may be asserted as broadly that R. M. Williamson was the revolution's chief orator and propagandist.

Long before Austin gave up hope of placating Mexico, Williamson, in league with such firebrands as Travis, F. W. Johnson, Mosely Baker, and William Wharton, was clamoring with magnificent indiscretion for independence. While Houston was romanticizing in Tennessee and drowning his resulting sorrows with the Indians, Williamson was in San Felipe getting the smell of the prickly pear in his nostrils and feeling the winds of the great prairie on his cheeks.

It may be that the technical nature of his work as a lawyer has tended to preclude an easy evaluation of his general worth. Judge Harbert Davenport, former president of the Texas State Historical Association and eminent Texas historian, states the theory thus:

> R. M. Williamson had a reputation as a lawyer with the "old bar" of Texas much greater than has survived in the books. Ability as a courtroom lawyer is very personal and evanescent; a compound of native ability, professional knowledge, understanding of men, force of character, and personal charm, in proportions which in no two cases are the same. Unfortunately there is, even now, no means of recording the qualities, or even the achievements, which make a trial lawyer great.[3]

Perhaps, too, the sober historian has been dismayed at the number of legends that cling to the man at every turn of his career, so that at times it seems impossible to distinguish myth from fact. However true some of the better known legends may be, many of the tales about him are spurious, although Williamson jokingly spread some of them himself. He was the kind of a man who engenders legends, for he was lively and a sad life bored him. He would have sentenced Falstaff to jail without a blink; then he would have slipped into Falstaff's cell to sip a bottle of sack with him.

A credulous historian could easily have lost his professional reputation by taking seriously all the talk about Williamson; but if he had recorded that talk faithfully, he would have added something to the world's folklore.

[3]Harbert Davenport to Thaddeus B. Rice, Greensboro, Georgia, July 22, 1937.

The gullible historian, J. W. Morphis, recites a prayer credited to Williamson before a battle in which he never participated. Just before the storming of Monterrey, Morphis says Williamson delivered himself as follows:

O Lord, we are about to join battle with vastly superior numbers of the enemy, and, Heavenly Father, we would mightily like for you to be on our side and help us. But if you can't do it, for Christ's sake don't go over to the Mexicans, but just lie low and keep dark, and you will see one of the damnedest fights you ever saw in all your born days.[4]

The battle prayer had no basis in fact, but it was easy to attribute it to the judge, who sometimes made amusing public prayers. No fool as a politician, at a preacher's invitation—according to his grandson, J. D. Williamson—he once prayed as follows before a crowd of rustics who were in the midst of a severe drought:

O Lord, Thou divine Father, the supreme ruler of the Universe, who holdest the thunder and the lightning in thy hand, and from the clouds givest rain to make crops for thy children, look down with pity upon thy children who now face ruin for the lack of rain upon their crops; and O Lord, send us a bounteous rain that will cause the crops to fruit in all their glory and the earth to turn again to that beauteous green that comes from abundant showers. Lord, send us a bounteous one that will make corn ears shake hands across the row and not one of these little rizzly-drizzly rains that will make nubbins that all hell can't shuck.[5]

But one great legend, the story of Williamson and his flourishing a revolver as the concrete expression of the constitution, actually happened, and it will be related in this biography in its proper setting.

Of Williamson one may say, in brief, that he came limping on the Texas scene in 1827, a young man of twenty-three, filled with the enthusiasm, courage, and generosity of youth. A born aristocrat, he made himself a champion of democracy; a lover of poetry and an erstwhile lover of a beautiful Southern woman, he probably found life in a rough frontier world crude, but he entered into the life without a trace of snobbery, making himself a boon companion of his fellows; legally trained, he analyzed the needs of a lawless republic,

[4]*Daily Democratic Statesman* (Austin, Texas), April 12, 1874.

[5]J. D. Williamson to D. W. R., interview, June 9, 1941.

and he became a force in establishing law and order in the infant state.

Williamson stood supreme as the dispenser of justice on the frontier. The victory of his revolver over the bowie knife of a border ruffain symbolized the triumph of technical civilization over the unrestrained simplicity of frontier life. Beside the cultivated and intelligent Williamson, Judge Roy Bean, with whom Williamson is often carelessly compared, was a mere jester. There was something organically primitive in Bean, but Williamson was a man of refinement and poise, and his clowning was on a grandiose scale.

Essentially, Williamson was a capable lawyer. It was no mere political gesture that brought about his election by the Texas Congress as one of the first district judges and as such a member of the Texas National Supreme Court. He was also one of the first important Texas editors, the first prosecuting attorney of Austin's colony, and one of the first legislators of the state when it entered the Union.

Williamson was first in another significant position: although crippled, he was the first major of the Texas Rangers. As such he earned a place in the hearts of a group of vigorous, homespun Texans who initiated a tradition of courage ably maintained by the ranger force ever since. From long before the time when Williamson was seen dashing towards San Jacinto—with the" coontails" from his coonskin cap flying over his shoulders—to the night of his death, when in a delirious dream he once again demanded of a phantom John Davis Bradburn the instant delivery of his old cronies, William Barret Travis and Patrick Jack,[6] he was a salty, virile man, and laughter bubbled out of him.

This then, at last, is the story of the famous old "Texian" who stirred up "one of the damnedest fights you ever saw."

—Duncan Robinson
North Texas Agricultural College
Arlington, Texas

[6]*Daily Ledger and Texan* (San Antonio, Texas), September 5, 1860.

Acknowledgments

For assistance in the preparation of this book the writer wishes to acknowledge the aid of several persons without whose services the manuscript could not have been finished. The initial assignment came from Professor Walter Prescott Webb of the University of Texas. Several persons were extremely helpful in gathering the scattered materials which have been employed. Miss Harriet Smither, archivist of the Texas State Library, Austin, discovered numerous documents by and about R. M. Williamson which she made available during the summer of 1941. E. R. Dabney, of the library staff of the University of Texas, found numerous pertinent newspaper articles, some of which apparently had never been consulted by any previous student of Williamson's career.

Others who helped round up the material were J. Frank Dobie, who made available the material on Williamson in his files; Miss Winnie Allen, archivist in the University Library, who furnished copies of documents comprising the R. M. Williamson Papers in the Bexar Archives; and last, but not least, Miss Ruby Mixon, of Fort Worth, authority on William Barret Travis, who permitted me to read her unpublished book on Travis and lent me a copy of Travis's Diary. Without this aid, Chapter V and parts of Chapter II of this work could not have been written with any approach to accuracy. One other indispensable aid, as the bibliography and the footnotes indicate, has been the published works of Dr. Eugene C. Barker.

The finished manuscript has been read and criticized by several persons, all of whom gave valuable suggestions or corrections. Thaddeus B. Rice, historian of Greene County, Georgia, a grandson of R. M. Williamson, who knows the geneaology of the Williamsons, was especially helpful. Professors W. A. Ransom, Cothburn O'Neal, E. C. Barksdale, C. D. Richards, and Lloyd Lassen, all of the North Texas

Agricultural College, also read all or parts of the manuscript and made corrections as to style, as did Professor Webb of the University of Texas. For these services I am sincerely grateful. I also wish to express appreciation to several students of the North Texas Agricultural College—Thelma Nix, Ruth Knox, Jo Ann Elliott, and Dollie Mae Slocum, who typed the manuscript.

A fellow-faculty member of the North Texas Agricultural College, Delmar Max Pachl, made two lithographs which are included and which give the book some artistic value. Pachl had planned to complete many more sketches; but, unfortunately, the war interferred, and he was killed in the invasion of Leyte in 1944.

Finally the writer wishes to express his gratitude to James D. Williamson of Waco, Texas, to whom the book is dedicated. This grandson of R. M. Williamson has furnished many of the documents he has gathered through a lifetime, has written numerous letters, has granted interviews, and has given financial assistance in the preparation of the manuscript. Knowing J. D. Williamson has given the writer a little of the flavoring of the Williamsons that he would otherwise have missed. Generous and blessed with a whimsical sense of humor, J. D. Williamson has consistently insisted that his grandfather's life be written in strict accord with the facts. At no time has Judge Williamson attempted to change an interpretation, and for this grant of liberty, for all the generous acts, and for the unfailing patience of this patron, the writer is genuinely appreciative.

D. W. R.

Contents

Illustrations

CHAPTER I

Family Background

The Williamsons in America had always been genteel and aristocratic, although one would not have guessed it if he had seen Three-Legged Willie in one of his lighter moments "patting Juba" at a frontier "love-feast."[1] His great-great-grandfather, the American male founder of the family, was a red-thatched Celt from the North of Ireland who had settled in Bedford County, Virginia, by 1670.[2] Little is known of him, but his descendants entitle him to recognition. One of his sons, John Williamson, journeyed to North Carolina, where he married Mary Davidson of the Davidson family from which Sam Houston descended.[3]

At least two sons of John Williamson and Mary Davidson won distinction. Hugh Williamson, a historian, was one of the Maryland signers of the Constitution of the United States, and Micajah Williamson was a lieutenant colonel in the American army during the Revolutionary War.[4] Micajah, as the founding father of the Georgia Williamsons, was the grandfather of Robert McAlpin Williamson.

Colonel Micajah Williamson had a colorful, war-torn career. Born in Bedford County in 1744, he married the beauteous Sarah Gilliam of Henrico County, Virginia, on February 25, 1765. Soon afterwards the couple moved to Georgia, where Micajah accumulated vast land holdings in the Indian territories, which, in 1773, were ceded to the

[1]Noah Smithwick, *The Evolution of a State*, 63.

[2]William H. Sparks, "Early Georgia," Atlanta *Constitution* (Atlanta, Georgia), January 23, 1881. Copied by Thad. B. Rice and included in J. D. Williamson Papers. Cited hereafter as Sparks, "Early Georgia."

[3]Judge Miles B. Lewis, Jacksonville, Florida, cousin of Sam Houston and R. M. Williamson, to J. D. Williamson, April 23, 1943.

[4]Judge M. B. Lewis to J. D. Williamson, May 19, 1943. See also Sparks, "Early Georgia."

United States. He bought a plantation in what became Wilkes County, and, since he was able to give sixty negroes for the property, was regarded as one of the wealthy men of Georgia.[5]

By 1776, the Williamsons had six children. The fourth, born in 1772, was Peter B., who was to be the father of Robert McAlpin. But for the American Revolution, the Williamsons might have led the leisurely life of prosperous Georgia planters. The war years, however, gave the staunch couple an ordeal of blood and fire.

After moving to Georgia, Micajah was a leader in repelling Indian attacks in the vicinity of his home where the town of Washington now stands. During the war he served as a lieutenant colonel under his friend, General Elizah Clark, in an army of scouts assigned to protect the western frontiers of the state. It is said that Colonel Williamson was often selected to command forays where "skill, caution, and perseverance" were essential and that he was wounded more frequently than any other officer in Clark's command.[6]

While Micajah was in the field fighting, his wife, born a Virginia aristocrat, showed the quality of her character. She managed the plantation, working in the fields with her sons and slaves. Once, during an attack of "English, Tories and Indians," the Williamson home and adjacent plantation buildings were burned. The distraught mother looked on as her eldest son, twelve-year-old William, was hanged for refusing to reveal the activities of the swamp fox, General Francis Marion. When the marauders left, Mrs. Williamson and her other children fled to the mountains, where they joined similar refugees. The ruffians later posted a reward for the head of Colonel Williamson.[7]

Micajah returned from the front to lead his stranded family to a desolate home, one shared with other raid-victimized neighbors. At intervals he continued his military service, probably operating in the vicinity of his home. He

[5]Thad. B. Rice to J. D. Williamson, June 22, 1946. See also Sparks, "Early Georgia."

[6]*Ibid.*

[7]*Ibid.*

was fighting as late as 1782, for in that year he wrote a terse letter requesting arms and ammunition of the governor.[8] In 1783 he made a start toward rebuilding the fortune that the lean years had shattered.

During the course of the war Williamson lost some of his lands, but he still had vast holdings including hundreds of acres in Washington and Wilkes counties.[9] Appointed one of the commissioners of Wilkes County by the state legislature in 1783, he helped to lay out the town of Washington, Georgia, where he built a new home. As he was pressed for cash, he soon added to the house a unit to be used as a tavern. This hostelry had a swinging picture of George Washington before its doors, and, according to legend, was once visited by General Washington himself. It played a part in shaping the destiny of the Williamson children.

Wilkes County in the 1780's contained more than half of the population of Georgia. Courts were held in Washington, and the Williamson tavern became the headquarters for judges and lawyers. The indomitable Sarah so skillfully guided the affairs of her beautiful daughters that all except one married lawyers. All of the Williamson boys who reached maturity became lawyers. Perhaps some of the tales of eloquent lawyers which Sarah later told to entertain her grandson, Robert McAlpin, may have helped to influence that young man in his choice of a career.

In any event, it is a fact that the tavern furnished Micajah with the money he needed so badly after the war. When he got a fresh stake, he went back to farming. At his death in 1796, he was the father of eleven children and had accumulated an estate worth $150,000 to be divided among his family.

In 1796 Peter B. Williamson, the fourth son, was twenty-four years old and probably already had been admitted to the bar. Certainly he was a seasoned soldier. Military records of Greene County of the early 1790's show him to have been

[8]Micajah Williamson to "his honour the governor," written from Fort Washington, Georgia, May 24, 1782, in J. D. Williamson Papers.

[9]Thad. B. Rice, Col. Micajah Williamson's Widow Marries Again, MS. in J. D. Williamson Papers.

an unabashed young captain. Sent to arrest a certain Captain Ferdinand Phinizy, presumably for incompetence, Peter was characterized by the bitterly complaining Phinizy as "that young upstart, Pitter Williamson." Phinizy confided to the adjutant general that he had wished to run his sword through Williamson for his impudence.

Peter was one of a group of veterans who trailed the Indian marauders who had ravaged Greensboro and Greene County. He personally captured eight of the Indians, turning them over to the county officers. In 1792 and 1793 he served with General Clark, his father's old commander, in a Florida campaign in the service of France against the Spaniards.

A few years after his father's death, Peter gained such prominence as a lawyer that he was engaged to represent the University of Georgia in considerable litigation concerning lands in Greene County. He entered suit against individuals who had defaulted on payments for property bought from the university.[10]

Peter was not only a soldier and lawyer; he was also a judge, a legislator, a farmer, and a lay-preacher of the Methodist Church. He became known as "the Marrying Parson" as much, perhaps, for his own marriages as for those he said for others. He was married five times. His first wife was Ann McAlpin, daughter of Robert McAlpin of Greene and Clark counties. The couple had three children, the third being Robert McAlpin, who was named for his maternal grandfather. Robert was born in Clark County in 1804; soon after his birth his mother died.[11]

In the following year Peter Williamson married Elizabeth Spullock, and the newlyweds moved to Jefferson, Georgia, where Peter took over the law practice of his brother Micajah, who had recently been murdered. In 1818, he moved to Alabama to begin a new legislative and legal career.

As he went his rollicking way, the three motherless children of his first marriage were left with relatives in Georgia. Historian Thad. B. Rice, of Greene County, asserts that it

[10]*Ibid.*

[11]Thad. B. Rice to J. D. Williamson, June 22, 1946. See also Rice, Col. Micajah Williamson's Widow Marries Again.

was Grandmother Sarah who took the infant Robert and his brother and sister under her wing. Her marriage in 1801 to Lamack Hudson, of whom nothing is known except that he had little property and was probably snubbed by Sarah's high-toned, well-married daughters, could hardly have changed her affection for her blood kin. This "mother of many children" was accustomed to trouble, and three additional youngsters underfoot around the place merely made her life seem normal. Unerringly she brought them to Milledgeville, the new capital of the state, where they could be associated with the class of society she had picked for her daughters in the old days and where, if anything happened to her, they could be cared for. Sarah's children were among the elite of the fledgling capital. Daughter Nancy had married Governor John Clark, and Daughter Susan, with whom Sarah may have lived, was the wife of Clark's staunch enemy, Dr. Thompson Bird. Susan's daughter, named for Grandmother Sarah, married L. Q. C. Lamar, and became the mother of a justice of the United States Supreme Court.

Then, too, there was Sarah's grandson, Charles Williamson, Jr., who was married to Mary Clark, the daughter of the old general. And not to be overlooked was Sarah's son, young William W. Williamson, recently graduated from the University of Georgia and married to the charming Mary Terrell. There were others nearly as prominent, and in this select company the infant Robert was cast.[12]

Little is known of the nature and quality of Robert's education, but it appears obvious that it was as good as the highest class of Georgia society could secure at the time. Noah Smithwick, who knew Robert in San Felipe de Austin and who was by no means an uncritical observer, refers to the young Georgian as "a member of a wealthy family, highly educated . . . ." His studies doubtless began in a simple elementary school, which Robert remembered with great amusement all his life. Many a stag party in the days when Smithwick and Robert were young men frolicking with lively companions at San Felipe was enlivened by an imitative monologue, in which Robert took all the parts. The per-

[12]*Ibid.*

formance was a spelling lesson in which the pupils studied aloud from Webster's elementary spelling book. Smithwick thus remembered the details of one of those side-splitting evenings more than seventy years later:

> Beginning in the low diffident tones supposed to belong to the tyro, Willie plodded his way doubtfully through the tedious length of the alphabet and gaining courage from the successful termination of the journey, tackled "a-b abs" . . . of "b-a ba, k-e-r ker, baker," thence to "c-r-u, cru, c-i cy, crucy, fi-x fix, crucifix," and so on through the successive increase of syllables gaining confidence with each rise till he finally arrived in triumph at in-com-pre-hen-si-bil-i-ty. To this succeeded the reading of the short proverbs at the bottom of the pages, the climax being reached when the star scholar shrilly piped out, "An old man found a rude boy up in one of his apple trees stealing apples, etc." So perfectly were the tone and manner varied to correspond with the successive stages that one might almost imagine himself in an old fashioned country school.[13]

This intimate knowledge of school ways doubtless grew from Robert's experiences, but his formal scholastic training suddenly ended when he was fifteen. He suffered an attack of "white swelling"—probably infantile paralysis—so acute that he was confined to his bed for months. The lower half of his right leg drew up at the knee and was useless to him for the rest of his life. When he walked again, it was with the aid of crutches and a wooden leg fastened to his knee cap. Later he got along without the crutches.[14]

It is evident, however, that Williamson was under competent instructors during his illness and the years immediately following, for his knowledge of mathematics, Latin, and literature was made evident later in his writings and his speeches. Dr. Thompson Bird, Aunt Susan's husband, is said to have had a hand in his general education.

From the time of his illness until his appearance as a colonist in Texas in 1827, the record of Robert's career is dim. The few available facts are intertwined with legends which are persistently asserted. All that is reasonably certain is that he was admitted to the practice of the law in

[13]Smithwick, *Evolution of a State*, 63.

[14]Statement, J. D. Williamson to D. W. R., June 9, 1941.

Milledgeville either in 1824 or in 1825 and that he left New Orleans, presumably for Texas, in 1826.

No one knows who presided over Robert's studies of law; but since a host of distinguished jurists were his kinsmen by blood or marriage, it is thought that he prepared for his profession under the guidance of his own people—probably in the offices of Judge John Griffen and Duncan Campbell, who was married to his Aunt Susan.[15] Evidence is strong that he practiced law for about a year in Judge Campbell's office in Milledgville. Most writers who comment on his practice as a Georgia lawyer say that he left a large and lucrative business when he shook the dust of the state from his heels.[16] This is debatable, but more puzzling is the question why he should suddenly pull up stakes and come to Texas. There are no known documents on this matter, but it has been widely related that he left because he killed a rival in a duel for the affection of a proud Georgia beauty, who thereupon spurned his love to marry a less belligerent suitor.[17]

The disgusted Robert is reported to have left Milledgeville in company with a crony, William Sparks, late in November, 1825. For a time he visited with his father in Alabama.[18] He may even have practiced a little law in that state, for he certainly stayed there long enough to make friends who thought enough of his judgment, five years after he left Alabama, to be influenced by it in deciding whether to emigrate to Texas. On December 2, 1832, Asa Hoxey, writing from Montgomery, Alabama, informed Robert that he might look for many of his "old acquaintances" in Texas next spring.[19]

[15]Sleeper, Three-Legged Willie.

[16]*Ibid.* Sleeper quotes several secondary sources, but personally doubts that Williamson, who was then only twenty-one, could have left behind a large legal practice.

[17]*Ibid.* Also cited in Marquis James, *The Raven*, and in other secondary sources. Sleeper quotes R. M. Williamson, Waco, Texas, brother of J. D. Williamson, as disagreeing with the duel story.

[18]Sparks, "Early Georgia."

[19]Letter, Asa Hoxey to R. M. Williamson, December 2, 1832, in *Quarterly of the Texas State Historical Association*, IX, 285.

Life in Alabama, however, proved unsatisfactory to Williamson. Accordingly, in 1826, in company with Sparks, he left Alabama for New Orleans. There the young men parted company, Sparks long afterwards recalling the parting scene thus: "Well do I remember too, our last parting upon the levee in New Orleans, when you went to unite your fortunes with the adventures and daring spirits, who were to strike for Texas liberty."[20]

What happened from the time Williamson left Sparks until he showed up on June 19, 1827, in San Felipe de Austin is as hazy as the story of his last days in Georgia. A headright certificate to three-fourths of a league and a labor of land, issued in 1838, states that Williamson had appeared before the board of land commissioners of Bastrop County and proved according to law that he had arrived in the country in 1826;[21] yet Volume A of the records of applications for land in Stephen F. Austin's colonies shows that Williamson arrived in Texas on June 19, 1827.[22]

A patently spurious legend, issuing from the tongue of an old duffer who purported to be quoting Williamson, only adds to the confusion. Robert is supposed to have said:

> I killed a man in North Carolina and then crossed over into Tennessee. I killed a man there. Then I went to Alabama and there I laid low my third man. This occasioned my visiting Mississippi, where I killed the fourth. Only after this fourth, gentlemen, did I consider myself sufficiently practiced to claim myself the honor of becoming a citizen of Texas.[23]

Since the sequence of Williamson's movements, as related by this story, are geographically illogical, the tale may be dismissed as a fanciful fabrication.

It is possible, however, that both records of the dates of Williamson's arrival in Texas are true. Mrs. Hallie Bryan Perry, great-granddaughter of Moses Austin, says she heard her father, Guy M. Bryan, and other relatives who knew

[20] Sparks, "Early Georgia."

[21] Record of First Class Certificates, General Land Office, Austin, Texas.

[22] Applications for Land, Date of Emigration, Stephen F. Austin's Colonies, A, 45-46, in Spanish Archives, General Land Office, Austin, Texas.

[23] Lanier Bartlett, *On the Old West Coast*, 219-220.

Williamson personally, relate the following tale a dozen times:

> When Williamson came to Texas from Tennessee, a group of his associates missed him one night for supper. He was found standing in his underclothes, whopping around on his peg leg, and beating his outer clothes with a hickory stick, saying, "You go back and give your own name, and you go to Texas under your real name."[24]

This may indicate that Williamson, upon parting company with Sparks, entered Texas as he told his friend he planned to do. He probably got no farther west than some border county, or perhaps Nacogdoches, when, after a few weeks of residence under an assumed name, he decided to see more of the world. He thereupon left the territory and, if the recollections of Mrs. Perry's kinsmen are correct, rode at least as far up the country as Tennessee. Authentic records show him to have been in Arkansas in May of 1827, by this time "very desirious of the acquaintance of Stephen F. Austin." To oblige, one Samuel Bridge of Hempstead, Arkansas, wrote Austin a letter of introduction for the young man who in a decade was to become a judge of the Texas supreme court.[25] Soon afterwards, Williamson tucked the epistle in his saddlebag and struck out for Texas to begin a career that would in truth make his "real name" known.

[24]Mrs. Hally Bryan Perry to D. W. R., interview, April 26, 1941.

[25]Samuel Bridge to Stephen F. Austin, in E. C. Barker (ed.), *Austin Papers*, Vol. I, Part II, pp. 1647-1648.

CHAPTER II

Citizen of San Felipe de Austin

High on a rolling prairie, sunning itself for half a mile on the west bank of the Brazos River at the lower Atascosito Road crossing, stood San Felipe de Austin, which was to be Williamson's home for the next eight years. Capital of Austin's colony, the town had been named by Austin in 1823 and formally established a year later.

In the summer of 1827, when Williamson arrived there, possessing little more than a horse, a broad smile, and Samuel Bridge's letter assuring Austin that the young Georgian was "quite unassuming, of a handsome education," the village had a population of two hundred persons, mostly male, and about twenty-five or thirty houses, built with but one exception, of "hewn logs." Near town, the Brazos was "scarce 100 yds in breadth," although elsewhere it was a river of "prodigious rapidity and great depth when full."[1]

The houses in the hamlet were erected irregularly along both sides of the road, "like Samantha Allen's funeral procession, pretty good as to length but rather thin." Entering the town by ferry from the east, the stranger first passed Noah Smithwick's "bachelor abode" and his blacksmith shop hard by. Then came Peyton's tavern, and next, Cooper and Cheeve's saloon and billiard hall, the only frame building. Farther down, third from the end, was the structure which was to become the office of the *Texas Gazette*, where Williamson took his fling at the trade of journalism.[2]

At the time, the place was not much to look at, but it was growing. Presiding over it was Austin, tired-eyed, care-

[1]For the description of San Felipe in 1827, see Smithwick, *Evolution of a State*, 55; for the quotation on the Brazos River, see J. C. Clopper, "Journal and Book of Memoranda for 1828," *Quarterly of the Texas State Historical Association*, XIII, 58.

[2]Smithwick, *Evolution of a State*, 56 ff.

worn, and slight, whose residence, a double log cabin with a wide dirt passage through the center and a chimney at each end, was considered "quite commodious and respectable." It was about a half-mile back from the river, on the west bank of Palmeto Creek. The empresario even then was showing the strain of his never-ending efforts, his stern self-denial, and his ceaseless attention to the minute details upon which the success of the colony depended. Looking a little dour upon the world, this "small, spare, little old bachelor" held himself aloof from the occasional horseplay of his friends. His duties had made him, despite his youth, a serious man.

Gathered about him in the embryo capital was a nucleus of colonists destined to write their names high in later days. Williamson could not have chosen a better place to start a career.

San Felipe was then the residence of David G. Burnet, who became the first president of the Texas Republic. Francis W. Johnson, who became one of Williamson's best friends and was to be Ben Milam's second in command in the assault on San Antonio in 1835, was in 1827 clerking in a store. Operating a blacksmith shop next to Smithwick's, was Gail Borden, who was also experimenting with a soup biscuit for seafaring men. Later Borden was to found and edit the Houston *Telegraph* and concoct a milk formula which would make his name known throughout the world.

There were many others worthy of the genial young Williamson's comradeship. Samuel Williams, Austin's hard-working secretary, who was later to become involved in gigantic land speculations and to atone by uniting with Thomas F. McKinney to aid in financing the Texas Revolution, became a friend of Williamson's. The town further had such personalities as Walter C. White, the leading merchant; Thomas Pilgrim, the colony's first schoolmaster; Nestor Clay, a "gifted nephew of a gifted uncle," educated, a master of logic and forceful English, but a drunkard; Godwin Bronson Cotten, the newspaper editor, a man as generous and gay as Williamson; Luke Lessassier, a lawyer and one of the best storytellers in the colony; and, in 1831, occasionally in town for a visit, Father Michael Muldoon, the priest of San Felipe and "Vicar General of all the foreign colonies of Texas," an amateur poet, a lover of Virgil and Alexander Pope, but not, withal, above an occasional tavern brawl.[3]

It would be a mistake to convey the idea that all the men in San Felipe were exemplars of talent. There were many of another sort, and Williamson often hankered for the company of that loudmouthed, lewd, frolicsome set, who were thoroughly fitted for frontier life and feared no man. Not far from town lived Brit Bailey, who was in Texas before Austin. He commanded his wife when he should die to bury him standing up because alive he had knelt to none; dead, he wanted men still to say, "There stands old Brit Bailey."

Some of the citizenry had no more culture than the wild mules running free on the prairie, but they had an acute sense of the comic, and they fended off monotony with a scornful disrespect for the dignity of their fellows. A man was likely to have a name bestowed by his comrades that was different from the one given him by his loving mother. "Pop Corn" Robinson was so called because he bought a big corn patch near Brazoria. "Mustang" Brown caught wild horses; "Waco" Brown had been captured by the Waco Indians; "Sheep" Brown owned many sheep, but "Dog" Brown acquired his monicker because he stole somebody's dog. Robert Williams, who wore store clothes, was called "Gentleman Bob." "Varmint" Williams captured animals for museums in the United States. "Pot" Williams, the town's first constable, had crashed a pot over a man's head in an argument. "Beaver Trap" Smith, of course, was a trapper.

There were two William Coopers. "Cow" Cooper had a large stock farm below San Felipe. The other, the merchant, was called "Sawmill" Cooper because he emerged mangled from an encounter with a sawmill. Robert Mitchell, one of the first colonists to engage in hog raising, was "Hog" Mitchell. "Ramrod" Johnson carried himself with too much dignity. A man from DeWitt's Colony, who had a few white spots in an otherwise rosy complexion, was known as "Old

[3]*Ibid.*

Paint" Caldwell. Losing an eye in an Indian fight caused a certain Wallace—no relation to "Big-Foot"—to be called "One-Eyed."[4]

When Robert M. Williamson showed up walking on a wooden leg with his right leg drawn back at the knee, it was inevitable that he should be called "Three-Legged Willie." It was unfortunate, in a way, that the crude appellation should have been attached to him, for despite his affliction he was a handsome man. About five feet nine inches tall, "of small bone and rather delicate frame," Williamson had broad shoulders and strong, lean hands. His deep, blue eyes flashed when he was angry. His forehead was high, and his eyebrows, a trifle heavy. His nose was long and straight, and he had a determined mouth with rather thin lips, the lower being a bit prominent. His chin was definitely prominent, and his hair was black, long, and inclined to wave, but it was not curly.[5]

In the early days at San Felipe he wore a coonskin cap and a buckskin garb when hunting or traveling. Sometimes, he donned homespun black clothes and wore a broad-brimmed black hat. Later, when he became prominent, he was a fashionable dresser, but in San Felipe his clothes at times looked "well-worn and dusty."[6]

Williamson readily adapted himself to the old town's everyday routine. Rural colonists, riding in on Saturdays or market days, found nearly all the necessities and a few luxuries for sale. Cooper and Cheeves were certainly forward-looking merchants. In 1830 they had just opened a general store and offered "low for cash" a general assortment of dry goods, hats, boots, shoes, crockery, glass and tinware. A little more elaborate was a new store put in by Perry and Hunter, who in February, 1831, received from New York, Philadelphia, and New Orleans an assorted stock of "broadcloths, cashmeres, casinetts, point and duffle blankets, rich bonnet and felt ribbons, linen and cotton diapers, bleached

[4]Noah Smithwick, "Early Texas Nomenclature," *Quarterly of the Texas State Historical Association*, II, 174 ff.

[5]J. D. Williamson to D. W. R., August 5, 1941.

[6]*Ibid.*; see also Houston *Post* (Houston, Texas), January 19, 1936.

sheetings and shirtings, and bed tuckings." They also offered "cutlery and hardware, plow arms, axes, groceries, gunpowder, Hyson tea, chocolate, coffee, ginger, Indigo raisins, and wines and liquors of all descriptions." The firm sold "low" for cash, but they would accept cotton or hides as payment for their wares.[7]

Apparently not fussy about the kind of payment he received was the merchant Lewis L. Veeder, who sold wool hats made by William B. Bridges, "warranted rain proof." He would take cash, beef hides, beeswax, cows, and calves in lieu of money. He sold "dry goods, cutlery, whiskey, sugar by the barrel, and coffee by the sack." But at times he demanded prompt payment. On May 26, 1831, for example, he got in "thirty barrels of Brazos salt; blue, brown, and black broadcloths; frock and dress coats; silk, velvet, valencia and marseilles vests, and cottonade and cotton pantaloons." In the same shipment he received a tempting assortment of "Collins and Co.'s axes, hatchets, drawing knives, knives and forks, butcher knives, fine Spanish dirks, pocket and pen knives, saws, candlesticks, razors, scissors, shovels and spades." These articles were to be sold for "prompt pay" only.[8]

Liquor and wines were for sale at several stores and at hotels and taverns. If one were a connoisseur, Thomas D. Hailes was an agent for the Genuine Liquor Store of New Orleans. Through him one could buy "for a moderate trade profit" cognac and Bordeaux brandy, Holland gin, Jamaica rum, and Scotch and Irish whiskey by the demijohn. By the dozen bottles the discriminating could purchase "Maderia and Teneriffe wines, London Porter, and Burton Ales." New York beer and common whiskey were available in barrels; and Philadelphia porter, ale, and cider, "bottled by a person well versed in that business," were also obtainable. In addition, Hailes took orders for the "best Havana Segars."[9]

Had Austin been able to change men's characters, the liquor part of the town's business would have gone begging, but

[7]*Texas Gazette* (San Felipe de Austin, Texas), October 24, 1830.

[8]*Mexican Citizen* (San Felipe de Austin, Texas), February 12, 1831.

[9]*Texas Gazette*, February 27, 1830.

many of the colonists were of a different disposition. The blunt truth is that some of the townsmen drank whiskey, and a number of them consumed it in enormous quantities. As a consequence, on July 31, 1830, the town fathers were inspired to decree that drunkenness was "prejudicial to the good order and tranquility" of the community. Thereafter, they ruled, the laws on the subject would be rigidly enforced. A little later they decreed that all houses, stores, shops, and other places selling spiritous liquors "positively must be closed at ten o'clock."[10]

In an attempt to promote the cause of temperance, Williamson "played" lawyer on occasion. A trifling drunkard was in the habit of going on a periodic spree in San Felipe, leaving his wife and children in a rural district to shift for themselves while he sought solace in his cups. On one such occasion, some of the lawyers organized a kangaroo court. Williamson made a characteristic oration as prosecuting attorney, and another barrister whetted a big machete with a menacing frown. As the defendant's horse was brought up, the defense winked. The drunkard quickly jumped in the saddle and was reportedly never seen again in San Felipe.[11]

On the tables, at least on those of the rural folk, "some of the fattest and most delicious beef and bacon in the world" were served, and buffalo, deer, and hog meat could be easily procured by hunting on the prairie. Oysters, fish, and produce of the countryside, including peas, potatoes, onions, cabbage, and beans, were available at the Brazos Hotel, situated at the mouth of the Brazos River and operated by William Chase. A special feature of this tavern was that it afforded a "very fine situation" for bathing. Near the printing office, Joseph White managed the Farmer's Hotel, where transients were boarded "either by the day or by the month." They were assured of every attention both to themselves and their horses. Here the tailor, John Mont-

[10]E. C. Barker (ed.), "Minutes of the Ayuntamiento of San Felipe de Austin, 1828-1832," *Southwestern Historical Quarterly*, XXII, 304.

[11]Rosa Kleberg, "Early Experiences in Texas," *Quarterly of the Texas State Historical Association*, II, 171.

gomery, "cleansed and repaired coats, pantaloons, etc., in the best style and on the shortest notice."[12]

In 1827 the Whiteside Hotel, operated by James Whiteside, was the tallest building in the town. It was a story and a half high, with a passage through the center, and a huge stick and mud chimney adorned each end. Jonathan C. Peyton and his wife operated one of the earliest small hostelries. This tavern had the distinction of being one of the early Texas residences of Robert M. Williamson, and, after 1831, of a young man who became one of Williamson's best friends, one destined to immortalize himself at the Alamo: William Barret Travis.[13]

It may have been at Peyton's that Williamson and his law colleagues played a mild joke on their landlady. She had a habit of reserving the delicacies and the better staple items of her menu for the ladies at her own table. Williamson once spread his coat wide to shield his stealthy companions, while he regaled the women with some of his choicest flatteries. During the droll conversation, Williamson's colleagues exchanged the plates so that the ladies had what the landlady intended for the lawyers.[14]

By 1830, San Felipe boasted several doctors. Two of these physicians, Robert Peebles and James B. Miller, informed the populace they had received "a large and general assortment of fresh and genuine medicines," some of these doubtless being strong enough to stir the vitals of a cast-iron dog. Dr. Peebles probably was not an eye specialist, but he advertised, nevertheless, that he "trepanned" one of his patients, causing his eyes, hitherto blind and dry, to water and redden. Before 1830, health, from a doctor's standpoint, was probably disgustingly good. Newcomers were sometimes troubled with chills and fevers. A few had severe bilious attacks, but no instance of death from stomach disorders

[12]*Texas Gazette*, February 13, 1830.

[13]Smithwick, *Evolution of a State*, 56-57. On residence of Williamson and Travis at Peyton's Hotel, see Ruby Mixon, The Life and Letters of William Barret Travis, MS., Fort Worth.

[14]Kleberg, "Early Experiences in Texas," *Quarterly of the Texas State Historical Association*, II, 171.

NO. 26. **THE TEXAS GAZETTE.** VOL. I.

SELECTED POETRY.

THE TORCH OF LIBERTY.

BY THOMAS MOORE

I saw it all in Fancy's glass—
  Herself the fair, the wild magician,
That bids the splendid day dream pass,
  And named each gliding apparition.

'Twas like a torch race—such as they
  Of Greece perfomed, in ages gone,
When the fleet youth in long array,
  Passed the bright torch triumphant on.

I saw the expectant nations stand,
  To catch the coming flame in turn;
I saw from ready hand to hand,
  The clear but struggling glory burn.

And oh! their joy as it came near,
  'Twas in itself a joy to see,
While fancy whispered in my ear—
"That torch they pass, is—Liberty!"

And each as she received the flame,
  Lighted her altar with its ray;
Then, smiling to the next that came,
  Speeded it on its sparkling way.

From Albion first, whose ancient shrine,
  Was furnished with the flame already,
Columbia caught a spark divine,
  And lit a flame like Albion's, steady.

The splendid gift then Gallia took,
  And like a wild Baccante, raising
The brand aloft, its sparkles shook
  As she would set the world a-blazing.

And when she fired her altar, high
  It flashed into the redening air,
So fierce, that Albion who stood nigh,
  Shrunk almost blinded with the glare.

Next Spain, so new was light [illegible],
  Leapt at the torch—but ere the spark
She flung upon her shrine, [illegible],
  'Twas quenched—and all again was dark!

Yet no: not quenched—a treasure worth
  So much to mortals, rarely [illegible]
Again its brilliant light put forth
  And shone a beacon in our eyes.

Who next received the flame? Alas!
  Unworthy Naples!—shame of shames—
That even though [illegible] hands should pass
  That brightest of all earthly flames.

Scarce had her fingers touched the torch,
  When frightened by the sparks it shed,
Not waiting even to feel its scorch,
  She dropt it to the earth and fled.

And fallen it might have long remained,
  But Greece, who saw her moment now
Caught up the prize, though prostrate, stained,
  And waved it round her beauteous brow.

"Shine, shine forever glorious flame,
  Divinest gift of God to men!
From Greece thy earliest splendor came,
  To Greece, thy ray returns again!

Take, Freedom, take thy radient round—
  When dimmed, revive; when lost, return;
Till not a shirne on earth be found
  On which thy glories shall not burn."

SURVEYING.

THE subscriber respectfully informs the public, that he has returned to the colony, and will attend to the duties of his appointment, viz: the partition of LANDS in this Municipality, by giving ten days notice at the Gazette Office.

THOS. H. BORDEN.

[illegible] 28, 1830.

IN conformity with a decree of the Constitutiona' Alcalde, of the Jurisdiction of Austin, bearing date 5th May, 1830,

A Public Sale

Of the property, moveable and immoveable, belonging to the estate of the late John R. Harris, deceased, will take place at the usual residence of the said John R. Harris, in the TOWN OF HARRISBURG, on the

8th day of June next.

The moveable property, for Cash, to be paid at the time of adjudication—the real estate, on a credit of twelve months from the day of sale, the purchasers giving approved personal security, with mortgage on the property until final payment.

The personal property consists of

Oxen, Cows and Calves,

Household and Kitchen Furniture, &c. &c.—The real estate is as follows—towit:—

The League of Land

Granted to the said John R. Harris, by the Mexican Government, situated on Buffalo Bayou, being the same on which the Town of Harrisburg is laid off—together with the

Steam Saw Mill

built at that place.

One Half of League

No. 3—which was granted by Government to James Scott, purchased at Sheriff's sale by the said John R. Harris, deceased, situated on the St. Bernard, below George Huff's. The

South 1-2 of a League

situated on the west side of Galveston Bay, at the Red Bluff's granted to John Cooke and Isaac Hughes, on the 10th August, 1824. The

South 1-2 of a Labor

situated on the west side of the San Jacinto, adjoining the lands of Amy White, adjudicated to said John R. Harris, deceased, by the Alcade of the jurisdiction of Austin. Luke Moore's Title Bond for

1-4th of a League

of land, situated on Bray's Bayou. John D. Taylor's Title Bond for

Two Labors of Land

situated at Pine Point. The Title Bond of Tabitha Jimes, administratrix of the estate of John Jimes, deceased, for

One Labor of Land,

at the mouth of Cedar Bayou.—Together with such other property as may be found, belonging to the estate of said Harris.

THOMAS BARNETT,
Alcalde.

Austin, May 6, 1830.

LAWS OF COLONIZATION,

FOR SALE AT THIS OFFICE.

Public Sale.

THE previous requisites of the law having been complied with to authorise a sale, I Thomas Barnett, constitutional alcalde of the jurisdiction of Austin, will on

Monday, 21st June,

1830, expose to public sale, at the last residence of the deceased Mary Sims near Bolivar, to the higest bidder, all the property real, personal and mixed, belonging to the estate of Warren Hall and Mary Sims, both deceased, payable on the first day of April next, the slaves remaining mortgaged until payment of the purchase money and purchasers giving personal security to the satisfaction of the administrator,

HENRY, aged about forty-four years,
NANCY, aged forty years,
BEN, aged about thirty-three years,
ROSE, aged about thirty-one years,
EVELINA, aged about twenty-nine years,
MARIA, aged about twenty-three years,
ELIZA, aged about sixteen years,
CHARLOTTE, aged about fourteen years,
GEORGE, aged about seventeen years,
VENICE, aged about twenty years, and her two children,
COJO, aged about thirteen years,
FANNY, aged about thirteen years,
CEASAR, aged about twenty years,
ADAM, aged about eighteen years,
FANEY, aged about twenty-five years, child six years old,
JINNY, aged about sixty years,
HENRY, aged about fifty-five years,
LYDIA, aged about forty years, and Lydia aged three years.
A Mare and Colt.
A few articles of clothing and other personal property.

THOS. BARNETT,
Alcalde.

Austin, 17th May, 1830.

NOTICE.

THE undersigned, being authorised to settle the estate of John R. Harris, deceased, hereby inform all persons indebted to the said estate, that it is requisite they do immediately come forward and make settlement.—And all those to whom the estate is indebted, are also notified that their claims must be presented legally authenticated, before the first day of August next, or said claims will be forever barred.

LESASSIER & WILLIAMS.
WILLIAMSON & HOLTHAM.

Austin, May 8, 1830.

LAW NOTICE

THE undersigned having associated themselves in the PRACTICE OF THE LAW, tender their services to the public. Business in the line of their profession entrusted with them, will be punctually attended to. They may at all times be consulted at their office, in the Town of Austin.

JOHN G. HOLTHAM,
ROBT. M. WILLIAMSON.

April 26

LAW NOTICE

THE undersigned having associated themselves in the PRACTICE OF THE LAW, tender their services to the citizens of this Colony, in the line of their profession. Every description of conveyancing will be done by them; and from their attention to business, hope to merit a share of public patronage.

L. LESIASSIER,
S. M. WILLIAMS.

April 10

NOTICE.—Persons who may wish to employ an agent to select Land for them, are notified that I offer my services to make selections for those who have received certificates of reception, as settlers in Austin's Colony. My charge, will be regulated on an interview with the person who employs me.

SETH INGRAM

Jan. 23.

JOB PRINTING,

DONE AT THIS OFFICE.

TEXAS GAZETTE, Containing Legal Notice Inserted by Williamson

was reported. Considering everything, the local paper confidently asserted that Texas had a "decided preference as regards health over any portion of the neighboring republic of the North." This, of course, was written before the terrible cholera epidemic of 1833.[15]

Slave sales were frequent, negroes being advertised for auction along with horses, corn, and farm utensils. Alcalde Thomas Barnett, on May 17, 1830, listed for public sale a mare and colt, a few articles of clothing, and eighteen negro slaves belonging to the late Mary Sims. Sheriff Sam Miller was directed by First Regidor Thomas Davis to expose to public sale on October 20 a negro named Slim, seized from his owner to satisfy a debt. On March 16, 1834, Williamson sold two slave girls, Rhode, aged nineteen, and Mary, aged sixteen, to John Brown for $1,050. If one kept his eyes open, he might get an occasional reward for capturing a runaway negro. John Random offered two hundred dollars to anyone who would return to him a negro named Will, six feet tall, and another named Adam, about five feet four inches tall, who was "inclined to be sour and look yellow."[16]

Although the *Texas Gazette* piously announced in 1830 that the colony since its foundation had witnessed but three thefts, one burglary, and four homicides, San Felipe was no seminary.[17] The editors of the paper, then Williamson and G. B. Cotten, were never ones to put the town's worst foot forward. Moreover, astute Stephen F. Austin did not believe in publishing news which the Mexican government might misconstrue.[18]

The town's administration of justice was sometimes prompt and severe. A man named Wilson, caught stealing clothing from the store of Cooper and Cheeves, was immediately hailed before Alcalde Barnett, and sentenced to receive "lynches law to tune of thirty-nine stripes, which was

[15]*Texas Gazette*, March 27, 1830.

[16]*Ibid.*, September 25, 1829; October 3, 1829; February 6, 1830. W. P. Webb to D. W. R., January 6, 1946.

[17]*Texas Gazette*, August 21, 1830.

[18]Austin to S. M. Williams, February 19, 1831, in Barker (ed.), *Austin Papers*, II, 599.

immediately struck up at the dead tree on the square."[19]

Occasional duels broke the long monotony of the recurring seasons. Noah Smithwick trained two men preparing to shoot at each other. At the encounter one missed his shot; the other fired a ball that broke both legs of his antagonist just above the ankles. A certain doctor when drunk had a habit of challenging anyone in sight. Falling out with Colonel Green DeWitt, he demanded satisfaction of that worthy, offering the colonel a choice of weapons. DeWitt chose his cane, and thereupon he gave the belligerent doctor "a drubbing that cured him of duelling."[20]

Williamson once used his persuasive powers to prevent a duel which was about to occur between Austin and Anthony Butler.[21] On the other hand, Williamson was one of several members of a "San Felipe Club" who encouraged William P. Jack to pick a fight with Major Ira M. Lewis. James Whiteside is authority for the statement that Williamson and his friends "put it on Jack to bring on the quarrell." Subsequently Jack struck Lewis a couple of blows with a cane but "retreated pretty fast" when Lewis drew his pistol. On the next day Lewis sent Jack a challenge to a duel. Of the duel, Whiteside observed that Jack "brought it on rather too rough," and that Jack's friends "all left him to fight by himself—except Wmson [*sic*] he stays . . . ." The other instigators allegedly fled to the safety of the "bufelo grange." The indignant Lewis was reported to have declared, "They shall all fight or knock under."[22]

Despite an affectation of community virtue constantly proclaimed by the newspaper, ayuntamiento officials (roughly the Spanish equivalent for city government) felt obliged to pass certain measures which warrant that the town had lapses from both civic pride and decorum. City fathers were

[19]*Texas Gazette*, January 23, 1830.

[20]Smithwick, *Evolution of a State*, 79-80.

[21]C. A. Gulick, Jr., and others (eds.), *Papers of Mirabeau Buonaparte Lamar*, VI, 180.

[22]James Whiteside to Anthony Butler, August 2, 1832, in Barker (ed.), *Austin Papers*, II, 829-831.

considerably vexed with the laxity of certain persons in tending their hogs. They decreed that after February 1, 1830, any hog or hogs over one year old found running at large might be deemed the property of those who might find and mark them. A little later the ayuntamiento ruled that no person should be permitted to fire any loaded gun, rifle, or pistol, within four hundred yards of the improved part of the town. This, of course, did not apply to the sounding off of the cannon "on days of solemn festival."[23]

The ayuntamiento in 1830 also was moved to ordain against gambling, which it held to be "pernicious and destructive to the good morals of society." Cards and dice machines were forbidden; but the decree did not "comprehend" horse racing and billiard tables, which were subject to separate rulings. Violators were subject to fines of not less than fifty dollars nor more than one hundred dollars. If they could not pay, they were to be required to work out their fines at "public labor, rate $3 per diem." This edict probably cut down gambling in public places only, for the playing of poker, euchre, faro, monte, and bragsome continued. The legal fraternity whiled away leisure hours at card games as they relaxed from court sessions in the evenings. In 1833-1834, William Barret Travis lost more than two hundred dollars playing the various gambling games then in fashion.[24]

Cases of violence and murder were rather frequent, but the loyal *Gazette* rationalized the situation by explaining that "the municipality was much exposed to inroads of fugitives of justice from the United States of the North." Probably one of these was Paul Daigle, for whose arrest fifty dollars was offered. Daigle almost murdered his wife and two women who were assisting her when she was in

[23]*Texas Gazette*, February 6, 1830.

[24]Ruby Mixon, The Life and Letters of William Barret Travis. Facts about Travis's gambling are also noted in the Diary of William Barret Travis, August 30, 1833-June 26, 1834, copied from the original in the Starr Collection, University of Texas Archives. Hereafter cited, Travis, Diary.

childbed confinement.[25] During Williamson's residence in San Felipe the town had no permanent jail; prisoners were either released on bail or guarded by duly appointed citizens. Sometimes they were kept in chains for months, since cases involving the possibility of a sentence of capital punishment had to be reviewed at Saltillo, Mexico, capital of the state of Coahuila and Texas. For such processes the Mexicans took a long time, and prisoners, as a consequence, sometimes broke custody. Hiram Friley, wanted for the murder of Fielding Porter, escaped, and a reward of one hundred dollars was offered for his capture. Noah Smithwick was banished from the colony for furnishing Henry Brown a file with which to cut his irons. Brown, according to Smithwick, had killed the alcalde at Gonzales and was kept in chains "until he was worn out."[26]

At least two shooting scrapes enlivened the year 1830. Thomas Jefferson Pryor discharged a pistol at Peter Andrew, who died in great agony after half an hour. A reward of two hundred dollars was offered for Pryor's arrest. On September 2, J. C. Holtham, Williamson's law partner, was killed in a "recountre" with Seth Ingram and H. H. League. Holtham died as a result of "a pistol ball passing through his body." Two years later the prisoners were still being held. A committee of reputable citizens asserted they could have escaped, but that they made no attempt to do so even when left alone.[27]

Ayuntamiento officials usually kept a close watch on the conduct of suspicious characters. In 1830 they reported to Empresario Austin that John Lytle was guilty of harboring Hiram Friley, the escaped prisoner, and they recommended the removal from the colony of four persons. They further avowed that John Williams on the San Antonio road was "a bad character," and they suggested that Henry P. Welch

[25] *Texas Gazette*, October 2; November 6, 1830. See also the proceedings of the ayuntamiento of San Felipe as described in Barker (ed.), "Minutes of the Ayuntamiento of San Felipe," *Southwestern Historical Quarterly*, XXII, 93.

[26] Smithwick, *Evolution of a State*, 84-85.

[27] *Texas Gazette*, September 6, 1830; January 10, 1832.

and his wife not be admitted as settlers. During the summer, Welch, who had been absent from Texas, gave notice in the *Gazette* that his attorney and agent during his absence was R. M. Williamson.[28]

But it would be a mistake to assume that the restraint of ruffians was the main concern of the town. The intellectual side of life was by no means neglected. On September 21, 1829, Schoolmaster Thomas Pilgrim announced the commencement of the third quarter of his school. He promised "particular pains to correct the chastity of the sentiments and the purity of the morals of scholars." Stephen F. Austin was a member of a committee attending examinations covering the Greek, Latin, and Spanish languages.

A little later Professor Pilgrim informed the public that his school had been removed to the settlement of McNeil and Westall in Gulph Prairie, where "being but 10 miles distant from the gulph and having no timber between to prevent a free circulation of the sea breeze" the health of the students would be "unimpaired." Scholars attending "from a distance" could be accommodated with "board and washing in a number of respectable houses from $6 to $10 per month." Terms of tuition per month "were reading and writing, $2; grammar, rhetoric and history, $2.50; moral philosophy and mathematics, $4."[29]

Pilgrim was not for long the lone voice of learning. Several other pedagogues soon appeared, among them Thomas S. Saul, who offered to teach reading, spelling, writing, and the "branches of education" for a fee of from two to four dollars per month. He, too, promised strict attention to morals and manners. Another was James Norton, who opened in 1830 a school, where for a term of one year, "on the most reasonable terms," orthography, reading, writing, arithmetic, geography, and English were to be offered along with the inevitable strict attention to manners and moral conduct.[30]

A little later, as if local academies lagged in their moral earnestness, there was a threat of competition from the

[28]*Ibid.*, November 6, 1830.

[29]*Ibid.*, January 23, 1830.

[30]*Ibid.*, February 6, 1830.

Gonzales, Texas, seminary, conducted by Professor D. B. Edwards, which had as a motto "Conduct not person creates distinction." There one could get certain rudiments of an English education for as low as "one dollar per month, half cash, half products." Orphans and persons in "indigent circumstances" received tuition "gratuitously."[31]

Despite the earnest efforts of the rising generation of these devotees of learning and virtue, the elders of the town had few opportunities to enjoy a literary atmosphere. Austin deplored his financial inability to order a few good books. Indeed, he said he had seen but few books in Texas, and most of these were of an intensely practical nature, closely related to his work. He would have liked, he wrote in a simple letter, tinged with unconscious pathos, "to read a few good Spanish and English works of a literary and historical character."[32] The newspapers, the *Texas Gazette* and the *Mexican Citizen*, were the intellectual fountains of the colony, and Williamson, as one of the occasional editors, selected from whatever was available such gems of literature and moral philosophy as suited his fancy. On March 20, 1830, the *Gazette* announced with becoming modesty that it had just received two books — Bonnycastle's *Arithmetic* and Murray's *English Reader*. As late as 1834, Travis could find no copy of the Bible to send to a rural woman who had befriended him. If anyone then could have found a book in San Felipe, it was Travis. In 1834, he managed to read Scott's *Rob Roy* and *Guy Mannering*, Smollett's *Roderick Random*, Kingsley's *Westward Ho!*, the *Spectator* papers of Addison and Steele, and a dozen or more other novels and histories less well known today.[33]

The *Gazette* office usually had a few borrowed books on hand. One of these was entitled *Laconics*, and the following quotation indicates its fate: "The Gentleman who 'borrowed' a small volume from this office, entitled 'Laconics,' is requested to return it immediately, as the owner has called for it."[34]

[31]*Ibid.*, October 16, 1830.
[32]E. C. Barker, *Life of Stephen F. Austin*, 294.
[33]Travis, Diary.
[34]*Texas Gazette*, November 7, 1829; April 17, 1830.

The newspaper's issue of November 7, 1829, quotes a pearl of wisdom from *Laconics*. Whatever else it may prove, the fragment reveals a tiny segment of a book read by Williamson as he prepared to make his fortune in Texas. It depicts the dreadful mental unrest of a monarch in these words:

> Hyden, like Richard the third, was observed by one of his most familiar companions to start frequently in his sleep; he once took the liberty to ask the despot "of what he had been dreaming." "My friend," replied Hyden, "the state of a beggar is more delightful than my envied monarchy: awake, they see no conspirators; asleep they dream of no assassins."

Notwithstanding the prevailing literary dearth, poets blossomed in the little capital. To be sure most of them sought a nobler theme than the one in whose honor a public demonstration was held soon after Williamson's arrival. This ill-fated bard was tarred, feathered, and ridden on a rail through the town. The fact that he had written a satire on the local citizenry was not his chief offense, but his lines certainly did not mitigate the feeling against him, for he had written:

> The United States, as we understand,
> Took sick and did vomit the dregs of the land.
> Her murderers, bankrupts, and rogues you may see,
> All congregated in San Felipe.[35]

Such realism was disliked by the citizenry, who doubtless felt, as readers have felt in all ages, that poetry need not confine itself to acute local observations. Indeed the pioneer was an incurable romantic, and the poets who caught his fancy most surely were those who conveyed a melancholy devotion to things "afar from the sphere of our sorrow."

Williamson himself was profoundly stirred by images of beauty. He was a singer and an expert banjo player. When he sang and played negro spirituals, he moved men's hearts. He sang hymns, too—old-fashioned ones he had learned in his childhood in Georgia. When he sang these songs, he was not clowning. His listeners were strangely impressed,[36] for

[35]Smithwick, *Evolution of a State*, 81.

[36]J. D. Williamson to D. W. R., interview, June 9, 1940.

this young man was considered as handsome as Lord Byron, and like Byron he was a cripple. He loved melancholy and poetic reflections on the inevitability of death, and so when he became an editor, the village poets had a champion in him. He may even have struck out a few lines of his own. One familiar with his style finds it is not unreasonable to assume that he could have been the author of the following, which appeared in the *Gazette* on February 27, 1830, signed "The Stranger."

TO THE RIO BRAZOS

As I gaze thy course, thou quiet, lone river,
Still pouring thy floods on the pirate's dark wave,
I think on the dream that is urging me ever,
Onward to the long quiet sleep of the grave.

I think of the years that are gone—and forever,
With time's restless tide to oblivion's shore—
Of ties and affections which fate bade me sever,
With parents and kindred, who meet me no more.

There was a Byron vogue in the *Gazette*. Included was a poem, probably issuing from the pen of a local author, praising Byron and lamenting his death. It was an obvious imitation of Byron's "Apostrophe to the Ocean" from *Childe Harolde*. A poem on liberty by Thomas Moore, Byron's bosom friend and the one to whom Byron dedicated a poem on the eve of his dramatic departure from England, was printed; and space was found for a poem by Lady Caroline Lamb, another of Byron's friends. Thus it is possible that the English poet who most influenced the Texas revolution was Byron, whose passionate lines so appealed to young Williamson.[37]

Thousands of poems appearing weekly in the newspapers of the times in North America indicate a generally unrecognized fact about the pioneer—he was a poetic creature although usually he lacked the talent to write first-rate verse. Essentially unrealistic in writing about his environment, he nevertheless unconsciously expressed observations of his locale even when his theme was the charm of life in Arabia or any similar subject about which he knew nothing.

[37] *Texas Gazette*, January 13, 1830; April 17, 1830.

Many of the poems in the colonial Texas newspapers were copied from exchange journals, often unsigned and uncredited; yet a considerable number bear evidence of home authorship. Phrases later used by Williamson in his speeches indicate that he may have been the pastoral poet who drew from the bird life on the prairies of San Felipe a simile about Byron, whose soul is imagined "free as a ring dove dancing on the summer air."[38] The best original poem appearing in the *Gazette* (signed F. W.—probably Francis W. Johnson who is known to have had literary inclinations) is one peculiarly inspired by the local environment. Although it has the restless melancholy of romanticism, it reflects certain physical features of the San Felipe community: the fordless Brazos, the tangled breaks and swamps, the black cypress, and the fresh horses. It follows:

MORNING

Mount and away! where the white man never
The free earth trod, our journey lies,
And we must swim the fordless river
Ere evening darken o'er the skies.

Mount and away! the path lies clear
We need not now the light of day
But tangled breaks and swamps are near
Where the black cypress clogs the way.

Our steeds are fresh, waste not the hour
They'll bear us o'er the creek 'ere night;
And safely then at evening's hour
We'll make our tent and strike our light.[39]

Like the noble literature of England, society in San Felipe was predominantly masculine. An old folk saying has it that Texas was all right for men and dogs, but it was "hell on women and oxen." The absence of women was regretted, but the general lack of feminine company did not lead such an exuburant male as Williamson to pine away. He and his friends, particularly his partner, Godwin B. Cotten, amused themselves with convivial stag parties. Noah Smithwick has preserved a little of the flavoring of these affairs as follows:

[38]*Ibid.*, January 13, 1830.
[39]*Ibid.*, February 6, 1830.

Godwin B. Cotten was the host in many a merry bout; love feasts, he called them. Collecting a jovial set of fellows, he served them up a sumptuous supper in his bachelor apartments at which every guest was expected to contribute to the general enjoyment according to his ability. Judge Williamson was one of the leading spirits on these occasions. Having a natural bent toward the stage, Willie was equally at home conducting a revival meeting or a minstrel show. In the latter performance his wooden leg played an important part, said member being utilized to beat time to his singing. One of his best choruses was:

Rose, Rose; coal black Rose;
I nebber see a nigger dat I lub like Rose,

a measure admirably adapted to the banjo which he handled like a professional.

Some sang, some told stories and some danced. Luke La Sascie [Lessassier], a Louisiana Frenchman, and by the way a brilliant lawyer, was our champion story teller; with Cotten and Doctor Peebles worthy competitors. I, being reckoned the most nimble footed man in the place, usually paid my dues in jigs and hornpipes, "Willie" patting Juba for me. Many a night was I dragged out of bed after a hard day's work in the shop to help out an impromptu "jag." The biggest time we ever had was on the occasion of a double wedding, the brides being a couple of grass widows who were domiciled together just out of town, their comfortable home and reputed bank account proving an irresistible attraction to a couple of good-looking young scamps who were hanging about; hence the wedding. The boys all got together and went out to charivari them. It was my first experience in that kind of performance; and was unquestionably the most outrageous din I ever heard; cowbells, cowhorns, tin pans and in fact everything that contained noise were called into requisition; and with their discordant sounds mingled hoots, howls and caterwaulings enough to make the hair rise on one's head. But all our efforts to bring out the happy quartette proved abortive. We overdid the thing and frightened them out of their wits.[40]

Yet despite the dominance of males, San Felipe was not wholly lacking in feminine charm. In the winter of 1827, "the young society" of San Felipe consisted of "two or three married ladies young and old, and three or four widows young and old." These comprised "the first class or higher circle," and were "very respectable and measurably interesting." Their leader was Mrs. James Long, the late

[40]Smithwick, *Evolution of a State*, 71-72.

General James Long's lovely widow, who was tall, graceful and had "a beautiful figure." With sparkling eyes, and a lively spirit, she was addressed by "the beau, the fop, or gallant," who found her "a gay widow . . . agreeable as the manner and disposition of her company require."

Leader of the most respectable portion of the male society was "Col. Austin," in whose circle moved "eight or ten married, batchelors, and young men," four or five of whom were lawyers.[41] By 1831, when the female population had increased considerably, young women on horseback would ride fifty miles to a ball, carrying in their saddlebags silk dresses made in Philadelpha or New Orleans.[42] Quite a lively social circle had developed by then. Travis was so enamored of a certain Miss Rebecca Cummings that he went across a swollen stream on a raft to visit her, after having been previously retarded by the flood. The rampaging river, he recorded, was the only thing that had ever caused him to turn back in his life.

At a ball at Miss Cummings' where "there was hell among the women about the party," Travis hired the fiddlers for an orchestra, paying "Indian John 12½c" and a certain "Burton 43¾c and 2 drinks at Connells."[43]

One of the chief diversions of the male population was hunting, an unbelievable variety of game being abundant in the vicinity of the town. Old Martin Varner had a lot of wild hogs running in the Brazos bottom lands on his place, and when he wanted pork, he simply went out and shot it. With several dogs, Noah Smithwick once flushed on Varner's estate a boar with tusks three or four inches long. Stealthy coyotes frequently stole equipment from sleeping hunters.[44]

When trailing wild game at night, the hunters usually carried a torch or firebrand which attracted the animals, whose shining eyes afforded the marksmen a shot. Black bears frequented the forests and canebrakes, and wolves

[41]Clopper, "Journal and Book of Memoranda for 1828," *Quarterly of the Texas State Historical Association*, XIII, 59-60.

[42]Mary Austin Holley, *Texas*, 145.

[43]Travis, Diary, entry for December 28, 1833.

[44]Smithwick, *Evolution of a State*, 73-74.

were commonly encountered. Running wild in the woods were the fierce peccari or Mexican hogs, and on the prairies roamed the gregarious buffalo. Deer were so common that every cabin had its deerskin rug. Foxes peeped from bush and brake, and it was considered a poor trip indeed if the hunter failed to encounter racoons, opossums, rabbits, and squirrels, or perhaps one of the large and innumerable flocks of wild geese. Infesting the bottom lands were brant, teal, and canvasback ducks, wild turkeys, partridges, pheasants, pigeons, turtledoves, prairie hens, snipe, and plover. When a shot resounded over the rolling grasses, these creatures uttered screams that resounded crazily through the prairie.

The hunter had to be careful going through the grasslands, for there lurked the deadly rattlesnake which grew to an immense size and frequently had fangs half an inch long. Its bite killed horses, cattle, and men. One of the rattler's most powerful enemies was the deer which stamped the reptile to death with its hoofs. Wild hogs also killed and greedily ate the snake. The Indians, lacking the scientific instincts of their white brothers, and thus being unacquainted with the efficacy of strong whiskey as a snake-bite cure, treated rattler-infected wounds by killing the snake, ripping it open, and placing its flesh tightly over the wound. The procedure was said to be a good remedy, as was the application of a root called "rattlesnake's master," growing in the piney woods. Of course, there were other snakes, including land and water moccasins, coach whips, and copperheads, as well as the chicken and garter varieties, but all these were as nothing compared to the deadly rattler.

Adding to the inconvenience of the encamped hunter were beetles, ants, wasps, spiders, red bugs, ticks, sand flies, and mosquitoes—the mosquitoes being a particular nuisance in the swamps and river bottoms.

Sometimes hunting was not entirely the relaxation the hunter might have anticipated. Wives frequently went along to perform exploits "which the effeminate men of populous cities might tremble at." It was not uncommon, Mrs. Mary Austin Holley observed, for ladies "to mount their mustangs and hunt with their husbands, and with them to camp out for days on their excursions to the sea shore for fish and oysters." One formidable Amazon, a Texas Diana, killed "eighty deer and one buffalo" with her rifle. Having to support a "canting husband, wanting industry and capacity," she was forced to assume a virile role.[45]

One of the mightiest hunters of all was Williamson. An amusing tale of his encounter with an enraged buffalo calf has been related by Smithwick, who, since he claims to have repaired the young man's wooden leg, should have been able to relate the affair with as much accuracy as one has any right to expect of a hunter. This is Smithwick's account:

> Being out alone on the prairie he [Williamson] espied a buffalo calf that had got lost from the band. Willie gave chase and coming up with the game, being otherwise unarmed, attempted to lasso it. Not being an expert with the lasso, however, he only succeeded in getting it on his own neck. The calf, being pretty well winded, came to a stop and thinking to slip a noose over its head, Willie dismounted, when seeing its persecutor within its reach, the calf turned on him and before he could get out of its way the Judge received a blow in the stomach which sent him to earth, and no sooner had he risen to his feet than the vicious little brute gave him another. Willie retained his recumbent position till the calf being apparently satisfied that its foe was effectually disposed of, started on its way. The calf so far had the best of it, but the majesty of the law must be vindicated. Casting about for a weapon with which to avenge the insult offered to the state in the assault upon an officer who was attempting an arrest, the judicial eye fell upon the great clumsy wooden stirrups. Quickly unbuckling one of the straps, Willie grasped it firmly in his hand and again running upon his adversary dealt it a blow on the head with the stirrup which in turn sent it to earth, continuing the application till life was extinct.
>
> I was aroused early one morning by hearing my name called by some one in the street. "O Smithwick; come here; here's a man with a broken leg." Recognizing the voice as that of Judge Williamson, I hastily donned my clothing, and, opening the door, found Willie sitting on the step with his wooden leg broken . . . ; I took the fractured limb to my shop and braced it up so that it was as good as new, and the Judge went on his way rejoicing.[46]

This remarkable adventure is one of the most persistent of the Williamson legends. William Sparks heard of it and

[45]Holley, *Texas*, 135.

[46]Smithwick, *Evolution of a State*, 63-64.

set forth a version of the anecdote in his memoirs.[47] The old Texan, R. J. Heard, who knew Williamson personally, had an account of it from Williamson, but writing in 1893, the aged gentleman got his dates confused. Heard's version follows:

When I arrived in Washington on the Brazos, about October 1, 1837, I put up at the Washington hotel. I was requested to visit Judge Williamson professionally. His office was just across the street in a shanty, and I found him in and ready to receive me. In the course of an hour or two, after we had concluded business, the Judge insisted that I, as a Georgian, should sit with him and talk for a while. I said:

"Judge, you have had much experience in this country, I wish you would give me some of it." He studied for a few minutes and then replied:

"Yes I have; but I hardly know where to begin to tell you. One little instance caused me more suffering than anything I can now remember. About June 1, 1835, I set out on my pony from San Felipe, armed and equipped with a brace of good pistols, two Mexican gourds—one filled with water and the other with whiskey—and started over the prairie for the Colorado. The air was cool and bracing and redolent with perfume, and the prairie was as green as ever emerald could be. I was happy. Some two miles ahead of me I saw a black object upon the prairie. I advanced upon it. It was a buffalo calf that had strayed from its mother.

"The creature was very gentle. It had come up and nudged my horse as if it wished to eat. I could not think of leaving the creature there to starve. So I thought I would carry it to the settlement. I dismounted and unloosed my lariat. How gentle it was! Yes, but as I attempted to put the lariat over its head, it backed a pace, then butted me right down! And there I lay with my three legs and could use none, for the calf stood right by my side and looked so gentle until I attempted to rise, when it would butt me down again. I was helpless. My horse was gentle and would not leave, but fed all around me. The sun rose higher and higher, the day grew hotter and hotter, my whiskey and water were within a few yards of me, but for the life of me I couldn't get to them.

"That day seemed to me like an eternity. I was on the wide prairie with no road near and no hope of rescue, and I had very little hope that the calf would die. Just about sunset I saw an object away in the distance, and I hollowed, for the object was a man. As he approached he called out: 'Is that you, Williamson? What are you doing there?' I replied: 'Ask that devil of a calf. He can tell you.'

[47]Atlanta *Constitution* (Atlanta, Georgia), January 23, 1881.

"He killed the calf and we then had water and whiskey and I felt better."[48]

A pioneer male society lacked many of the sensitive spiritual manifestations of more settled communities. Although most of the colonists were religiously inclined, their Catholicism was rather lukewarm. The Mexican Colonization Law of 1825 required of colonists already in the state an oath to observe the Catholic religion. Newcomers were required to give evidence of "Christian and good moral character."[49] The Catholic Church was the authorized church of Mexico, and as such, it naturally became the official church of Texas. But San Felipe's Catholicism, despite the integrity of Empresario Austin, who believed in keeping his word, was, at the best, of the nonparticipating variety. Attempts to organize Protestant Sunday schools and the efforts of self-appointed preachers, particularly in the rural districts, made little headway. Without Austin's endorsement, the Protestant faith struggled forlornly for years. Yet, strangely enough, Catholic officials seem to have made relatively little effort to endoctrinate the San Felipeans. Only at intervals did a priest come over from San Antonio. Between his visits the colonists were left to minister to their own spiritual needs. Couples wishing to marry registered with the alcalde and set up housekeeping. The nuptial ceremonies waited the arrival of the priest.[50]

In 1831, however, Father Michael Muldoon was made "parish priest of Austin and vicar general of all the foreign colonies of Texas." One of the committee named to wait on him on his arrival was Williamson. By this time Williamson was city attorney and editor of the *Mexican Citizen*, which for an interval had replaced the *Gazette*. The *Citizen* issue of May 20 contains an interesting letter from the facile pen of Father Muldoon. It was written partly as a poem which the Father admitted might fall "under the lash of criticism,"

[48]Galveston *Daily News* (Galveston, Texas), June 11, 1893.

[49]Barker, *Life of Stephen F. Austin*, 137.

[50]*Ibid.*, 261. See also Henry Smith, "Reminiscences of Henry Smith," *Quarterly of the Texas State Historical Association*, XIV, 34.

but, he contended, "home manufacture should always be preferred to foreign finery."

The letter reveals some of the Father's adventures in Texas. On May 16, he spent the night at the residence of a Mr. Edwards, a tenant of Austin's, where he viewed a spring storm, the lightning and thunder seeming to "convulse asunder the earth." Of this the Father said:

> The zig zag dart! the astounding crash
> Made hairs to stand and teeth to gnash.

But in the morning, the sun revealed the green fields, with grapes clustering on the vines and the deer advancing to stare fearlessly.

At Edward's residence an old gentleman revealed that he had been in the habit of preaching not only at home but also in different places in the colony. Father Muldoon attributed this less to the old man's arrogance than to "the imbecility of his great age." The Father proceeded to give the patriarch a reprimand, the gist of which was recounted to the public in verse, reading much like Pope's "Essay on Man."

At the residence of Joseph Kuykendall, one of the first settlers of the colony, the Father baptized one hundred persons and married four couples. He describes the wedding festivities with relish. Whole steers were roasted on turning spits. After the feast, the musicians brought out their fiddles, and the young folks danced out the stars.

A little later Father Muldoon encountered another preacher, but the man seemed an obvious charlatan. The Father said this parson had his eyes on a rich widow and wanted personal lands.

On the whole, however, Father Muldoon was favorably impressed with his parish. He was "gratified to discover such a general and voluntary adhesion to the Catholic Church." Enemies might claim otherwise, but Father Muldoon was sure the colonists were people whose religious pretentions had been grossly misrepresented.

To the Father's lasting credit, it must be recorded that during the subsequent trouble that occurred at Anahuac in 1832 and 1835, the priest offered his own person as security to the Mexican authorities in an effort to have several prominent Texans released from jail, and during Austin's imprisonment in Mexico, in 1833-1835, Father Muldoon bestowed upon the languishing empresario many personal kindnesses.[51]

If, however, the opinion of Henry Smith, who was to be the first provisional governor of Texas, but who in 1831 was a resident of Austin's colony at Brazoria, was typical, many of the colonists concluded that Father Muldoon was "nothing but a common man—and an Irishman at that." Indeed, Smith considered him "vain, vulgar and very a scamp as ever disgraced the colony," despite the fact that it "took up half a column of a newspaper" to list his titles. He was observed to have "a snug little money making business, charging two dollars for baptism and twenty-five for marriage."

Smith recalled that following the Father's entrance into the Brazoria community, he issued an edict forbidding provisional marriage, "which made it very inconvenient to the people who lived scattered over a district . . . several hundred miles in extent." It furthermore "really looked dry and odd" to Smith to see "those who had for years been living together as man and wife, and had perhaps a large family, step forward to the marriage altar." Many of the colonists, particularly the oldsters, considered the idea of being baptized by a Catholic priest "an everlasting stigma and disgrace."

A ceremony designed to be a mass baptism and marriage of many Brazoria citizens, Smith vividly recalled as follows:

> The baptism commenced first, as heretics could not be lawfully joined in matrimony until they were baptized in the true faith. Next commenced a kind of liturgy—that finished, the marriage ceremony, which was short and a mere conjoining in lawful wedlock closed the scene. . . . They had all been conjoined but one couple and the lone woman, when her husband made his appearance quite out of breath, his hair flying, his eyes walling with a wild and frighted look. He did not know how much harm he had done nor realy what it all meant, for he had been raised with hue and cry and told to hurry, or the Priest would take his wife from him. The scene, take it all in all, was truly ludicrous in the extreme. Most of them had children and some five or six. To see brides on the floor, and while the marriage rites are performing, with bosoms open and little children sucking at the breast, and others in a

[51]Mixon, Life and Letters of William Barret Travis.

situation realy to delicate to mention, appeared to me more like a burlesque on marriage than a marriage in fact.[52]

San Felipe's transportation problems were solved in the main by everyone's riding horseback, but ox wagons, rare four-wheel carriages, pack mules, and loaded horses were also used. There were few roads—none in the modern sense of the term. Surveyors were appointed by the ayuntamiento to lay out paths to adjacent communities. In 1830 routes for roads from San Felipe to Harrisburg and Marion were ordered surveyed. Surveyors were asked to report the best route from Harrisburg to Retor's point at the mouth of the San Jacinto, and from Jenning's crossing on the Colorado to Brazoria. In 1831 the citizens of Harrisburg petitioned the ayuntamiento to appoint commissioners to lay off a road from Harrisburg to New Kentucky; and in a meeting of the San Felipe city council, Williamson moved that a road be surveyed from San Felipe to Brazoria, some eighty miles away. In 1831 Gail Borden was the municipal surveyor of Colony District No. 5.[53]

San Felipe was about eighty miles from the Gulf, and many colonists came into Texas by sea. In 1830 the sloop *Nelson*, bearing fifty passengers from New Orleans, arrived at the mouth of the Brazos. During the same year the new schooner *Pocahontas*, which was advertised to have "fine accommodations," left Brazoria for New Orleans, but the schooner *Augusta* was forced to delay its departure a few days owing to the illness of its master, Captain Dunn. The sloop *Jackson* arrived from New Orleans at the mouth of the Brazos after a voyage of twelve days. On "coming over the bar it missed the channel, it having changed, and beat violently on the sand bank for three hours." Ultimately the boat succeeded in getting over, but she "drifted ashore hard and fast." All passengers and the cargo were saved.[54]

[52]Smith, "Reminiscences of Henry Smith," *Quarterly of the Texas State Historical Association*, XIV, 34 ff.

[53]See scattered references in Barker (ed.), "Minutes of the Ayuntamiento of San Felipe," *Southwestern Historical Quarterly*, XXII, 78-95; 180-196; 272-278; 353-359.

[54]*Texas Gazette*, February 27, 1830. See also issue of October 24, 1830.

Getting across the Brazos was a problem. In 1829 the condition of the ferry was so "abandoned" that the city fathers ordered the person holding the ferry lease to put into operation immediately a sufficient number of boats to accommodate travelers, and to "make safe the approaches to the ferry by filling the gullies in the river bank." At the end of the year, John C. Reed, the ferryman, had not paid his rent. This negligence may have influenced the council when it fined Reed one hundred dollars for having failed to deliver "a good and substantial ferry flat boat."

The city fathers interposed further by fixing ferry rates. A pack mule or a loaded horse went across for 12½ cents, a man for 6¼ cents, and a hog for 2 cents. A loaded wagon and four animals were ferried for $1.25, but a wagon and two animals crossed for one dollar flat. All rates were double when the river was out of banks, an almost annual occurrence in the spring.[55] Doubling the rates was a futile gesture, for when flooded the bottom lands surrounding the town were impassable, and travel through those regions halted abruptly until the "Mississippi of Texas" resumed its normal flow.[56]

The Texans' comparison of the Brazos with the Mississippi was inept, for beside the Mississippi, drawing its water supply from an "area spread of forty-five degrees of longitude," the brackish Brazos, running eastward from the interior of Texas some nine hundred miles to the Gulf, suffers by contrast. Yet in its own right, the Brazos is a remarkable river. Rising in a salt region in the Texas Panhandle near the New Mexico border, the river near its source was in the 1830's so salty that in dry seasons, when the water evaporated, immense quantities of salt were deposited along the river bed. The water carried a fine red clay, "slippery as soap and as sticky as putty," until fresh tributaries dissipated it.[57]

The color of the river varied from deep red to chocolate,

[55]Barker (ed.), "Minutes of the Ayuntamiento of San Felipe," *Southwestern Historical Quarterly*, XXI, 113.

[56]Clopper, "Journal and Book of Memoranda for 1828," *Quarterly of the Texas State Historical Association*, XIII, 58.

[57]Holley, *Texas*, 31.

according to the prevailing freshet, and it was generally from 20 to 30 feet deep and about 150 feet wide. In 1834 the river went on a mighty rampage causing terrible destruction to property. In some places the overflow was ten miles wide. Today the Brazos divides ten Texas counties and intersects six, emptying into the Gulf at Freeport.

Even as early as 1827, the San Felipe district on the Brazos had cotton gins in operation, the raising of cotton being the tedious process which made the colonists touchy about Mexican attempts to restrict slavery. Salt beds being scattered throughout the territory, salt was made abundantly and sold "remarkably low." Several planters were already erecting sugar mills and planning to vend their wares at ten cents a pound, a sum cheaper than the prevailing price of the commodity when it was transported from New Orleans.[58] These mills, however, did not prosper, for in 1829 the *Texas Gazette* announced that the cane was not being extensively cultivated. In that year, a particularly fine one for agriculture in general, only about one hundred acres in the San Felipe district were planted to the crop. Although the *Gazette* assured its readers that if well handled the Texas product would "greatly exceed the best average of Louisiana cane," the colonists found it difficult to "procure persons informed in the process of sugar milling." But the corn and cotton in 1829 exceeded anything seen in "the southern climate," and the paper informed the public that since Austin came to Texas seven years before, not one year had been bad for crops if the seeds were planted in time and the plants tended properly. The harvest was short in 1826, but that, the paper explained, was because the civilian militia had to turn out in the spring to combat the Indians.[59]

Nor was the *Gazette* alone in hailing the agricultural paradise to be found along the Brazos bottoms. An elderly colonist from Kentucky wrote a letter for the March 27, 1830, issue of the paper, reflective of the enthusiasm which since that time has been so characteristic of Texas that it is

[58]Clopper, "Journal and Book of Memoranda for 1828," *Quarterly of the Texas State Historical Association*, XIII, 59.

[59]*Texas Gazette*, October 13, 1829.

matched in the United States only by the arrogance of New Englanders in discussing their locale. The correspondent wrote:

> . . . Texas is without doubt the finest portion of the inhabitable globe. Everybody says so Messrs. Editors; and *an experimental residence*, of something like three years in the country, satisfies me that the broad assertion above, is true.
>
> I can raise larger and better pork in Texas, than I could in Kentucky with all the corn I could give them. I can raise *ten calves* in Texas with *less trouble* than I could *one* in Kentucky!! I can kill a better and fatter beef from among my stock, in the winter, than I ever saw butchered from the *stall* in Kentucky!!! I can raise horses, *in proportion to cattle*!!!! I can raise more *corn* to the acre in Texas than I could in Kentucky and with *less labor*!!!!! My peas grow longer, and the hulls fill better *here* than I ever had them to do in Kentucky!!!!!! . . . Hemp, I dare say would grow better here than in Kentucky, but I think for cables or strong ropes, the *cabrista*, or rope of the wild horse hair, preferable to those made of hemp!!!!!!! For comfortable and lasting apparel, give me the well dressed Texas buckskin in preference to all the *rotted* hemp, in Kentucky!!!!!!!! My wife, Messrs. Editors, has not yet got *under way*, at gardening, but I pledge you my word I never have seen, in Kentucky, or elsewhere as large, beautiful white cabbage as I saw in Mrs. ——'s garden in August. I was compelled to dine with her—*I ate up the subject*!!!!!!!!![60]

Even if the native Kentuckian's assertions are to be dismissed as the effusions of one born too soon to take his place on the board of directors of the East Texas Chamber of Commerce, Austin's colony was in fact a fertile area. In addition to producing cotton, corn, and sugar cane, previously mentioned, the virgin earth yielded abundantly of maize (Indian corn), wheat, rye, oats, barley, and other small grains. Although not extensively planted, flax and hemp were suited to the soil, and rice was grown in considerable quantities. Tobacco also could be "grown luxuriantly," and the indigenous indigo was considered superior to the indigo cultivated in the United States. Beans, peas, Irish and sweet potatoes grew in amazing quantities and were of the quality to make a man's mouth water. The vanilla bean, then esteemed as a perfume and also adapted in "Mexico,

[60]*Ibid.*, March 27, 1830.

Madrid, Paris and London for use with chocolates, ices, and jellies," grew wild. Some of the sweet potatoes weighed from four to seven pounds, and pumpkins, as large as a man could lift, grew in a manner to delight a "genuine Yankee."

The region further yielded an abundance of fruit. Native grapes of several varieties, ranging from the large fox-grape to what was called the chicken-grape grew in profusion. Olives, oranges, lemons, figs, prunes, peaches, and melons "of the richest gusto," could be raised even by a lazy farmer who spent too much time in San Felipe, for the delicacies required but little care. Available for the picking were blackberries, dewberries, and May apples.

In the spring the whole countryside bloomed with yellow, blue, and purple varieties of stellaria stretching as far as one could see. Dahlias, geraniums, lilies, and lobelias were "exceedingly common." The ground apple produced a white flower exquisitely beautiful, and the violets so carpeted the meadows that the stranger might have thought himself in fairyland. Multiflora and other varieties of roses grew without care, as did primroses; and in April when the delicate mimosa made the prairie a sea of pink, the furtive poets of San Felipe felt their "hearts leap up," although no Wordsworth was among them to acclaim the flowers of Texas.

Forest lands, containing most of the varieties of trees found in North American states—live oaks, hickory, ash, wild cherry, mulberry, elm, red cedar, yellow pine, linn, gum, pecan, willow, chinaberry, sycamore, and wild peach—were abundant. Peculiarly "Texian" was the nopal or prickly pear plant, forming at places an "impenetrable thicket," and producing an immense quantity of fruit for "vast herds of cattle and wild horses." The Texan army during the revolution was at one time "preserved from famine" by the fruit of the prickly pear.

If a man liked stock raising, this was his country. The cost was absolutely nothing, for the pastures produced acorns, pecans, hickory nuts, and a variety of nutritious grasses with many kinds of roots for the animals to feed on. All one had to do was to brand the stock he wanted, and he could "rear a hundred as well as a half dozen." Horses, mules, cattle, hogs, sheep, and goats were thus raised annually without much effort on the farmer's part. Out on the great prairie, to the south, mingled with herds of wild mustangs were numerous jacks, jennies, and mules, the jacks bringing twenty dollars each and the mules from two to five dollars each on the home market.

The log cabins in town and country alike usually consisted of two rooms, a kitchen and bedroom, and were rarely plastered. As a rule the furniture was homemade, although for the more ornate residences it was shipped in piecemeal from the United States. When built by the colonists, furniture patterns were extremely simple: the tables were of plain board construction, and chairs usually had seats of stretched deer skin, buffalo hide, or hemp rope. Later some of the residences were of better construction, finished boards and even brick replacing unhewn logs as sidings; but until 1830 such luxurious building was rare.[61]

When Major H. H. League advertised in 1829 that he had repaired and cleansed "his well of warter" and that the water was free to all who would draw it, the offer was by no means regarded as a mere pleasantry by the San Felipeans, many of whom had to fetch their water from the river or near-by branches. Underground water was about thirty feet deep, and the soil, being sandy in some places, continually caved in during the process of well digging. In one instance it required ten thousand bricks to wall a well, and the total cost to the owner was about three hundred dollars.[62]

Public entertainers occasionally appeared in San Felipe. On August 1, 1830, Victor Pepin presented a grand and brilliant display of fireworks, set off for "the gratification and amusement of the populace." Included were a changeable wheel, the windmill of Don Quixote, the cross of St. Andrew with four revolving suns, and as a grand finale, a naval engagement between two Spanish war cruisers. This display was lighted at the rear of the *Gazette* office, and the

[61]Holley, *Texas*, Chapters IV and V.

[62]See *Texas Gazette*, October 24, 1830, for League's advertisement. Information on walling a well is in letter, James Whiteside to Anthony Butler, Barker (ed.), *Austin Papers*, II, 829.

paper assured the community that entertainments so highly moral should be encouraged.[63]

In such a town and under such conditions the fathers of Texas spent their youth. Their reveries might be suddenly broken off and their wrath aroused as they hastily stepped aside to avoid a litter of pigs scurrying through the muddy street; but the thought of an evening's frolic at one of Cotten's "love-feasts" would soon restore tranquillity, for there the convivial bottle would be passed freely. At the party Luke Lessassier might be in one of his discursive moods, and the stories would be worth listening to, or Bob Willamson would be sure to have his banjo going.

In the summer when a man felt the breeze whipping in from the sandy prairie where the dried-up grass afforded the parched soil no protection, he thought he was feeling gusts from a furnace and wished the city fathers would require land purchasers to plant trees,[64] but there was vast, unutterable beauty on the prairie in the spring when, clothed with grass "from one to two feet [in] height," it had the resemblance of a boundless ocean, bending in swards like billows, its canopy a cloudless sky or "a dark pavilion of the threatening storm." Then it was alive with "deer, mustang, and wild horses," gamboling loftily and executing "manoeuvers . . . unshackled by the thraldom of man."[65]

San Felipe, on the whole, afforded a rough, coarse life. The quarrels that strong-willed men, handy with their shooting irons, were frequently engaged in, the brawling in the taverns, and the lack of any but the simplest accommodations in the hewn log dwellings all made the community somewhat violent and primitive. But kindness and sensitivity dwelt unsuspected in many a heart. As a traveler, stricken with high fever on the road to San Antonio, lay unconscious, his brother, realizing the youth was dying, tearfully bade him farewell, "in a far distant land . . . with no mother, no sister, no gentle voice of womankind to smooth the passage to the

[63]*Texas Gazette*, July 31, 1830.

[64]*Ibid.*, August 31, 1830.

[65]Clopper, "Journal and Book of Memoranda for 1828," *Quarterly of the Texas State Historical Association*, XIII, 57.

tomb."[66] When the owner of an ox left the animal tied for several days near the *Gazette* office without food or water, someone wrote a letter to the paper protesting the brutality of the deed.[67]

In his home on Palmeto Creek, Stephen F. Austin would often be sitting up late writing for the thousandth time to prospective colonists the advantages of Texas, after having listened all day to the endless complaints of men who wanted more than their share of the colony's property. In 1833 young William Barret Travis, like as not, could be found reading *Roderick Random* and contemplating the purchase of two bottles of cologne water and an ounce of cinnamon to give to a certain young lady for Christmas, little guessing then he would have the honor of lending her bridegroom "a shirt and drawers" for the wedding ceremony.[68] And Robert M. Williamson in his law office would be mightily obliged if someone would find and return a deed which he had mislaid or lost, but just having bought a horse from Travis,[69] and being for the moment out of funds, the young lawyer would be sitting, chin on hand, gazing at the Rio Brazos and composing, in a nostalgic mood, a poem about friends he would never see again in this world.

[66] *Ibid.*, 63.

[67] *Texas Gazette*, April 17, 1830.

[68] Travis, Diary. See entry for December 25, 1833, and January 5, 1833.

[69] *Ibid.*

CHAPTER III

Lawyer and Newspaper Editor

When Williamson first settled in San Felipe, opportunities for a young lawyer to display his talents were few, particularly in private practice. Although more than five years had passed since Austin began distributing lands to the settlers, Mexican jurisprudence functioned very inefficiently in Texas. In 1821, Governor Antonio Martínez made Austin head of the Anglo-American colony in Texas until the federal authorities should organize a governing plan. Two years later, still trying to get a definitive statement of his powers, Austin was informed that in criminal offenses carrying capital punishment he was to report the trial to the superior government and work the prisoners concerned on public roads until a final decision was returned. In all other respects, however, Austin was to be personally responsible for local government.[1]

In August, 1822, the colony was divided into two districts, each having an alcalde (a sort of mayor and justice of the peace) to dispense justice and look after local administration. Austin made additional divisions in the succeeding years, so that seven were in operation when the official ayuntamiento, prescribed by Mexican law, was established in San Felipe on February 12, 1828.

Until 1828 neither the alcaldes nor the citizenry knew whether or not the Mexican laws applied to the colonies; they did not even know what the statutes were. To create some semblance of order, therefore, Austin, without benefit of form books or precedents, issued a set of "Instructions and Regulations for the Alcaldes." It was in the courts of these alcaldes that young Robert M. Williamson, trained

[1]E. C. Barker, "The Government of Austin's Colony, 1821-1831," *Southwestern Historical Quarterly*, XXI, 225.

under the supervision of several of the leading lawyers of Georgia, first displayed his legal abilities in Texas.

Austin's criminal code provided for dealing with the offenses of Indians and fixed penalties and punishments for the crimes committed by the colonists. Cases involving murder, theft, robbery, gambling, profane swearing, drunkenness, and counterfeiting all had to be examined by the alcalde and tried by a jury of six. For minor offenses, fines were to be the usual penalties, but whipping and banishment from the colony were allowed. All records and verdicts were submitted to Austin for approval.

Under Austin's civil code, an appointed sheriff executed the empresario's processes as judge, and a constable served for the alcalde. If acting alone, the alcalde was final authority in cases involving less than ten dollars. Acting with arbitrators he had final jurisdiction in cases involving sums up to twenty-five dollars. He had primary jurisdiction in cases involving sums up to two hundred dollars. Austin made it incumbent on the alcaldes to attempt an agreement out of court as the first step in settling a case. Only after failing in this, were they to hold a trial.

With a sharp rise in immigration after 1825, Austin found increasingly less time to attend to appeals from the alcalde courts. In 1826 he ordered each of the six districts then existing to elect a representative to meet with him to form a new judicial system. As a result, a court composed of any three alcaldes thereafter heard appeals at three annual sessions in San Felipe.[2] Williamson's practice before this group was so impressive that in 1830 he was chosen to be the first prosecuting attorney for the San Felipe district. Unfortunately, however, the position paid no salary.[3]

After March 11, 1827, when a constitution for Coahuila and Texas was adopted, Mexican legal procedures somewhat modified the conduct of the colonial courts, the extent depending upon the mood and legal knowledge of the prevailing ayuntamiento officials. Indictments were unnecessary in

[2]*Ibid.*, 227-231.

[3]Barker (ed.), "Minutes of the Ayuntamiento of San Felipe," in *ibid.*, XXII, 193.

criminal trials, and petty offenders could be punished without formal trial or right of appeal. For serious offenses, the accused could be held for forty-eight hours without formal charges. The constitution required the state congress to provide statutes for the establishment of trial by jury in criminal cases and to extend it gradually to civil cases. This was the first mention of a jury in any law ever in force throughout the whole Texas territory, although locally, as in Austin's colony, almost from the beginning, juries had been employed.[4]

It required more than three years for the state congress to comply with the constitutional mandate validating jury practice in criminal trials, and even then the decree, dated September 1, 1830, had no application to civil cases. The articles of the decree, summarized by John C. Townes, reveal the striking contrast between Mexican and Anglo-American concepts of jury trials, and they further show the conditions of practice governing many of the cases which Williamson pled before the alcalde courts. Judge Townes's summary follows:

> The ayuntamiento in each district capital was to select yearly from among the citizens of the district from twenty-one to eighty-four jurors, who should possess the same qualifications as members of the ayuntamiento. The persons so selected were to be the jurors for one year. The preliminary examination of criminal offenses was to be conducted as heretofore by the primary courts of justice, but whenever the evidence introduced satisfied the primary judge that the crime was proved, he was to desist from further investigation of the case, and send the prisoner and the proceedings had before him, to some alcalde of the capital of the district. The proceedings were to be continued before this alcalde who should at once require the prisoner to choose his counsel, and immediately thereafter the trial should begin. The prisoner then selected from the list of jurors seven to sit in his case. The prosecution could make objection to two jurors, provided this was done within twenty-four hours after they were chosen. The places thus made vacant were to be filled by selection by the prisoner from the other jurors. The seven jurors were then to be notified by the alcalde and were to meet within four days and were to be sworn to try the case. From these jurors a secretary and a fiscal were to

[4]John C. Townes, "Sketch of the Development of the Judicial System of Texas," *Quarterly of the Texas State Historical Association*, II, 29 ff.

be selected. The fiscal thus selected was to make an examination of the proceedings up to that time and form a "recapitulation" thereof, and express his opinion as to the guilt or innocence of the prisoner. For this he was allowed eight days, and immediately thereafter the jury was to meet again publicly, and the proceedings and recapitulation were to be read in the presence of the prisoner and his counsel, and the record was to be delivered to them, and upon the 6th day after such delivery the jury was to reassemble and proceed with the investigation, having the right to examine the prisoner and his counsel. The case was then to be discussed by the jury until all of them signified that they were prepared to vote. Each juror was then to vote by ballot, signifying his judgment as to the guilt or innocence of the prisoner, and if he believed him guilty specifying the punishment to be inflicted. If a majority concurred in the innocence of the prisoner, he was acquitted; if a majority concurred in his guilt and as to the punishment, he was adjudged guilty, and the punishment was fixed as specified in the ballots. If a majority found him guilty, but differed as to the punishment, the question of punishment was reconsidered until a majority should agree on it. If the prisoner were acquitted, this ended the proceedings; if he were found guilty, judgment could not be pronounced in that tribunal, but all the proceedings were passed to the first hall of the tribunal of justice, which was required to pass upon the question of punishment; and if the punishment as fixed by the jury was moderated or approved, judgment to that effect was rendered by that court, and from this no appeal could be taken. If, however, this tribunal should increase the punishment as fixed by the jury, an appeal lay to the second hall of the tribunal of justice. If this second appellate court concurred in the increase of the punishment, this should be final. In case the punishment assessed were capital, an appeal lay to the tribunal of justice, composed of all three halls of the supreme court.[5]

The activities of the lawyers in attempting to impose these practices upon colonists accustomed to North American procedure caused considerable discontent in San Felipe. With the rural population, ayuntamiento officials were at one time so unpopular that the farmers would not trust them even to manage funds being solicited to establish an academy.[6] Austin himself considered that lawyers made life unnecessarily contentious in the colonies. The fact is that Austin was not greatly impressed with lawyers as a class.

[5]*Ibid.*, 134-135.

[6]J. H. Bell to Stephen F. Austin, March 13, 1829, in Barker (ed.), *Austin Papers*, II, 183.

Williamson, he certainly liked, but "hot-headed, fractious, abusing and contentious" lawyers, he considered a curse. For his part, Austin thought men should settle their differences by an arbitration of neighbors.[7]

That Williamson had hard sailing during the first months of the ayuntamiento's existence is evidenced by the fact that in the latter days of 1829 he was serving as assistant to the editor of the *Texas Gazette*. This would indicate that he found the law practice so dull he required a supplement to his income.

Indeed, while Williamson was waiting for San Felipe to grow big enough to permit him to devote all of his time to the law, neither his law practice nor his ventures in newspaper publishing occupied his full time. A part of his energies went to the accumulation and sale of real estate, and he contemplated becoming a stockbreeder. On June 29, 1830, his petition, written in Spanish, to the state of Coahuila and Texas for a quarter of a section of land below San Felipe on the Brazos "for the raising and breeding of cattle and horses and for agriculture," was granted.[8] The official deed shows the land was surveyed on April 23, 1831, by Thomas H. Borden, brother of the famous Gail. It was on the right bank of the Brazos, beginning with a box elder tree, eight inches in diameter, marked No. 9. What happened to this land is not known. Williamson spent little time either in farming or raising fine cattle and horses.

Ayuntamiento records of December 21, 1829, show that Williamson's associate, G. B. Cotten, editor and publisher of the *Texas Gazette* bought city lots 44 and 50 for forty-five dollars. Two months later Cotten offered to publish all decrees and advertisements of the ayuntamiento for one year as payment for these lots. He requested that the titles be made to himself and Williamson. The records of May 15, 1830, show that Williamson bought city lots 142, 143, and 144 for ninety-nine dollars. Much of the property accumulated by Williamson did not long remain in his possession.

[7]Barker, *Life of Stephen F. Austin*, 275-276.

[8]Titles to Austin's Second Contract for 500 Families, Vol. III, in Titles in Spanish Archives, General Land Office, V, 1142-1149.

SELLO TERCERO: DOS REALES

HABILITADO POR EL ESTADO DE COAHUILA Y TEXAS PARA EL BIENIO DE 1828 Y 29. 30 y 31

Williams

Señor Comisionado

Villa de San Felipe de Austin 15 de Marzo de 1831

Al Agente del C. Empres.o [illegible] para que se sirva informar si el terreno es baldío y si puede ó no darse legua. [illegible]

[illegible]

Robert M Williamson uno de los Colonos introducidos por el Señor Empres.o Austin ante V. con el mayor respeto hago presente Que por el Supremo Gobierno del Estado se me concedió como poblador un sitio de tierra de los baldíos en esta Colonia cuya concesión lleva la fecha de 29 de Marzo del pasado año de 1830. En cuya virtud, y con la aprobación del mismo Señor Empresario he escogido un sitio de tierra que está situado sobre el Río de los brazos abajo de esta Villa y sobre la misma margen colindante y abajo del sitio de John Little por cuya razón me presento á V. para que se sirva posesionarme de dicho terreno conforme á la concesión referida á cuyo fin le acompaño la copia testimoniada de ella. En la inteligencia de que ofrezco poblarlo y cultivarlo de conformidad con la ley y á cumplir con las demás obligaciones de la misma, por tanto.

A V. pido se sirva hacer como dejo referido á que en ello recibiré gracia.

Villa de Austin 15 de marzo de 1831

Robt M Williamson

Señor

Petition to Commissioner for a Grant of Land Located by Williamson in Austin's Colony on Brazos River

Title to lot No. 50, owned jointly with Cotten, was transferred to Thomas Gay, probably in payment either for carpenter work or for lumber furnished to the *Gazette*. Titles to the lots which Williamson bought in May were transferred to Samuel Townsend on December 6.[9] Advertisements in issues of the *Mexican Citizen* of March, 1831, reveal that Williamson offered for sale "a league of land, situated on the east side of the Brazos river, precisely at the head of the tide."

The practice of law, however, was Williamson's first love. On May 8, 1830, a *Gazette* advertisement announced the formation of a law partnership between Williamson and J. B. Holtham, who, at the time, had been in San Felipe only a few weeks. Holtham, described by Austin as a "vagabond in Texas," reportedly left behind him an unsavory reputation in the United States, but he was somewhat redeemed in Texas by his knowledge of the Spanish language. While Williamson's partner, he served for a time as the secretary of the ayuntamiento.[10]

Williamson and Holtham established an office, but only scant records of the business they transacted survive. Jointly with the firm of Lessassier and Williams, they were authorized to settle the estate of John R. Harris, deceased. In July, 1830, Williamson was authorized to act as attorney for Henry P. Welch during his absence from Texas, but Williamson lost this client permanently a few months later when the ayuntamiento recommended to Austin that Welch and his wife not be admitted to the colony as settlers.[11] The partnership ended on September 2, when Holtham, as previously related, was killed in a shooting scrape with Seth Ingram and H. H. League.

There is no record of Williamson's reaction to the murder of his partner, although the prisoners were held in chains for months, and the affair was a topic that long buzzed in

[9]Barker (ed.), "Minutes of the Ayuntamiento of San Felipe," *Southwestern Historical Quarterly*, XXII, 88, 190; XXIII, 75.

[10]Barker, *Life of Stephen F. Austin*, 219.

[11]Barker (ed.), "Minutes of the Ayuntamiento of San Felipe," *Southwestern Historical Quarterly*, XXIII, 70.

the town's conversation. Williamson had little chance to brood over it, for in this month his first real legal opportunity came to him. The ayuntamiento conferred an honor on him by choosing him over all others who had offered their services to be city prosecutor (gratis) for a period of six months.[12] At the meeting in which Williamson was made prosecuting attorney, the ayuntamiento passed an ordinance prohibiting gambling. Persons found "establishing cards, dice, or hazards on their premises" were subject to a fine of from $50 to $150. Among the first luckless gentlemen to be caught violating the law were Stephen Brown, Noah Scott, Jesse Clift, John Williams, and John McGee. Later, with Williamson as prosecutor, the alcalde fined each of these men fifty dollars. They promptly petitoned the ayuntamiento for a remission of their fines; and, when that body unanimously rejected their pleas, the *Gazette* editorially championed the defendants' cause, arguing "the ordinance was new and the offenders ignorant of it."[13]

This stand of the *Gazette* is curious. Williamson wrote some of the paper's editorials, but he certainly must not have written this one since the article disapproved his accomplishment as prosecutor. Occasionally Austin wrote the *Gazette* editorials, but it is incompatible with all knowledge of that austere gentleman to imagine him pleading leniency for gamblers. The only other plausible author is Cotten. His stand on the matter may have been an instance that later prompted Austin to write that the *Gazette* had been "badly conducted."[14]

Despite the implied disapproval of the *Gazette*, Williamson proceeded resolutely on his course, well prepared for whatever legal problems might arise. In 1830, he had access to a law library of many volumes. On August 14, 1830, a *Gazette* advertisement listed a forthcoming public sale at the office of Williamson of "a law library belonging to A. B. Clark, deceased, subject to a lien of $120, in favor of R. M. William-

[12] *Ibid.*, XXII, 193.

[13] *Texas Gazette*, October 2, 1830.

[14] Stephen F. Austin to Samuel M. Williams, February 19, 1831, in Barker (ed.), *Austin Papers*, II, 599-600.

son." It is improbable that Williamson would have sold these books had he not possessed similar volumes in his own library. To be sold were twenty-two volumes of Vesy's *Chancery Reports* and various other volumes including Morgan's *Essays*, Robertson's *Fraudlent Conveyance*, Bayard's *Evidence*, Montagu's *Law of Lien*, Chitty's *Criminal Law*, Gaydon's *Justice*, Park's *Insurance*, and similar legal books. In all, a total of eighty volumes were to be vended.

Williamson evidently pleased the citizenry with his services as prosecutor, for in December at the annual ayuntamiento election he was chosen to be San Felipe's *sindico procurador* (roughly, city attorney) by a vote of 250 to 56 over Stephen Richardson, his nearest rival.[15] He served in this capacity throughout the year of 1831.

As *sindico procurador* Williamson plunged into the busiest period of legal and civic activity he had yet known. In the first ayuntamiento session, he was commissioned to examine the list of fines due the municipality, and he was also requested to make a study of the taxes due the city government on town lots.[16]

By March the young Georgian had so impressed his colleagues that they passed a very flattering resolution concerning him. It was rumored that the Mexican government was contemplating the formation of several circuit courts for the colonies. The council, in one of its lengthiest sessions, recommended "in consideration of the moral and political virtues and also the knowledge of the laws as found in the person of R. M. Williamson" that he be appointed prosecuting attorney of the proposed circuit court to function for San Felipe. Nominated for judge was Luke Lessassier, who was to become Williamson's law partner in 1832.

Williamson also was appointed a member of the board of health for San Felipe along with Drs. Robert Peebles, James B. Miller, Socrates Moseley and Luke Lessassier and William H. Jack, lawyers. They were supposed to take preventive steps against a small pox "contagion" which had

[15]Barker (ed.), "Minutes of the Ayuntamiento of San Felipe," *Southwestern Historical Quarterly*, XXIII, 150.

[16]*Ibid.*, 220.

broken out in Bexar and Goliad. In the same session Williamson was made one of a committee with Lessassier and Samuel Williams to welcome Padre Muldoon and "to provide such conveniences for his comfort as the circumstances and situation of the place will admit."

Activities as recorded in the minutes of the San Felipe ayuntamiento seem trivial, but upon reflection one will see that the sessions of this pioneer council gave Williamson his first experience in the formation of laws, lessoned him in simple but essential workings of the democratic process, and, above all, associated him with men who were to be his lasting friends and associates in the years ahead when together they would assume roles in shaping the course of a sovereign nation rather than a village.

For example, Alcalde Francis W. Johnson, treasurer of San Felipe on Williamson's motion, was later to be Williamson's commander at Anahuac, and his friendship for Williamson—evident in such instances of the ayuntamiento session as that in which Johnson moved that Williamson be "a committee to make a settlement with Nicholas Clopper for a house which the ayuntamiento had purchased in town—"[17] had become so firm during the revolution that it was to Williamson, whom Johnson called "Dear Willie," that the erstwhile alcalde turned during the siege of San Antonio with the plea, "For God's sake have the battering piece forwarded. . . ."[18]

Ordinances introduced by Williamson indicate his comprehension of the town's problems. It was he who moved that a safety patrol be formed for the town and neighborhood and that the council make an arrangement with Tom Borden or someone else to survey a road from San Felipe to Brazoria.[19] The committees on which Williamson served gave him a variety of experiences: he was named one of the group to devise a plan of taxation to run the city govern-

[17] *Ibid.*, 302-303.

[18] F. W. Johnson to R. M. Williamson, November 18, 1835, in Army Papers, No. 926, File Box 10, State Archives, Austin, Texas.

[19] Barker (ed.), "Minutes of the Ayuntamiento of San Felipe," *Southwestern Historical Quarterly*, XXIII, 303-304.

ment and to finance the building of a city hall and jail; he was twice appointed "to examine the true situation of the taxes due on town lots"; and he was chosen to preside as the judge in an election of officers for the civic militia.[20]

By midsummer Williamson completed his assignment as tax examiner. On July 4, 1831, he moved that Walter C. White, *regidor*, be authorized to collect the amount due the municipality on town lots. Williamson made no motions at the September meeting and was absent at the October sessions. At the meeting of November 7, the council took up most of its time nominating officials to preside over the election for the ayuntamiento of 1832. By this time the population of the colony was in excess of five thousand, and because of this growth, San Felipe's officials, under the law, were henceforth to be two alcaldes, six *regidors*, and two *sindico procuradors*. In the December election of 1831, Jesse Grimes, many years later Williamson's rival for a seat in the Senate of the Texas Republic, was elected one of the *regidors*.[21]

While Williamson was thus participating in the civic life of the community, practicing law in the courts of the alcaldes, and dealing in real estate, he avoided monotony by working on the town's newspapers. During the latter part of 1829, for the first five months of 1830, and for an unknown length of time in 1831, Williamson was a newspaper editor. His associate, at the start, was G. B. Cotten, who started the *Texas Gazette* on Friday, September 25, 1829. Not the first Texas newspaper and not even the first to have been issued in Austin's colony,[22] the *Gazette* was nevertheless the most important pre-revolutionary journal to be published in Texas.

Cotten, judging from his role in the social life of San Felipe, was a genial soul. He was thirty-eight—older than Williamson by thirteen years—when he arrived in Austin's colony on August 10, 1829. Physically he was a big man.

[20]*Ibid.*

[21]*Ibid.*, XXIV, 162.

[22]Barker, "Notes on Early Texas Newspapers, 1819-1836," *Southwestern Historical Quarterly*, XXI, 127.

Signing himself G. B. Cotten, he was asked by an inquiring individual what his initials stood for.

"Why, damn it, can't you see?" replied Cotten. "Great Big Cotten, of course." Williamson and Cotten soon became cronies, Williamson serving as assistant when the paper was launched.[23]

When the *Gazette* was only six issues old on January 23, 1831, Cotten relinquished the editor's role to Williamson. Cotten remained with the paper, according to the inscription under the masthead, as printer and publisher. No one knows why Williamson rose so rapidly, but the chances are that Cotten recognized in the learned young Georgian talents which might be used to popularize the paper. Then, too, Cotten was not overly prosperous. The distinction of the position he gave Williamson may have been a part of Williamson's reward for his labors. Another consideration may have been that Williamson, rising rapidly in public esteem, was in a position to serve the paper's interests with the city council.

Williamson edited the paper for about three months—until May 8—when issue No. 22 announced the resumption of the editorship by Cotten. The issues edited by Williamson offer an insight to his personal philosophy and his sense of humor. In general, they further reveal that Williamson had a fine nose for what then passed for news.

No less an authority than Eugene C. Barker, Austin's biographer, attributes many of the major editorials of the *Gazette* to Austin.[24] During Williamson's conduct of the journal, there is much internal evidence to sustain the assumption. A *Gazette* editorial of March 13, for example, in urging the local ayuntamiento to petition the Mexican government for translations of the laws under which the colonists were to be governed, cites the fact that there were competent Mexican translators. The writer based his opinion upon "the circumstance of our having seen an important decree, published in Saltillo in English, French, and Cas-

[23]Smithwick, *Evolution of a State*, 127-128.

[24]Barker, "Notes on Early Texas Newspapers, 1819-1836," *Southwestern Historical Quarterly*, XXI, 134.

tillion." Austin was then a member of the state legislature of Coahuila and Texas which met at Saltillo. Williamson, at the time the appointed prosecutor for the ayuntamiento, would have been undiplomatic to have belabored his elderly colleagues with an enlightening article on their duties. But Austin was accustomed to lecturing the city fathers without compunction.

As a whole, the editorials published during Williamson's supervision are shrewd, cagey, and placatory when the Mexican government is concerned. One interprets the proposed march of General Manuel de Mier y Terán with 2,100 soldiers into the colony as a measure designed to afford the inhabitants protection from Indian attacks.[25] Another calls for a better translation of the laws, thus implying that any local actions offensive to the Mexicans may have resulted from an imperfect understanding of the laws.[26] Still another praises the activities of Ramón Músquiz, the Texas political chief, who had written a petition to the Mexican government requesting the exemption of Texas from the slave emancipation decree.[27] In general, every action of the Mexican government is interpreted in the best possible light.

How Williamson regarded these editorials, if he was not actually the author of some of them, we have no way of knowing. In later years he was to speak with supreme contempt of the Mexican character, but in 1831 he deferred to the views of Austin, who was more experienced in Mexican relationships and whose support was essential to the success of the paper. Later Austin was one of the owners of the *Mexican Citizen*, which Williamson edited. It is improbable that Austin would have consented to Williamson's editorship of the *Citizen* had his associations with Williamson on the *Gazette* been disagreeable.

The question remains, then, if he was not the *Gazette's* mouthpiece, what did Williamson do as editor? In the first place, he actually wrote some of the editorials—those Austin would have considered light—but the ones which the read-

[25]*Texas Gazette*, March 27, 1830.

[26]*Ibid.*, March 13, 1830.

[27]*Ibid.*, April 17, 1830.

ers, unless they were more ponderous than they are now, enjoyed more than they did the sager ones. It was Williamson who held up to the admiration of the public the account of a surgical feat in which Captain Robert Kuykendall, totally blind for several years from a supposed depression of the brain, was "skillfully operated upon and trepanned" by Dr. Robert Peebles.[28] It was doubtless Williamson who proclaimed the spring of 1830 to have been the most successful immigration period of the colony's existence. "We can not give," he wrote, "the precise number of families that have arrived, . . . but we have no hesitation in saying that the aggregate number of souls may be estimated at *one thousand*."[29] Austin could certainly have given the exact number.

It was also probably Williamson who hailed the establishment of a sawmill as a long step in the direction of progress.[30] After a little coaching by Austin, it would not have been beyond Williamson's capacities to have turned out some of the political editorials.

The bulk of Williamson's duties on the paper, however, were a source of pleasure and amusement. Cotten's role as "publisher" meant that G. B. was the mechanical foreman as well as proprietor. Setting all the type by hand and printing the paper from stone forms were tasks which required hard physical labor. Since Williamson had a "white-collar" job, it was to help Cotten that the editor inserted in the issue of February 6, 1830, an advertisement stating the paper's need of an apprentice, "a lad from 14 to 16 years of age who can read and write and is somewhat acquainted with English grammer."[31]

An article, lifted from an unacknowledged source, sets forth an exaggerated account of an editor's tribulations at the time, but doubtless there was some truth in the description:

[28] *Ibid.*, March 27, 1830.

[29] *Ibid.*

[30] *Ibid.*, March 13, 1830.

[31] *Ibid.*, February 6, 1830.

THE TEXAS GAZETTE.

"DIOS Y LIBERTAD."

PRINTED AND PUBLISHED, WEEKLY, BY GODWIN BROWN COTTEN, AT SIX DOLLARS, PER ANNUM, IN ADVANCE.

VOL. I. AUSTIN, SATURDAY, JAN. 23, 1830. NO. [illegible]

EDITED BY
ROBERT M. WILLIAMSON.

From the Philadelphia Album.

PRIZE ESSAY,

On the Importance of Mental Resources.—"Stand out of my sunshine," said Diogenes to Alexander, when the emperor asked what service he could do him. And, haughty as the philosopher's reply may sound, it implies only the honest independence which every highly gifted, and well balanced mind may feel towards those who merely possess the accidental distinctions of rank and fortune. He must be reduced to pitiful extremities, who needs the condescending smile of the proud, or the heartless flattery of the vain, either to rouse him to exertion, or to warm him into happiness. The power of self excitement, is the most desirable of all attainments; and it is the most rare. To love knowledge only for its usefulness, and thus convert it into a source of happiness—to form and strengthen virtuous dispositions, only for the sake of the deep tranquillity they bring—is a task performed by few. Yet experience constantly proves to us that there are no other means of attaining permanent happiness. He to whom nature is an open volume, where truths of the loftiest import are plainly written, may smile at the thwarting influence of external circumstances; and he who can find, in the fall of an apple, or the hues of the wild-flower, abundant food for reason and for fancy, may well say the officious world, "stand out of my sunshine."

I do not mean that selfishness is bliss, even where enjoyment is of the most dignified kind. An eminence, which placed us above the delightful sympathies of social life, would indeed be unenviable; but surely that which places us above the ever-changing tide of circumstance and opinion is very desirable. The study of nature, more than any other study, tends to produce this internal sunshine, across which the vexatious cares of the world are, at the most, but flitting shadows. Politics, love of gain, ambition of renown,—every thing, in short, which can be acted upon by the passions of mankind, have a corrosive influence on the soul. But nature pursues her course with the same majestic step, the same serene smile, whether a merchant is wrecked, or an empire overthrown. The evil feelings of our nature cannot defile her holy temple. They may indeed close its portals against the restless and the bad; but the radiant goddess is ever within the altar, ready to smile upon those who are pure enough to love her quiet beauty. Ambition may play a mighty game—it may crack the sinews of a whole nation, and make the cringing multitude automaton dancers to its own stormy music.—But sun, and moon, and stars, go forth on their sublime mission, independent of its powers; and its utmost efforts cannot alter the laws which produce the transient glory of the rainbow. Avarice may freeze the genial currents of the soul; but it cannot diminish the pomp of summer, or restrain the prodigality of autumn. Fame may pursue glittering phantoms, until the diseased heart loses all relish for substantial good; but with all its eager aspirations, it can neither change or share the immortality of the minutest atom.

Here then is a sequestered spot where the weary may rest, safe from the whirlwind of its own passions. Here is a mirror made to reflect heaven alone, and which the Proteus forms of human pollution can never darken.

He who has steered his bark, ever so skilfully, through the sea of politics, rarely, if ever, finds a quiet haven. His vexations and his triumphs have all been of an exciting character. Both depended on outward circumstances, over which he had very limited power; and when the precarious breeze had subsided, he finds, too late, that he has lived on the breath of others, and that happiness has no empire within him. And what is the experience of him, who has existed only for wealth,—who has safely moored his richly freighted vessel into the spacious harbour of successful commerce? Does he find that happiness, like modern love, can be bought with gold? You see him hurrying about, purchasing it in small quantities, wherever taste and talent offer it for sale; but the article is too etherial to be baled for future use, and it soon evaporates into the vacuum of his intellectual warehouse. He who has lived for fancy only, will learn that happiness and renown are scarcely speaking acquaintance. Even if he grasps the rainbow he has so madly pursued, he will find its tints fading with every passing cloud, and flickering at every changing ray. Nor is he, who has wasted the energies of his youth in disentangling the knotty skein of controversy, more likely to find the evening of his days cloudless and serene. The demon of dogmatism, or of doubt, will grapple him closely, and convert his early glow of feeling, and elasticity of thought, into rancourous prejudice, or shattered faith. But the deep stream of philosophical knowledge is untinged by one drop of bitterness. Its gurgling waters constantly speak of the heaven from which they flow, and the quiet sound lulls the listening soul into peace.

If age, like infancy, must have its playthings, what can be so dignified as battery and barometer, telescope and prism? Electric power may be increased with less danger than the power of man; it is safer to weigh the air than a neighbor's motives; it is less agitating to fix the eye upon volcanoes in the moon, than upon tempests in the political horizon;—it is far easier to separate and unite the colours in a ray of light, than it is to blend the many coloured hues of truth, turned out of their courses by the three cornered glass of [illegible].

He who drinks freely at the fountain of natural science, will reflect all around him the light which beams on his own tranquil spirit. If the sympathy of heart and intellect is within his reach, he will enjoy it more highly than any other man; but if he is alone in the world, no man can, with so much sincerity, say to the incitements of fame, the glitter of wealth, and the allurements of pleasure, "stand ye out of my sunshine."

The conjugating Dutchman.—We know not where the following story came from, but as it gives a droll picture of a methodical and persevering Dutchman, it may not prove unentertaining. "Two English gentlemen once stepped into a coffee house in Paris, where they observed a tall, odd-looking man, who appeared not to be a native, sitting at one of the tables, and looking around with the most stone-like gravity of countenance, upon every object. Soon after the two Englishmen entered, one of them told the other that a celebrated dwarf had arrived at Paris. At this the grave looking personage above mentioned, opened his mouth and spake: 'I arrive' said he 'thou arrivest, he arrives, we arrive, you arrive, they arrive.' The Englishman whose remarks seemed to have suggested this mysterious speech, stepped up to the stranger, and asked, Did you speak to me, sir? 'I speak,' replied the stranger, 'thou speakest, he speaks, we speak, you speak, they speak.' 'How is this?' [illegible] the Englishman, 'Do you mean to insult me?' The [illegible] replied, 'I insult, thou insultest, [illegible] insults, we insult, you insult, they insult.' 'This [illegible] [illegible]' said the Englishman; 'I will have satisfaction—If you b[illegible] any spirit with your rudeness, come along [illegible].' To this defiance the imperturable stranger replied, 'I come, thou comest, he comes, we [illegible] come, they come,' and thereupon he a[illegible] with great coolness and followed his challenger. In those days, when every gentlemen wore a sword, duels were speedily despatched.—They went into a neighboring alley, and the Englishmen unsheathed his weapon, said to his antagonist, 'Now sir, you must fight me'—'I fight,' replied the other, drawing his sword, 'thou fightest, he fights, we fight,'—here he made a thrust—'you fight, they fight,' and here he disarmed his adversary. 'Well,' said the Englishman, 'you have the best of it, and I hope you are satisfied.' 'I am satisfied,' said the original, sheathing his sword, 'thou art satisfied, he is satisfied, we are satisfied, you are satisfied,—'I am glad every body is satisfied,' said the Englishman, 'but pray leave off quizzing me in this strange manner, and tell me what is your object, if you have any in doing so.' The grave gentleman now for the first time, became intelligible.—'I am a Dutchman,' said he 'and am learning your language. I find it very difficult to remember the peculiarities of the verbs, and my tutor has advised me, in order to fix them in my mind, to conjugate every English verb that I hear spoken. This I have made it a rule to do; and I don't like to have my plans broken in upon while they are in operation, or I would have told you of this before.' The Englishman laughed heartily at this explanation, and invited the conjugating Dutchman to dine with them.—'I will dine,' replied he, 'thou wilt dine, he will dine, we will dine, you will dine, they will dine, we will all dine together." This they accordingly did, and it was difficult to say whether the Dutchman ate or conjugated with the most perseverance.

Nature.—The Empress Josephine used to send from Paris bales of toys, playthings, puppets, &c. to her grand children; among others Napoleon, the little son of Louis, used to receive an ample share while at the Hague. One new year's day, the queen Hortense received an immense case full of the most ingenious toys that the invention of Granchey, and Giroux could devise. Young Napoleon was sitting looking out of a window into the park, and appeared to receive with indifference all the presents spread out before him; he still preserved in gazing down the long avenue that led from his window. The queen disappointed at not seeing him so happy as she expected, asked him if he was not grateful to his grandmama for having taken such pains to procure him all the pretty things before him? 'Oh! yes, mama, I am very grateful;' 'but do not all these pretty playthings amuse you?' 'yes, mama, but—' 'but what?' 'I want very much—something else.' 'Tell me what it is, I promise it you, my boy.'—'Oh mama, but you would not I am sure.' 'Is it money for the poor?'—'Papa gave me that this morning, and it is already distributed; it is—' 'Come, speak out, you know how much I love you, so you may be sure that I would begin the new year with something you would like; come then, my dear darling, what is it you want?'—'Mama, I want to *walk in that pretty mud*, which I see out of the window; that would amuse me more than any thing.'

NOTICE.—The Subscriber respectfully informs his friends, and the Public, that he has lately removed his *SCHOOL*, for its better accommodation, to the Settlement of McNeil, and Westall, in Gulf Prairie. A commodious House, has been erected, very eligibly situated being surrounded by beautiful shades, and but ten miles distant from the Gulf shore, with no timber between to prevent a free circulation of the Sea Breeze, and no stagnant waters near, to render it deleterious to health. Scholars wishing to attend from a distance, can be accommodate with board and washing, in a number of respectable families, from six to ten dollars per month. Terms of Tuition.—Reading and Writing, $2, per month; English Grammar, Geography, Rhetoric, History, Composition, Aritometic, Natural Philosophy, $2,50 cents, per month; Moral Philosophy, Languages, and Mathematics, $4, per month. A strict attention to the interests of the School is faithfully promised, and public patronage humbly solicited by THOMAS J. PILGRIM.

Jan. 15, 1830.—3t.

TO RENT, for the Term of one year, the *PLANTATION*, belonging to the estate of the late Alexander Jackson, on Peach Creek. For terms apply to James Whitesides, Esq. at Austin, or the subscriber on the San Jacinto.

Jan. 15 [illegible] B. JACKSON.

TEXAS GAZETTE, January 23, 1830, Showing Williamson as Editor

A Country Editor—Is one who reads newspapers, selects miscellany, writes articles on all subjects; sets type; reads proof; works at press, folds papers; and sometimes carries them; prints jobs, runs on errands; cuts wood; toats water; talks to all his patrons who call; patiently receives blame for things that never were nor can be done; gets little money; has scarce time or materials to satisfy his hunger, or to enjoy the quiet of "nature's grand restorer" sleep; and esteems himself peculiarly happy, if he is not assaulted and battered, (or bulletted and his ears cut off) by some unprincipled demagogue, who loves puppet shows, and hires the rabble with a treat of corn whiskey, (and that burnt), to vote him into some petty office.—A man who does all this and much more, not here recorded, you well know is rather a busy animal; and as he performs the work of so many different persons, he may justly be supposed their representative, and to have an indisputable right, when speaking of himself, to use the plural number, and to say "we," on all occasions and in all places.[32]

Notwithstanding all this, Williamson's chief duty was to furnish edited copy to the printers. The little three-columned *Texas Gazette*, of course, was severely restricted as to its news sources. Like all American journals of the day it published relatively few accounts of local happenings; what would now appear on the pages devoted to city news was then either ignored or included in the editorial columns. There was practically no distinction between an editorial and a news story. The writer flavored whatever local happenings he wrote about with his own comment—a tendency universally practiced at the time. For example, a *Gazette* story of January 23, 1831, telling of a man named Wilson caught stealing clothing from the store of Cooper and Cheeves and receiving thirty-nine lashes following his conviction, concludes: "This suit of stripes, thus acquired by Wilson, ought to be a caution to others, that have an inclination to clothe themselves in the same way."

But such stories were rare. The main criticism which may be made of most early American papers is that they overlooked local happenings to publish gems of philosophy, devout essays, anecdotes of famous men, short stories, and sage observations upon life in Europe and the United States. The techniques of local reporting were not developed, probably

[32] *Ibid.*, May 15, 1830.

because it was customary to publish edifying or romantic stuff. The pioneer was as much a romanticist in his journalistic preferences as in his choice of poetry. The consequence is that much of Williamson's job was to select from his reading of other newspapers and books such gems of thought and entertainment as might give the reader food for meditation or diversion. Probably the main thing that irked Williamson about the articles from which he selected items for reprinting in the *Gazette* was their consistent veneer of piety.

Williamson clipped his extracts to reprint according to tradition and current taste, but he developed a keen eye for the exciting, the unusual, and above all for the comical. That which would cause a chuckle, or, better still, a roar of laughter seemed invariably to attract him. Doubtless in this he had been tutored by Cotten, but Williamson required little encouragement on things humorous. A few typical instances of the articles he selected to amuse the *Gazette* readers may be noted here.

In the issue of February 6, 1830, from a New York paper, Williamson chose the article: "A Life Saved by Brandy." It tells of a headwaiter returning to his room with a kettle of burning charcoal to protect himself from the cold. Dozing off, he was soon almost suffocated and would have died had not a boarder been in want of brandy and entered the man's room for a key to the liquor cellar. He applied himself to the waiter, and after two hours of exertion the poor fellow was revived. The article argues that if the boarders had been members of a temperance union, the waiter would have died; it concludes, "We therefore pass this life perserved to the credit of spirituous liquor, which deducted from the 30,000 annually lost from the same cause, leaves a balance of 29,999."

Exchange articles depicting the foibles of the legal fraternity were frequently used. From the *New England Farmer* the following doggerel was taken:

An upper and a lower mill
Fell out about their water.
To war they went, that is to law
Resolved to give no quarter.

A lawyer was by each engaged,
And hotly they contended;
When fees grew slack the war they waged
They judged were better ended.

The heavy costs remaining still
Were settled without pother.
One lawyer took the upper mill
The lower took the other.[33]

The story of a judge's verdict in a queer case involving a man named Page charged with the attack of a Mrs. Anne Bray is related from the New York *Mirror*. The jury found the defendant guilty, and a sentence of death was imminent, when the defending lawyer, with the inspiration of genius, persuaded Page to marry Mrs. Bray. When the judge learned of the wedding, he announced there would be no sentence since "Mrs. Anne Bray had changed her asinine name to sweet Anne Page."[34]

Correspondents sending letters to Williamson were certain to have them published if they told a good hunting story. A story signed "The Traveller," an original composition of some local citizen concerning the greed of Turkey Buzzard, should be included in the tall tales of Texas. The author gravely asserts its truth as follows:

The voracious disposition and nature of the "Turkey Buzzard" is well known. Yet some *facts* in relation to this bird, have been within my hearing, since my residence in this province, that must excite the wonder of the brethren of this gormandizing biped, who take their *savory* meal in a more northern latitude. A gentleman of this place, a few weeks ago, being in search of his horses, chanced to kill a fine large buck; and, as the practice is with hunters, in such cases, he suspended the deer between two trees with its lower extremity several feet from the ground. In this situation he left his game and came home. On his return, which was within an hour and a half, he found the bones of his buck where he had left them, but they were completely stripped of hide, flesh, muscle and sinew —dry and smooth "as a hickory pole with the bark off." The hide had fallen to the ground and was not materially injured. The buzzards, who had thus unceremoniously divested these bones of their outward covering, were seated quietly and contentedly on

[33] *Ibid.*, February 13, 1830.

[34] *Ibid.*, November 7, 1829.

the branches of the neighboring trees, picking their teeth, and smiling at the disappointment of the amazed hunter.

On another occasion, a hunter came suddenly upon two deer lying down in the prairie; he fired and killed one—the other fled two or three hundred paces and stopped—the hunter pursued through the high grass and killed this one also—He then looked back to the place where the first deer lay, and saw a number of these buzzards flying and alighting in that direction. Suspecting their purpose he ran to his deer and frightened the plunderers away—they had, however, made good use of their time and devoured most of the carcass. Whereupon, (although truly astonishing, *yet true it is 'tis true*) these winged prowlers of the desert waste, took their course with rapid flight to the place where the other deer lay, and ere our hunter could reach the spot, and contend for his right, notwithstanding he had posted there with all due speed, his hungry adversaries had completely divided the spoil, leaving him the hide and bones. Our adventurer thought this *short work*, without knife or fork—and having some apprehensions that these hereditary proprietors of the prairies of Texas might have a relish, by way of *dessert*, for some of the sweet meat that covered his own joints—he shouldered his rifle and made long strides for his cabin.

These, gentle reader, are not "Fish Stories" nor "Snake Stories" —but real Turkey Buzzard Stories!!![35]

Williamson could not forbear clipping an item relating the sad death of a gentleman named D. C. Fellow, who committed suicide "by putting his head directly in the way of a barrel of vinegar, which was rolled down the steps of his cellar." Neither could he overlook the announcement that "Messrs Moon & Gunn of *The Waterloo Observer*" had sold out. "Mr. Moon had changed his residence and Gunn had gone off," the notice concluded.

Nor did society notices escape his eye. A notice of the marriage in Salem of Mr. Lewis Plum of Newark and Miss Elizabeth P. Lemon of Salem contained the comment, "This is certainly a fruitful match, but we hope none of the little plums will inherit their mother's acidity," and a short quatrain thus wished the couple wedded bliss:

For matrimony sweetens life
So changed the sourest maids become
They drop the Lemon in the wife
And ever after cherish plum.[36]

[35] *Ibid.*, February 27, 1830.
[36] *Ibid.*

Williamson probably was not personally advertising for a wife when he accepted an article in which the writer requested "a little wife who can milk the cow, rock the cradle, sleep at night, work all day—that can discourse music on the cheerful spinning wheel," nor was he alarmed when he used a filler proclaiming, "The present times are too unnatural and luxurious. Our ancestors were simple. No fidgets, fainting, fits, or frightful blues, no painful corns from wearing Chinese shoes."[37] Judging from his future willingness to speak out against executive authority, one would suppose that Williamson's own thinking was more exactly reflected in such an insertion as the following:

> Electric power may be increased with less danger than the power of man; it is safer to weigh the air than a neighbor's motives; it is less agitating to fix the eyes upon volcanoes in the moon than upon tempests in the political horizon.[38]

In general, even after over a hundred years, the reader of the yellowed pages of the *Gazette* feels that it must have been fun being editor of that paper.

During Williamson's editorship, the *Gazette's* motto was "God and Liberty," but Cotten, resuming the editorship early in May, changed it to, "Where light is, there is liberty . . . where liberty is, there is my Country." Under both editors each edition contained four pages, each type page being 9½ by 12 inches. Subscription rates were six dollars per year in cash or produce. Later the six-dollar rate applied only to those who paid in advance. The subscriber who waited until the end of the year to remit had to dig up eight dollars. There were frequent pleas to the reader to consider the travail of the printer and pay the subscription rates promptly.[39]

Williamson's abrupt departure from the staff of the *Gazette* has never been explained, but a simple reason appears probable—Cotten could not afford to pay Williamson's salary. There was no serious break between the two friends, for Cotten announced about seven months later, when he

[37] *Ibid.*, January 30, 1830.

[38] *Ibid.*, January 23, 1830.

[39] A typical example of such a plea appears in *ibid.*, January 30, 1830. See also issue of September 25, 1829.

relinquished his publishing burdens to go into the hotel business, that the proprietorship of the *Gazette* had been "disposed of to R. M. Williamson Esqr . . . whose talents are recognized by all."[40]

The first thing Williamson did in 1831, upon the resumption of his editorship, was to change the name of the *Texas Gazette* to the *Mexican Citizen*. This may have been Austin's idea, for the father of the colony had decided opinions on the proper conduct of a newspaper. Writing to Sam Williams from Saltillo on February 19, Austin declared:

> I am much pleased with the new arrangement of the paper, though I do not like the motto—*Mexico es Mi patria*, would do better, for it will be as much as to say to people abroad, "we have a country and are proud of it, and we are ready and willing to defend her rights," and it will remind our *home folks* whom they belong to. I recommend that [the] motto I have suggested be adopted, or something like it.
>
> That paper must be conducted with great prudence, you have no idea there, what importance is attached even to trifles coming from the *Austinians*.[41]

Williamson's partner in publishing the *Mexican Citizen* was John Aitken, who came to Texas from Pensacola, Florida, where he had been copublisher of the Pensacola *Gazette*.[42] Aitken, judging from the neat appearance of the four issues of the *Mexican Gazette* which have been preserved, was a better printer than Cotten. At any rate, Sam Williams was enthusiastic over the prospects for the new journal. He wrote to Austin:

> You will perceive . . . that a change has been made, and I assure you it is an important one, and must prove beneficial to the country. Williamson's partner, Mr. Aitken, is an excellent workman, and quite a gentleman, and they must succeed.[43]

Too few issues of the handiwork of Williamson and Aitken are available to afford any accurate comparisons of the

[40] *Ibid.*, January 15, 1831.

[41] Austin to S. M. Williams, February 19, 1831, in Barker (ed.), *Austin Papers*, II, 599-600.

[42] Barker, "Notes on Early Texas Newspapers, 1819-1836," *Southwestern Historical Quarterly*, XXI, 136.

[43] *Ibid.*

MEXICAN CITIZEN

Terms.—Six dollars per annum, in advance, if payment is deferred twelve months, eight dollars will be required.

VOL. 1. PRINTED WEEKLY, BY AITKEN & WILLIAMSON. AUSTIN, MARCH 17, 1831. NO. 5.

Advertisements inserted at Two dollars for every 10 lines or less, for the first three insertions, and 50 cents for each continuance.

POETRY.

THE BLIND MOTHER.

Gently, dear mother, here
The Bridge is broken near thee, and below
The waters with a rapid current flow—
Gently, and do not fear.
Lean on me mother—plant thy staff before thee,
For she who loves thee most is watching o'er thee.

The green leaves, as we pass,
Lay their bright fingers on thee unaware,
And by thy side the hazels cluster fair,
And the low forest grass
Grows green and lovely where the woodpaths wind—
Alas, for thee, dear mother, thou art blind!

And nature is all bright;
And the faint grey and crimson of the dawn,
Like folded curtains from the day are drawn;
And evening's dewy light
Quivers in tremulous softness on the sky—
Alas, dear mother, for thy clouded eye!

The moon's new silver shell
Trembles above thee, and the stars float up
In the blue air, and the rich tulip's cup
Is pencilled passing well,
And the swift birds on brilliant pinions flee—
Alas dear mother, that thou canst not see!

And the kind looks of friends
Peruse the sad expression in thy face,
And the child stops amid his bounding race,
And the tall stripling bends
Low to thine ear with duty unforgot—
Alas, dear mother, that thou seest them not!

But thou canst hear—and love
May richly on a human tone be poured,
And the slight cadence of a whispered word
A daughter's love may prove;
And while I speak thou knowest if I smile
Albeit thou dost not see my face the while.

Yes—thou canst hear—and He,
Who on thy sightless eye its darkness hung,
To the attentive ear, like harps, have strung
Heaven, and earth, and sea!
And 't is a lesson in our hearts to know
With but one sense the heart may overflow!

[*Token for* '31.

MISCELLANEOUS.

DUELLING.

From Blackwood's Magazine for September.

I had been invited by young Lord ——, the nobleman mentioned in my former chapter, to spend the latter part of my last college vacation with his lordship at his shooting box in ——shire. As his destined profession was the army, he had already a tolerably numerous retinue of military friends, several of whom were engaged to join us on our arrival at ——! so that we anticipated a very gay and jovial season. Our expectations were not disappointed. What with shooting, fishing, and riding, abroad—billiards, songs, and high *feeding*, at home, our days and nights glided as merrily away as fun and frolic could make them. One of the many schemes of amusement devised by our party was given a sort of military subscribtion ball at the town of———, from which we were distant not more than four or five miles. All my Lord ——'s party, of course, were to be there, as well as several others of his friends, scattered at a little distance from him in the country.

On the appointed day all went off admirably. The little town of —— absolutely reeled beneath the unusual excitement of music, dancing and universal feating. It was in short, a sort of miniature carnival, which the inhabitants, for several reasons, but more especially the melancholy one I am going to mention, have not yet forgotten. It is not very wonderful, that all the rustic beauty of the place was there. Many a village belle was there, in truth, panting and fluttering with delighted agitation at the unusual attentions of their handsome and agreeable partners; for there was not a young military member of our party but merited the epithets. As for myself, being cursed—as I once before hinted—with a very insignificant person, and not the most attractive or communicative manners—being utterly incapable of pouring that soft delicious nonsense—that facinating, searching, small talk, which has stolen so often right through a lady's ear, into the very centre of her heart—being no hand, I say, at this, I contented myself with dancing a set or two with a young woman, whom nobody else seemed inclined to lead out; and continued, for the rest of the evening, more a *spectator* than a partaker of the gaieties of the scene.

There was one girl there—the daughter of a reputable retired tradesman—of singular beauty, and known in the neighbourhood by the name of '*The Blue Bell of* ——.' Of course, she was the object of universal admiration, and literally besieged the whole evening with applications for 'the honor of her hand.' I do not exaggerate, when I say, that, in my opinion, this young woman was perfectly beautiful. Her complexion was of dazzling purity and transparence—her symmetrical features of a placid bust-like character, which, however, would perhaps have been considered insipid, had it not been for a brilliant pair of fine, languishing, soft, blue eyes resembling,

——'blue water-lilies when the breeze
Maketh the crystal waters round them tremble,'

which it was almost madness to look upon. And then her light auburn hair, which hung in loose and easy curls, and settled on each cheek like a soft golden cloud flitting past the moon!

I observed one of our party, a dashing young captain in the Guards, highly connected, and of a handsome and prepossessing person and manners, and a gentleman, of nearly equal personal pretentions, who had been invited from———Hall, his father's seat, to exceed all present in their attentions to sweet Mary——; and as she occasionally smiled on one or other of the rivals, I saw the countenance of either alternately clouded with displeasure. Captain —— was soliciting her hand for the last set—a country dance—when his rival, (whom for distinction's sake I shall call *Trevor* though that, of course is very far from his real name,) stepping up to her, seized her hand, and said, in a rather sharp and quick tone, 'Captain —— she has promised me the last set; I beg, therefore, you will resign her—am I right Miss ———?' he inquired of the girl, who blushingly replied, 'I think I did promise Mr. Trevor—but I would dance with both if I could. Captain you are not angry with me; are you?' she smiled appealingly.

'Certainly not, madam,' he replied, with a peculiar emphasis; and after directing his eye, which kindled like a star, to his more successful rival, left the room. A strong conviction seized me, that even this small and trifling incident would be attended with mischief between those two haughty and undisciplined spirits; for I occasionally saw Mr Trevor turn an inquiring glance around the room, as if in search of Captain ——. I saw he had noticed the haughty frown with which the Captain had retired.

Most of the gentlemen who had accompanied Lord —— to this ball were engaged to dine with him the next Sunday evening. Mr Trevor and the Captain (who, I think, I mentioned, was staying a few days with his lordship) would meet at this party; and I determined to watch their demeanour. Captain ——was at the window, when Mr Trevor, on horseback, attended by his groom, alighted at the door, and on seeing who it was, walked away to another part of the room, with an air of assumed indifference; but I caught his quick and restless glance invariably directed at the door through which Mr Trevor would enter. They saluted each other with civility—rather coldly, I thought—but there was nothing particularly marked in the manner of either. About twenty sat down to dinner. All promised to go off well—for the cooking was admirable—the wines first rate and the conversation brisk and various. Captain —— and Mr Trevor were seated at some distance from each other—the former was my next neighbour. The cloth was not removed till a few minutes after eight—when a desert and a fresh supply of wine were introduced. The late ball of course, was a [illegible] topic of conversation; and after a few of the usual bachelor toasts had been drank with noisy enthusiasm, and we felt all the elevating influence of the wine we had been drinking, Lord —— stood up and said, 'Now, my dear fellows—I have a toast in my eye, that will delight you all—so, bumpers, gentlemen,—bumpers!—up to the very brim,—so make sure your glasses are full—while I propose to you the health of a beautiful—ay, by —! the most beautiful girl we have any of us seen for this year.—Ha! I see all anticipate me—so, to be short—here is the health of Mary——, the Blue Bell of ——!' It was drunk with acclamation. I thought I perceived Captain ——'s hand, however, shake a little, as he lifted the glass to his mouth.

'Who is to return thanks for her?' 'Her favourite beau to be sure.' 'Who is he?' 'Legs—rise—legs—whoever he is!' was shouted, asked, and answered, in a breath. 'Oh—Trevor is the happy man—there's no doubt of that—he monopolized her all the evening—I could not get her hand once,' exclaimed one near Mr Trevor. 'Nor I'—'Nor I'—echoed several. Mr Trevor looked with a delighted triumphant air around the room, and seemed about to rise, but there was a cry—'No—Trevor is not the man—I say Captain ——— is the favourite!' 'Aye—ten to one on the Captain!' roared a young hero of Ascot. 'Stuff—stuff!' muttered the Captain, hurriedly cutting an apple to fritters, and now and then casting a fierce glance towards Mr Trevor. There were many noisy maintainers of both Trevor and the Captain

'Come—come, gentlemen,' said a young Cornish baronet, good humouredly, seeing the two young men appeared to view the affair very seriously—'The best way, since I dare be sworn the girl herself does not know who she likes best, will be to *toss up* who shall be given the credit of her beau?' A loud laugh followed this dull proposal; in which all joined except Trevor and the Captain. The latter had poured out some claret while Sir —— was speaking, and sipped it with an air of assumed carelessness. I observed, however, that he never removed his eye from his glass—and that his face was pale, as if from some strong internal emotion. Mr Trevor's demeanour, however, also indicated considerable embarrassment; but he was older than the Captain, and had much more command of manner. I was amazed, for my own part, to see them take up such an insignificant affair so seriously; but these things generally involve so much of the strong passions of our youthful nature—especially our vanity and jealousy—that, on second thoughts, my surprise abated.

'I certainly fancied you were the favourite, Captain; for I saw her blush with satisfaction when you squeezed her hand,' I whispered. 'You are right, ——,' he answered, with a forced smile,—'I don't think Trevor can have any pretentions to her favour.' The noisiness of the party was now subsiding—and nobody knew why an air of blank embarrassment seemed to pervade all present.

'Upon my honor, gentlemen, this is a vastly silly affair altogether' and quite unworthy such a stir as it has excited,' said Mr Trevor; 'but as so much notice has been taken of it, I cannot help saying, though it is monstrously absurd, perhaps, that I think the beautiful "Blue Bell of ———" is mine—mine alone! I believe I have good ground for saying I am the sole winner of the prize, and have distanced my military competitor,' continued Mr Trevor, turning to Captain ———, with a grim air which was very foreign to his real feelings, 'though his bright eyes—his debonair demeanour—that fascinating *je ne sais quoi* of his.'

'Trevor! Don't be insolent!' exclaimed the Captain sternly, reddening with passion.

'*Insolent!* Captain!—What the deuce do you mean? I'm sure you don't want to quarrel with me—oh, it's impossible. If I have said what was offensive, by———, I did not mean it—and, as we said at Rugby, *indictum puta*—and, there's an end of it. But as for my smart little Blue Bell, I know—am perfectly certain—aye, spite of the Captain's dark looks that I am the happy man. So gentlemen, *de jure* and *de facto*—for her, I return you thanks.' He sate down.—There was so much kindness in his manner, and he had so handsomely disavowed any intentions of hurting Captain———'s feelings that I hoped the young Horspur beside me was quited. Not so, however.

'Trevor,' said he, in a hurried tone' 'you are mistaken—you are, by ———! You don't know what passed between Mary ——— and myself that evening. On my word and honor she told me she wished she could be off her engagement with you.'

'Nonsense! nonsense! She must have said it to amuse you, Captain—she *could* have had no other intention. The very next morning she told me'———

'The very next morning!' shouted Captain ———, why, what the——— could you have wanted with Mary ———the next morning?'

'That is my affair, Captain—not yours. And since you *will* have it out, for your consolation, Mary and I have met every day since!' said Mr Trevor, loudly, even vehemently. He was getting a little *flustered*, as the phrase is, with wine, which he was pouring down glass, after glass, or of course he could never have made such an absurd—such an unusual disclosure.

'Trevor, I must say you act very meanly in telling us,—if it really is so,' said the Captain, with an intensely chagrined and mortified air: 'and—if you intend to ruin that sweet and innocent creature,—I shall take leave to say, that you're a—a—a—curse on it, it will out—a villain,' continued the Captain slowly and deliberately. My heart flew up to my throat, where it fluttered as though it would have choked me. There was an instant and dead silence.

'A *villain*—did you say, Captain! and accuse me of meanness?' inquired Mr Trevor, cooly, while the colour faded from his darkening features; and rising from his chair, he stepped forward and stood nearly opposite to the Captain, with his half-emptied glass in his hand, which, however, was not observed by him he addressed.

'Yes, sir, I *did* say so,' replied the Captain, firmly—'and what then?'

'Then, of course, you will see the necessity of apologizing for it instantly,' rejoined Mr Trevor.

'As I am not in the habit, Mr Trevor, of saying what requires an apology, I have none to offer,' said Captain———, drawing himself up in his chair, and eyeing Mr Trevor with a steady look of composed intrepidity.

'Then, Captain, don't expect me to apologize for *this!*' thundered Mr Trevor, and at the same time hurling his glass, wine and all, at the Captain's head. Part of the wine fell on me, but the glass glanced at the ear of Captain——, and cut it slightly; for he had started aside on seeing Mr Trevor's intention. A mist seemed to cover my eyes, as I saw every one present rising from his chair. The room was, of course, in an uproar, the two who had quarrelled were the only calm persons present. Mr Trevor remained standing on the same spot with his arms folded on his breast; while Captain —— calmly wiped off the stains of wine from his shirt-ruffles and white waistcoat, walked up to Lord——, who was at but a yard or two's distance, and inquired, in a low tone of voice, 'Your Lordship has pistols here, of course? We had better settle this little matter now, and here. Captain V——, you will kindly do what is necessary for me?'

'My dear fellow, be calm! This is really a very absurd quarrel—likely to be a dreadful business, though!' replied his Lordship, with great agitation. 'Come, shake hands, and be friends!—Come, don't let a trumpery dinner brawl lead to bloodshed—and in my house, too!—Make it up like men of sense.

'That your Lordship of course knows, as well as I do, is impossible. Will you Captain V——, be good enough to bring the pistols? You will find them in his lordship's shooting gallery—we had better adjourn there, by the way, eh? inquired the Captain, coolly—he had seen many of these *affairs!*

'Then, bring them—bring them, by all means.' 'In God's name let this quarrel be settled on the spot!' exclaimed—— and ———, and ———.

'We all know they *must* fight—that's as clear as the sun—so the sooner the better!' exclaimed the honorable Mr ———, a hot-headed cousin of Lord ———,

'Eternal curses on the silly slut!' groaned his lordship; 'here will be blood shed for her!—My dear Trevor!' said he, hurry-

MEXICAN CITIZEN, MARCH 17, 1831, SHOWING WILLIAMSON AS CO-EDITOR

Citizen with the *Gazette*. The issue of March 17 carries what may have been the first forerunner in Texas of stories now appearing on modern sports pages. Under the title "Sporting" the article proceeds as follows:

> An old man who was never accused of being a wizard went out with his gun one day to hunt squirrels, accompanied by his son. Before they approached the ground where they expected to find the game, the gun was charged with a severe load and when at last the old gentleman discovered one of the animals, he took a rest and blazed away, expecting to see him fall of course. But not so did it happen, for the gun recoiled with such force as to kick him over. The old man got up and while rubbing the sparks out of his eyes inquired of his son, "Alpha, did I point the right end of the gun at the squirrel?"

In general, Williamson seems to have carried on in the easy, colloquial manner of his old partner, Cotten. In view of the fact that the *Mexican Citizen* ceased publication by December, 1831, one may assume that it was not altogether the success Sam Williams thought it would be. Williamson's relationships with the owners, particularly Austin, probably became a trifle strained as time progressed. Williamson in 1831 had become *sindico procurador* of the ayuntamiento, and as he grew more experienced in the affairs of the community, he probably found Austin's supervisory habits and his policy of conciliating the Mexicans irksome.

On April 6, 1830, the Mexican Congress had enacted a series of laws particularly objectionable to the colonists. They forbade further colonization from the United States and made illegal the further introduction of slaves. Austin, brilliantly and prudently circumventing the intent of the decrees by his own interpretations, was forever watchful lest the newspapers of his colony give offense to the authorities. He thought the best way the people of Texas could give proof of their "fidelity and attachment to Mexico . . . is through the newspaper." With regard to the potential role of the *Citizen* in getting the laws repealed he wrote:

> But what is deemed to be the dignity of this Govt. will not suffer it to move the repeal of the law of 6 April unless some prominent reason can be given for so doing. I wish the people of Texas to give such a reason by proofs of fidelity and attachment to Mexico

and the best way of manifesting these proofs is through the newspaper—Let it be what its title [the *Mexican Citizen*] professes. A *Mexican* defends everything that is Mexican—but in gen[eral] terms, without being in favor of or against political parties.[44]

That Austin was Williamson's friend is instanced by Austin's ordering Sam Williams to give Williamson as many certificate blanks containing Austin's signature—good as passports into Texas despite the Law of April 6, 1830—as Williamson wanted. This showed supreme confidence in Williamson, for Austin had specifically cautioned Williams to be careful with his signature. "Let none know of this but Lessassier and Williamson . . . . Don't put me in the power of the printer or his boys," Austin requested.[45]

But Williamson was not of Austin's temperament. Austin was a man of peace, a realistic compromiser, a statesman. Williamson followed him in the beginning, for both men were intelligent, generous, and honest; but Williamson was never impressed with the Mexican character; ultimately Williamson described the Mexicans as "semi-civilized savages."

Grateful as he was to Austin for his favors, it was with a sense of relief that Williamson retired from newspaper work permanently when Cotten, late in 1831, rebought the paper. No matter how noble his mentor may be, the young man of spirit eventually follows the dictates of his own mind.

[44]Austin to Williams, February 19, 1831, in Barker (ed.), *Austin Papers*, II, 599-600.

[45]Barker, *Life of Stephen F. Austin*, 320.

CHAPTER IV

Leader at Anahuac

Since ayuntamiento officials were not eligible for reelection on consecutive years,[1] Williamson, at the beginning of 1832, relinquished his council office and devoted himself exclusively to the practice of law. For a time he was the partner of Luke Lessassier, but the association was of short duration.[2] Williamson soon established an independent office and began to develop a thriving practice. Among his more famous clients was the bushy-browed Ben Milam, who was killed at the siege of San Antonio in 1835, but who gained a lasting place in the hearts of all fighting Texans by roaring to a dispirited army on the verge of disbanding, "Who will go to San Antonio with old Ben Milam?" Williamson became the agent for Milam's colony, and one of his acts in that capacity was to introduce William Barret Travis for a land grant.[3] It was about this time that Williamson began a friendship with Travis that was to be increasingly cordial and intimate until Travis died in the Alamo. In 1832 Travis was involved in an affair at Anahuac that sent Williamson "cursing in a style peculiar to himself" into the middle of his first scrap with the Mexicans.[4]

The trouble that flared at Anahuac was the first violent expression of the discontent smoldering in the colonies as a result of the Texan disapproval of Mexico's reversal of her liberal policies as expressed in the colonization laws of January 4, 1823, and August 14, 1824. The generous spirit

[1]H. P. N. Gammel (ed.), *Laws of Texas*, I, 167.

[2]*Court Advocate and Texas Public Register* (Brazoria, Texas), September 5, 1832.

[3]John Henry Brown, *History of Texas*, I, 319.

[4]N. D. Labadie, "Narrative of the Anahuac or Opening Campaign of the Texas Revolution," *Texas Almanac for 1859*, p. 31.

of these national laws was specifically codified in the law of colonization of the state of Coahuila and Texas on March 24, 1825. Articles of the state law provided that each family whose occupation was to be farming should be given one labor (177 acres) of land. If the family should also desire to raise stock, twenty-four labors of grazing land, enough to complete a sitio (4,428 acres), should be added to the labor to be used for farming. Should stock raising be the sole occupation, the family would receive "a superfice of grazing land equal to twenty-four million square bars."

Unmarried men were to get the same grant only when they entered upon the estate of matrimony. If they persisted in remaining single, they got only one-fourth of the allotment given to a family. If they married native Mexican women, however, they were to get one-fourth more than a foreign family received.

Charges to the colonists for these grants were extremely slight. The cost of 177 acres of nonirrigable land was $2.50, and for the same amount of irrigable land, $3.50. For 4,428 acres of grazing land only $30 was required, and the money could be paid in three installments beginning on the fourth year after settlement.[5]

These provisions led to the settlement in the various Texas colonies of such a steadily rising stream of emigrants from the United States that by 1833 the Anglo-American population had reached an estimated total of twenty thousand persons, an increase in less than a decade of over 500 per cent.[6] The government of the United States, aware of this movement, made three proposals to the Mexican government, between 1825 and 1829, for the purchase of all or a part of Texas. But these offers were not taken at face value, for even then suspicion of the "Northern Mammoth" disturbed the Latins in their dreams. North American proposals and the growing numerical strength of the Texas colonists led Mexican officials to imagine interventionists or revolutionists lurking everywhere beyond the purple sage breaks of the Nueces River. Lucas Alamán, Mexican secre-

[5]Gammel (ed.), *Laws of Texas*, I, 99 ff.

[6]Barker (ed.), *Readings in Texas History*, 132.

tary of state, saw in the Texas experiment a typical American scheme to annex the territory. He even reduced the American design to what he thought was a formula: exploration, settlement, protest, and diplomatic management. The phase of diplomatic management, he surmised, was commencing.[7]

Both as a result of Alamán's disturbing report and also upon the recommendations of General Manuel de Mier y Terán, a man of considerable experience in Texas, the Mexican Congress reversed its former liberal policies. In the decree of April 6, 1830, the Congress passed the articles which embraced the gist of General Terán's recommendations into a law which legalized the military occupation of Texas and proposed a counter-colonization movement by Mexicans and Europeans and the development of an economic bond between Texas and Mexico by coastal trade. From the Texan viewpoint, the worst features of the articles were the prohibition of further introduction of Anglo-American colonists and the provision for regulating trade by the establishment of military posts and customhouses. When these phases of the law became known, the "ebullition of public feeling" in San Felipe was "fearful."

Austin, as previously indicated, remained cool amid the general uproar, interpreting the law advantageously to his colony. He reasoned that Article 10, which read in part "no change shall be made with respect to colonies already established . . . ," meant that the edict forbidding further North American settlement was not binding on either his colony or Green DeWitt's, since these areas were already established and proceeding according to prior agreements. Williamson doubtless concurred with Austin's interpretation, for, as noted before, he was one of two men who were informed of Austin's plans to issue certificates to emigrants on their way to the colony.

What actually caused physical violence was the Mexican method of administering military control. With unusual promptness for them, the Mexicans showed the earnestness of their resolves by establishing, in 1831, garrisons at Ana-

[7]Edna Rowe, "The Disturbances at Anahuac in 1832," *Quarterly of the Texas State Historical Association*, VI, 266.

huac, Arroyo de la Vaca, Tenoxtitlan, Fort Terán, and Fort Velasco. Troops were also stationed at Nacogdoches, Bexar, and San Felipe.[8]

The Mexican commander at Anahuac was a tyrannical busybody named John Davis Bradburn, a renegade American who had become a colonel in the Mexican army. Even the dispassionate Austin considered him half-crazy. In February, 1831, Bradburn ordered the arrest of J. Francisco Madero, a special land commissioner, who had been instructed by the state governor to issue land titles to certain settlers who, being outside of any colony, were actually squatters, but who had long cultivated the lands and had made considerable improvements to the properties they held. Bradburn had further caused complaints by impressing slaves for labor without compensating their owners, by stirring up discontent among slaves by promising to free them, by disbanding the ayuntamiento and subjecting the territory of Liberty to martial law, by refusing to surrender runaway slaves to their owners, and, above all, by arresting several colonists and holding them for military trial without bail.[9]

Williamson had been aware of Bradburn's presence in Texas since November 6, 1830, when the *Texas Gazette* announced "with great pleasure" the arrival of the officer "in Galveston bay . . . to establish a military post." The newspaper proceeded to point out that all harbors required protection and also intimated that the Mexican soldiers would be useful in repressing the Indians who were troublesome in some sections of the territory. The newspaper interpretation doubtless reflected the view Stephen F. Austin wished to have accepted.[10]

In the spring of 1832 Williamson spent some time in Anahuac on business concerning the land titles being issued to the settlers. Williamson's close friend, Patrick C. Jack, another San Felipe lawyer, was then practicing his profession

[8]*Ibid.*, 267-270.

[9]R. N. Richardson, *Texas, the Lone Star State*, 102.

[10]This reference seems justified in view of Austin's influence on the editorial policies of the *Gazette*. The arrival of Bradburn is announced in the issue of November 6, 1830.

at Anahuac, as was the newcomer, Travis. On May 18, Williamson, having returned to San Felipe, received a disturbing letter from James Lindsay of Anahuac. It was a message calculated to arouse Williamson to a fighting pitch, for it read:

Friend Willey

our friends P. C. Jack & travis are in the Calobouse and entirely prohibited from speaking to any of their friends the Charge that Travis was taken up on was that he gave a letter to the guard some time last week—what was in the letter I know not but tis said that it stated there was one hundred Americans coming here from the u. s. of the North for to take the place. Jack was taken up for nothing at all Such a state of things will not do I think, there fiscal (pacho) is taking Declerations every day in his own house and the boys in the Calabous they understood that you were still on Trinity & sent there *Pug Mouth* prisoner after you when I heard of it I was in hopes that you were but lo when he returned we found that you had left we will know in a day or two what is to be done with our friends. every person has left Town Doct Patrick takes his wife away this afternoon to Cloppers point if you have any knews let me know it by the oppertunity. Yours & c.

James Lindsay.

N B.

The boys are not even allowed to write to there friends as one of the Soldiers were punished the other evening for allowing them to speake to some of there friends and a letter taken away from Hannah the black girl from Travis to Maj. Burnett on some particular business.[11]

Lindsay's request for "knews . . . by the oppertunity" shows that Williamson's friends were expecting some sort of help from him. Williamson's bellicose mood was further inflamed by a letter written six days later by the more prolific and vigorous Monroe Edwards, also of Anahuac.

Edwards gave a specific reason for the arrest of Travis by informing Williamson that while Bradburn was in a state of great excitement over the prospect of an invasion he received a letter purportedly "from a creature by the name of McLaughlin, a well known Sycophant of Bradburn's." This letter must have been extremely uncomplimentary and sarcastic. When Bradburn discovered it to be a hoax, he, "being

[11]James Lindsay to R. M. Williamson, May 18, 1832, in Gulick (ed.), *Lamar Papers*, I, 90.

very much martafied," arrested Travis as the suspected author. P. C. Jack, Edwards continued, went to Bradburn in an attempt to learn his intentions as to Travis. During the interview some heated words took place, and, as a result, Bradburn angrily ordered Jack "to the Calibouse forth with." Although Colonel James Morgan offered all his property as security, Bradburn refused bail for the prisoners.

Edwards further disclosed that he had been in correspondence with the pair since their arrest until "today [May 24] when a letter was detected which they had written to me." In this letter, the prisoners directed Edwards to convey a message to Austin's colonists soliciting their rescue from "the claws of thirty rascally and convict soldiers."[12] As a consequence of the interception of the letter, Edwards was fearful of his own immediate future, for he said:

> Happyly i in my corrispondence with them assumed a ficticious name and by that means eluded immediate imprisonment. An investigation is now going on and I am strongly suspisioned. they can produce no evidence against me but I have no doubt I shall be a tenant of the Calibose before 10 o'clock tomorrow.

Williamson's temper boiled as he read on. He learned of the impending fate of his friends and the spiritless inactivity of the settlers of Anahuac. Edwards continued as follows:

> It is the avowed purpose of Bradburn to send these two young men to Matamoris immediately & for what!—Mearly because they have incured the displeasure of a damed insignificant Military despot who without any evidence or any good grounds for what they are suspected percecutes them to the utmost of his power.
>
> I have made several vain attempts to arrouse the feelings of the people of this place and neighborhood in their behalf but am sorry to say that there is not more than 5 persons in this place that can be depended upon. It is generally believed here that they will be sent to Mattomoris in a very short time and if there friends do not releas them they must inevitably go. I have made several propositions to a few persons here to releas them by attacking and dispercing the guard but I can not find numbers sufficient to attempt such an enterprise.

[12]Rowe, "Disturbances at Anahuac," *Quarterly of the Texas State Historical Association*, VI, 281.

In closing, Edwards stated that he did not intend to "run off" and requested Williamson to act as his feelings dictated.[13]

Williamson acted immediately. D. L. Kokernot, who commanded the schooner, *The Red River*, one of "a fleet" of three Texas vessels which blockaded the town in sympathy with the prisoners, said that as soon as Williamson learned Bradburn's plan to send the prisoners to Mexico the young lawyer recruited a company of fighting men to oppose Bradburn. Here is Kokernot's version of Williamson's venture:

> The brave and noble Willie went to work to raise a company to liberate our friends, we having first gone to Bradburn to see if he would release them; but he told us he had chartered a schooner to send them as prisoners to Matamoras; whereupon a company of about forty was organized under the command of Willie. That night Bradburn put the men aboard of a schooner to send them off, as he had threatened to do; but Willie, with his command of brave men was out on the morning following, determined to rescue our friends or die in the attempt.[14]

As soon as Williamson arrived in Anahuac, he made two unsuccessful attempts to interview Bradburn, but a third effort, made a few hours later, was successful. In company with Dr. N. D. Labadie, surgeon to Bradburn's forces, Williamson confronted the petty commander. As the conversation progressed, according to Dr. Labadie, Williamson became very heated and swore "in a manner peculiar to himself." He shouted to Bradburn, "Dr. Labadie and I are determined that Jack shall have his liberty."

Bradburn was on the point of making a noncommittal answer, when Williamson interrupted him by pounding his fists and roaring: "I tell you, sir, Jack must come on shore or you or I will be a dead man by tomorrow. I tell you, Colonel, that all hell will not stop me. Dr. Labadie is a witness that what I say is true. There are many more besides us to make my words good. Blood will flow if Jack is not released by tomorrow."

The astounded Bradburn paled, but he managed to mum-

[13]Monroe Edwards to R. M. Williamson, May 24, 1832, in Gulick (ed.), *Lamar Papers*, I, 91-92.

[14]D. L. Kokernot in Galveston *Daily News*, May 12, 1878.

ble that he had given orders that the prisoners were to be brought ashore and freed by three o'clock in the afternoon. Williamson and Dr. Labadie then bowed haughtily and stalked out.[15]

They immediately galloped to the landing, close to the prison ship, where presently Travis and Jack were brought ashore. The triumphant Texans gave "three hearty cheers" and, after a little back slapping, dispersed, Williamson and his force soon returning to San Felipe. But Bradburn was not finished. The armed invaders had hardly left Anahuac before he again arrested Travis and Jack and jailed Lindsay for good measure. Warrants were also issued for the arrest of Monroe Edwards. Williamson's wrath, when he learned of Bradburn's duplicity, was so violent that he rattled the rafters with his explosive rage. Other recent belligerents of San Felipe, also in no mood to be trifled with, soon perfected "a plan of operations." First of all, men had to be recruited, and Williamson was selected to gather them in from the settlements of Mill's Creek, Coles on the Goliad road, and Washington.[16] Making short work of his assignment, on June 4 he wrote a passionate appeal to the citizens of Brazoria, urging them to rally out for a forced march "to the theater . . . of misfortunes." He announced his intention of leaving San Felipe by "light in the morning," and revealed that a group of men would assemble at Lynch's ferry on the San Jacinto River on Tuesday evening. His closing words show that Williamson fully realized the seriousness of the undertaking. He declared:

> I consider it of the utmost importance that on this occasion our Brassoria turn out strong. We have been solicited to do so not only by the unfortunate and suffering victims of the wrath of a Military despot shut up in the Calabose and crowded upon by a host of rable convicts thieving from them the comforts their friends may contrive to them but we have been invited to cooperate with the citizens of our Colony in general to purchase their release—Let us effect it if we can—and do it we can; if their is unanimity

[15]Labadie, "Narrative of the Anahuac or Opening Campaign," *Texas Almanac for 1859*, p. 31.

[16]F. W. Johnson, "Further Account by Col. F. W. Johnson of the First Breaking out of Hostilities," *Texas Almanac for 1859*, p. 37.

—if we make the attempt and fail we are done forever and therefore I repeat my solicitude and anxiety that on this occasion WE TURN OUT STRONG—I shall Join you, Fellow citizens of Brassoria, at the point designated.[17]

After consulting the alcalde and other citizens of Liberty, Texan leaders decided to make their headquarters at Minchey's, a few miles below Liberty. Recruits coming in from Austin's colony were directed to Minchey's as soon as they arrived in Liberty. After a force of about sixty men had gathered, the insurgents voted to march on Anahuac. Francis W. Johnson, the erstwhile alcalde of San Felipe, was elected commander of the forces. Soon an advance guard of sixteen men, commanded by Williamson, rode forward. Williamson's patrol had not gone more than half the distance to Turtle Bayou when it surprised and captured a party of Mexican cavalry without firing a gun. Securing their prisoners, the Texans camped at White's Crossing on the west side of Turtle Bayou for the night. The next morning they resumed the route and by midday were in sight of Anahuac. When the main force arrived, the leaders appointed a committee—of which Williamson, thoroughly disgusted with the idea of further conversation with Mexican officials, was not a member—to confer with Bradburn. The committeemen were conducted through the Mexican guard to the fort, where Bradburn informed them he was no longer the commander but that Colonel Suberan, lately arrived, was the new chief official. This gentleman was present at the parley, but the committee was unable to obtain any satisfaction from him. Thereupon they informed the Mexican officers that the Texans "would try what virtue there was in force."

When the committee returned to camp, the news they conveyed brought a roar of anger from the insurgents, who readied their long rifles. Next day some skirmishing took place between Texan and Mexican horsemen, but no casualties resulted. The Texans made several feints in an attempt to draw the Mexicans out of the fort, but Bradburn was too wily to risk a rough-and-tumble fight with the invaders.

[17]Gulick (ed.), *Lamar Papers*, I, 92-93.

On the third day, Commander Johnson decided to surround the Mexican garrison. On the opposite riverbank, earth mounds afforded excellent protection from the fort's fire. Just as the Texans were preparing to take positions there, an American, John A. Williams, rode up and informed them that Colonel Suberan was not in sympathy with the policy of the Mexican government. Williams said that the colonel, a follower of the rebel, General Antonio López de Santa Anna, had said the present troubles could be "amicably and satisfactorily arranged through commissioners." Accordingly, Captains John Austin, Hugh B. Johnson, and Wyly Martin were sent to converse with Suberan.

In the parley the Mexican officers agreed to exchange Travis and Jack and all other American prisoners for the Mexican prisoners whom Williamson had captured. The Mexican captives were to be released first, and the Texans were to retire to Taylor White's, on Turtle Bayou, a distance of about six miles from Anahuac. On the next day the Texan prisoners would be delivered to their friends.

The rank and file of the Texans greeted the announcement of these terms with skeptical derision. It required all the oratorical skill of Captain Martin to answer the consensus that it would be bad business to surrender the Mexicans before the Texans were set free. But Martin argued that a Mexican officer "wearing an epaulet" would not be "base enough to forfeit his plighted honor," and in deference to him, the Texans elected to abide by the agreements.

The majority of the Texans consequently wheeled about and set off for Turtle Bayou, while a small detachment remained with the commissioners. Williamson was with the main force at Turtle Bayou the next morning when the Texans heard firing from the direction of Anahuac. Soon a rider galloped up to inform the men that the Mexicans had repudiated the agreement and were marching out to attack the commissioners and their guards.

Once again the indignant Texans hurried back toward Anahuac. They had galloped about two miles when they met the commissioners and their party "retreating in good order." Commissioner Austin said he had received a letter from Bradburn declaring the treaty had been violated by the Texans. Bradburn threatened, as a consequence, to pillage the countryside.[18]

In the opinion of Williamson, Bradburn's actions were typical of the Mexican character. Writing of the affair in later years, he asserted: "Here let the historian observe the first treaty of Mexicans and Texans broken, and point out one that has been subsequently made that has been inviolate by the Mexicans."[19]

Bradburn, after abrogating the treaty, marched his men into the positions formerly accessible to the Texans and brought out his artillery to cover his lines. The Texans, seeing their disadvantage, returned to Turtle Bayou.[20] There on June 13, a consultation adopted the "Turtle Bayou Resolutions." At this meeting, Williamson, as one of a committee of seven which drafted the terms, shared in a diplomatic move as clever as any ever conceived in the Texas colonies. It was well known to the Texans that Mexican reinforcements were en route to Anahuac. A pitched battle with the forces Bradburn had in Anahuac might be won, but, the insurgents reasoned, they probably could not defeat all the Mexican forces which were in, or might be sent, to Texas. In Mexico the tottering government of President Anastacio Bustamente was in the throes of a revolution led by General Santa Anna, who was proclaiming liberal policies.[21] A declaration of sympathy with the liberalism of Santa Anna and a denial of the intent to revolt from Mexico would obviously be a fine move, if Santa Anna won.

As a consequence, four declarations were drafted and signed by the seven committeemen. Williamson's signature was last, a fact which may indicate that he wrote the document. The resolutions were read to the army by Luke Lessassier, unanimously adopted, and sent in a letter to

[18]Johnson, "First Breaking Out of Hostilities," *Texas Almanac for 1859*, p. 37.

[19]R. M. Williamson, "Historical Notes," in Gulick (ed.), *Lamar Papers*, V, 373.

[20]Johnson, "First Breaking Out of Hostilities," *Texas Almanac for 1859*, p. 38.

[21]Richardson, *Texas, the Lone Star State*, 104.

Colonel José Antonio Mexia of Santa Anna's army. They read:

RESOLVED That we view with feelings of the deepest regret, the manner in which the Gover't of the Republic of Mexico is administered by the present dynasty—The repeated violations of the constitution—the total disregard of the law—the entire prostration of the civil authority; and the substitution in the stead of a military despotism, are grievances of such a character, as to arouse the feelings of every freeman, and impel him to resistance—

RESOLVED That we view with feelings of the deepest interest and solicitude, the firm and manly resistance, which is made by the highly talented and distinguished Chieftain—General Santa Anna, to the numberless Incroachments and infractions, which have been made by the present administration, upon the constitution and law of our adopted and beloved country.

RESOLVED That as freemen devoted to a correct interpretation, and enforcement of the Constitution, and laws, according to their true Spirit—We pledge our lives and fortunes in support of the same, and of the distinguished leader, who is now so gallantly fighting in defence of Civil liberty.

RESOLVED That the people of Texas be invited to cooperate with us, in support of the principles incorporated in the foregoing resolutions.—[22]

Williamson regarded the expressions with pride. "Copies," he wrote, "were published and circulated throughout Mexico. They produced a powerful effect in re-establishing order and the constitution throughout the country." In the letter to Mexia which enclosed the resolutions the committee also set forth a detailed account of the trouble between the Texans and Colonel Bradburn.[23]

But the support of Santa Anna could not bring immediate results. Meanwhile Bradburn was supreme at Anahuac, and the prisoners still chafed in jail. Accordingly, in the evening the insurgents moved up to Dunman's residence, where a consultation decided to send a large detachment under Captain John Austin to Brazoria for the purpose of securing artillery and munitions to be brought by boat on the Brazos to a point near Anahuac. A small group was left to watch the Mexicans and to strike a blow at them if a favorable oppor-

[22]Gulick (ed.), *Lamar Papers*, I, 142-143.

[23]*Ibid.*, V, 373.

tunity came. Williamson and Colonel William Pettus were sent to San Felipe to solicit reinforcements.

They lost no time, for in a few days the force encamped near Anahuac was joined by Captain Abner Kuykendall and a company of from forty to sixty men from Austin's colony. Smaller parties trickled in daily. The Texans were now waiting only for the arrival of their cannon from Brazoria to resume the offensive.[24]

But once again a series of parleys prevented bloodshed. By this time Bradburn's frantic appeals for reinforcements had brought to Anahuac a detachment of Mexican troops under the command of Colonel José de las Piedras from Nacogdoches. Commissioners from Piedras visited the Texans and arranged a conference to be held within the next few days.[25]

Meanwhile, with the enemy in their front and rear, the Texans moved to Moss Spring to improve their position. The first conference between the Texan commissioners and Colonel Piedras accomplished nothing, but the Mexican colonel was warned that any movement of his forces would be considered as an act of hostility. After arranging for another conference, the Texans then moved to a position near Martin's to prevent a junction of the forces of Piedras and Bradburn.[26] At this time they received news by rider of a splendid victory by their comrades at Velasco, where Austin's detachment had given battle to the forces of Colonel Domingo de Ugartechea, who had attempted to prevent the vessel bearing the cannon for Anahuac from sailing. A nip-and-tuck scrap in which both sides sustained casualties continued until Urgartechea ran out of ammunition. Then he surrendered, agreeing to withdraw his troops from Texas.[27] By this time Williamson was back with the forces at Anahuac.

[24]Rowe, "Disturbances at Anahuac," *Quarterly of the Texas State Historical Association*, VI, 288.

[25]Johnson, "First Breaking Out of Hostilities," *Texas Almanac for 1859*, p. 39.

[26]*Ibid.*

[27]Rowe, "Disturbances at Anahuac," *Quarterly of the Texas State Historical Association*, VI, 292.

While recruiting, he had kept in touch with John Austin's progress and had reported that a battle at Velasco was inevitable.[28]

News of the outcome of the Velasco fight may have had some influence on the decisions of Colonel Piedras, for after a few conferences, he agreed to release the Texan prisoners, to pay for the private property Bradburn had commandeered, and to attempt to relieve Bradburn of his command. The colonel kept his word. Amid great jubilation, Travis and Jack were released, and Bradburn was persuaded to resign. Fearing violence at the hands of the Texans, he soon made his way in ignominy to Louisiana. The Mexican troops in the garrison at Anahuac declared for Santa Anna; and a few days later, under the command of Suberan, they sailed to join their new chieftain in Mexico.[29]

The war against Bradburn thus concluded, the victorious Texans returned to their homes. Their actions, however, were not fully approved by all the colonists. Indeed, a considerable number highly disapproved them. While the insurgents were encamped before Anahuac, an ayuntamiento meeting held in San Felipe, attended by sixty citizens, adopted a resolution expressing "regret, sorrow, disapprobation for the imprudent and precipitate action." The insurrectionists were urged to return to their homes so that civil authorities could adjudicate matters. Similar disapproval was expressed at meetings held at Bastrop, the lower Colorado and Lavaca settlements, the lower Brazos, Liberty, and Ais. During the campaign, the armed forces had encountered active opposition from Texan colonists near Anahuac. Only at Brazoria did a convocation sustain the actions of the belligerents.

The insurgent leader, William H. Wharton, was vigorous in his denunciation of the opposition. He railed at "the tory spirit" of San Felipe and said the colonists there were opposing the insurgents as much as they opposed the Mexicans.

[28]Johnson, "First Breaking Out of Hostilities," *Texas Almanac for 1859*, p. 39.

[29]Rowe, "Disturbances at Anahuac," *Quarterly of the Texas State Historical Association*, VI, 297.

He wrote that he would like to spend a few days in the town to "reason some of these fellows into sense and cowhide the balance into rags."[30]

During the excitement, Stephen F. Austin was in Mexico. When the news of the disturbance reached him, he reacted calmly. He wrote to Sam Williams: "Pray try and keep the people there from any acts that may be construed into opposition against the government, for that will turn all parties against us," and he also wrote to Mexican officials condemning Bradburn and interpreting the actions of the insurgents as resentment against that official rather than as disloyalty to the Mexican government.[31] A little later, however, Austin expressed the opinion that it would be better for the Texans to uphold no party in the Mexican civil war.[32] This, of course, was a view which did not coincide with the sentiments of the Turtle Bayou Resolutions; but since Austin had always urged allegiance to the Mexican constitution he maintained, by his advocacy of neutrality, a position which would allow him to deal with either party in power. Had Santa Anna lost, the insurgents, by contrast, would certainly have found themselves in a precarious situation.

But fortune sometimes favors the bold. On July 2, loyalist General Terán committed suicide.[33] Everywhere the forces of Santa Anna were proving victorious. Colonel José Antonio Mexia, of Santa Anna's staff, deciding to study the situation in Texas at first hand, arrived, on July 16, at the mouth of the Brazos, where he conferred with Captain John Austin, the victor of Velasco. Following the conference, Colonel Mexia issued a statement assuring the colonists of his cooperation and unity with them if they were sincere in their allegiance to the principles of Santa Anna's party.[34]

Colonel Mexia's statement was a mighty prop for the insurgents, for, as we have seen, but for the outcome of the struggle in Mexico in favor of Santa Anna, the invaders of

[30]Barker, *Life of Stephen F. Austin*, 389.

[31]*Ibid.*, 395 ff.

[32]*Ibid.*, 399.

[33]*Ibid.*

[34]*Ibid.*, 400.

Anahuac would have been considered by the Mexican government, even as they were already regarded by a considerable number of Texans, as a group of lawless ruffians. Now they could assert themselves as patriots. The difference in attitude between the insurgents and the colonists who shaped the various ayuntamiento resolutions was significant. It indicated a cleavage which later would divide the Texans into members of "war" and "peace" parties, and incidentally it identified Williamson as a man who would be an outstanding member of the war party.

When Williamson got home from the Anahuac campaign, he viewed with contempt the opposition of his erstwhile friends in San Felipe. The scorn of Williamson's associates in fiery Brazoria mounted so high that Sam Williams and Thomas Jefferson Chambers, who had been instrumental in effecting the San Felipe resolutions of disapproval, were hanged in effigy.[35]

Williamson was a prime mover of the Brazorians, probably not in their gesture toward Williams and Chambers, but certainly with regard to resistance of whatever Mexican authority he considered noxious. At Nacogdoches, Colonel Piedras, following the affair at Anahuac, still commanded a garrison of troops loyal to the Mexican government which Santa Anna was rapidly dissolving. Piedras's concessions to Texans at Anahuac may have been dictated more by expediency than sympathy, for upon his return to Nacogdoches he set about recruiting Indians to supplement his forces. The colonel's activities were regarded by Williamson as designed for revenge upon the Austin colonists and the settlers at Liberty. Hence, on August 2, Williamson once again called the Brazorians to arms. This time the villain was Colonel Piedras and the enemy the federal garrison at Nacogdoches. Williamson thus sounded the alarm:

> It will be seen by reference to the inclosed documents that; *you* who have ever been attentive, to the cries of the weak and opressed; are *again* summoned to the Scenes of difficulty, which at present surround your Fellow Citizens of the Districts of Nacogdoches and Aysh, who have espoused the cause of civil liberty as guaranteed

[35] *Ibid.*, 403.

to them by the constitution and Laws of our adopted country.

Since the return of Col. Piedras to Nacogdoches, his every movement seems to have been characteristic of mortification at, and revenge towards the inhabitants of Austins Colony and Liberty who he says compelled him to treat with them on their own terms near Anahuac. He has consequently ever since, been Studiously occupied in converting over, and making allies, of the different tribes of Indians evidently with the view of making a fatal and final blow at the people of that Section of Texas. His language is "let every Son of God that is capable of bearing arms and who will array himself in our lines be equipped": Thus inviting and receiving under his banners the blood thirsty savage whose mode of warfare knows no distinction in age or Sex, and whose courage is alone commensurate with their prospects of plundering their mangled and butchered enemies. To check this monster then Brazorians, in his contemplated *inhuman career*; I consider the next interprise before you; and shall indulge the pleasing hope that on *this*, as on all other occasions a goodly number of you will be found at your posts, ready to share *with the friends of Santa Ana* the honor and glory of routing this *unholy alliance of deluded Mexicans* and *merciless* Indians—I am your friend

Williamson

Col. Austin left San Felipe on Tuesday last for Anahuac without any knowledge of the Situation of affairs at Nacogdoches. The information inclosed came to hand this morning by express, only three days from Nacogdoches and copies have been made out and despatched to him wherever he may be found—A Company will be immediately organized in this place holding themselves in readiness to march in a few hours warning, after hearing from Austin who it is supposed can inform us, whether Col. Mejia will need our services or not, or whether we can arrive in time to act in concert with him or not. Austin is instructed to send an express to you to inform you what may be wanting at the same time he despatches one for this place. You will all, therefore, see the propriety of holding yourselves in readiness in case you should be called on, which reason has influenced me to favor you with all the information I have on the subject—I remain your friend and obt. servant.

R. M. Williamson[36]

But the services of the Brazorians were not needed in Nacogdoches, for after a sharp battle there on July 31, between the forces of Piedras and colonials loyal to Santa Anna, Piedras was defeated and forced to withdraw from the garrison. His soldiers then declared for Santa Anna and

[36]Gulick (ed.), *Lamar Papers*, I, 146 ff.

soon were evacuated from the country.[37] Williamson, exhorting the Brazorians on August 2, evidently had not received the latest information from Nacogdoches.

A final postscript which Williamson added to his appeal shows that he had broken publicly with Stephen F. Austin. It reads: "P. S. You shall have information of what we do hear, should Austin happen to neglect you. We must raise [?] that fellow off the land if he don't come to."[38]

What Williamson meant by the sentence, "We must raise that fellow off the land if he don't come to" is unknown, but probably it was written in a mood of resentment at Austin's habitual policy of placating the Mexicans. Probably it meant merely to say that should Austin continue to appease the Mexicans, the colonists must not listen to him. Flushed by the triumph at Anahuac, Williamson had youth's typical impatience. Only twenty-eight at the time, his season was spring. Later events show that the hostility Williamson's sentence reveals toward Austin was not to be a permanent attitude toward an old friend. After the early years in San Felipe, Williamson never approved Austin's Mexican policy, as a reflection he wrote long after the Anahuac disturbance had been forgotten plainly shows:

> Recourse was had to the State Authorities to check these high-handed measures—and the people were advised by their representative S. F. Austin, that there was no remedy but "to conciliate the military." Worn out with repeated and daily outrages, the people resolved to remedy their wrongs by force.[39]

Yet when, in 1835, Austin favored war with Mexico, he was characterized by Williamson as "this distinguished citizen" and commended for assuming a decisive tone "unknown to him before."[40]

[37]Barker, *Life of Stephen F. Austin*, 400.

[38]Gulick (ed.), *Lamar Papers*, I, 146 ff.

[39]R. M. Williamson, "Historical Notes," in Gulick (ed.), *Lamar Papers*, V, 372.

[40]*Ibid.*, 374.

CHAPTER V

Alcalde under the Mexican Government

After the excitement at Anahuac subsided and Williamson returned to his practice of law, he was finished forever with all enthusiasm for things Mexican. However composed he might become as the violence of the nervous days of 1832 receded in memory, he kept henceforth a wary eye upon his superiors in the government. For the next two years Texas was to enjoy a period of comparative peace, during which Williamson, already experienced in colonial affairs, rapidly developed the maturity and skill that were to make him one of the leaders of the coming revolution. He had a vital role in the Convention of 1833, developed a prosperous legal business, and became the alcalde of San Felipe, the highest political office in the community.

Shortly after the Anahuac disturbance, the San Felipe ayuntamiento issued a call for a meeting of representative citizens on October 1 to draft a list of reforms to be asked of the Mexican government. This convention requested separation of Texas from Coahuila, repeal of the law forbidding further land grants to citizens of the United States, extension of tariff exemptions, protection from Indian attacks, reform of the judicial system, and changes in other matters of less urgent concern. William H. Wharton and Rafael Manchola were named to present the petitions to officials in Mexico.

All this labor, however, was soon frustrated by the reactions of the officials at Bexar. Ramón Músquiz, the political chief there, concurred with his associates that petitions to the federal government should stem from regular or official channels—ayuntamiento declarations. Furthermore, the Bexar leaders, although agreeing in substance with the requests, were inclined to be hesitant about memorializing the government since, as they pointed out, the recent Turtle Bayou Declarations endorsing Santa Anna had deeply offended the Bustamente government, then in power. In consequence Wharton and Manchola did not make their contemplated trip, and the convention's desires thus remained officially unexpressed.[1]

To encourage the Bexar leaders to take the initiative in presenting the reform program, Stephen F. Austin, in the fall of 1832, toured the colonies as an advocate of the measures; but during his absence from San Felipe aggressive members of a central committee appointed by the recent convention, issued, without Austin's knowledge or consent, a call for another assembly. Despite Austin's opposition when he learned of the proposal, the second parley gathered, more than fifty delegates strong, in San Felipe on April 1, 1833. The selection of Wharton, who had been one of the meeting's instigators, to be president rather than Austin signified the beginning of an active coalition, including Williamson, soon to be known as the war party.

Williamson had not been an official delegate to the convention of 1832, his late adventure at Anahuac having lost for him at the time the support of many San Felipe citizens. But in 1833 he was a member of a convention committee which drafted a constitution for the proposed separate state of Texas. The committee chairman was a delegate from Nacogdoches and a recent arrival in Texas, Sam Houston. The document drafted by Williamson and his associates was clearly an Anglo-American rather than a Spanish instrument. It incorporated a bicameral legislature, which was required to elect judiciary officials subject to removal by legislative vote, and provided for a governor who would be elected for a two-year term and who would not serve more than four in a given period of six years. The governor's veto could be overridden by a majority of the legislature.

In addition to reiterating the requests of the meeting of 1832, the later convention petitioned repeal of the tariff provisions of the law of April 6, 1830, and asked the establishment of an improved mail service.[2]

[1]Barker, *Life of Stephen F. Austin*, 404-408.

[2]*Ibid.*, 409 ff.

Partly as a balm to Austin's injured feelings but more certainly out of respect to his superior ability in dealing with the Mexicans, the convention named Austin as one of three delegates to present the constitution and the convention's requests to the national government for approval. Had Austin been petty or vindictive, he might with perfect justice have declined the assignment with the strong language an ordinary human being would have used in reply. But the welfare of Texas transcended all things else in Austin's mind, and with an objectivity somewhat magnificent, the tired empresario began his labors in behalf of the convention. For these, he was to be imprisoned for nearly two years, and his fate was to be of grave concern to Williamson, who in 1834 became the alcalde of San Felipe.

Williamson's elevation to the highest office within the gift of the local voters came at a time when his law practice was flourishing and when he was more consistently occupied in courtroom pleading and legal business than at any other period of his career. The diary of Travis, settled as a lawyer in San Felipe following the Anahuac incident and by 1833 both a legal associate and a close friend of Williamson, indicates the surprising amount of legal business transacted in San Felipe a few years before the revolution.

By 1834 the department of Brazos, which contained the San Felipe district, had a population estimated at eight thousand, the local district being credited with two thousand persons.[3] At the time, in addition to Williamson, Lessassier, and Travis, such competent lawyers as Wyly Martin, Thomas J. Chambers, Moseley Baker, Ira Lewis, and the Jack brothers, Patrick and William, were all profitably engaged in their practices at San Felipe. Rent for an office even when combined with a lodging was not high, Travis paying $8.33 per month and getting for the sum a promise from his landlord, Dr. J. B. Miller, to put a new roof on the house and a fence around the stable.

Drawing up land deeds was probably the most prolific source of business, but, in addition, innumerable civil suits

[3]Homer S. Thrall, *A Pictorial History of Texas*, 172. The figures are based on General Juan N. Almonte's estimate.

on debt collection, contract violation, and property line disputes, as well as criminal cases were filed. Williamson, better known than Travis at the time, frequently directed clients to his friend, and occasionally he employed Travis to assist him in important cases. For example, as chief attorney for William H. Wharton in a suit against William T. Austin and others, Williamson engaged Travis as an assistant and paid him a fee of fifty dollars. In "favor his claim to Maylam's [Milam's] colony," Williamson also retained Travis as his personal attorney and promised him a league of land for his work. Later Williamson hired his friend to represent the Alabama Company "about the 11 league grants" in case Sterling C. Robertson should "attack" them.[4]

The studies of Miss Ruby Mixon, the outstanding contemporary authority on Travis, reveal considerable information on the fees colonial lawyers usually charged. If Travis was a representative example, lawyers asked as much as two dollars for drawing up a power of attorney, ten dollars for writing a bill of sale in Spanish, twenty dollars for writing a will, and twenty-five dollars for representing a client in a minor criminal case. In a damage suit involving a sum of fifteen thousand dollars, Travis once received a fee of five hundred dollars.

In the fall of 1833 Travis was engaged to represent fifty-seven clients at the forthcoming court term, and by the following spring his business was so good that he hired a young man to assist in paper work. Williamson, sometimes sending business to Travis, was equally busy. But neither lawyer had instincts of thrift. So far as money was concerned, it was "easy come, easy go" with them. When out of cash, they borrowed small sums from each other. On October 5, 1833, when Williamson announced his candidacy for alcalde, he borrowed five dollars from Travis, and a little later he again borrowed the same amount. On November 1, he paid Travis six dollars on account. Subsequently Travis got possession of a note which Williamson had made to Thomas Davis for twenty-two dollars by giving Davis a note against Abram Roberts for twenty-five dollars, Davis

[4]Travis, Diary, entry for June 16, 1834.

being obligated to pay the extra three dollars to Travis when Roberts should pay his debt. Travis gave Williamson this note, to be credited on a sum Travis had previously borrowed from Williamson, amount unspecified. On January 31, 1834, Williamson paid Travis thirty dollars, and two weeks later Travis borrowed twenty-four dollars from Williamson. Thus did the two cronies favor each other against the harsh demands of society, although friendship was temporarily set aside once when Williamson as alcalde fined Travis five dollars for contempt of court.[5]

Sometimes both attorneys practiced in neighboring jurisdictions. In April of 1834 Williamson accompanied Travis to a court held under the live oak trees in the rural region near Stafford's Point, where Travis defended a man accused of marking and branding his neighbor's yearlings. Representing the plaintiff was Travis's erstwhile jailmate, Patrick C. Jack. The judge was David G. Burnet, and other lawyers present were W. H. Jack and John W. Moore, the Mexican alcalde.

The lawyers were well known to a local citizen, Ben Fort Smith, for previously he had gone hunting with some of them and had contributed two calves to be barbecued for their dinner. Dr. P. W. Rose was host to the lawyers, who slept in a playhouse, built by the doctor's small daughters, under four giant live oak trees. Each member of the legal fraternity was equipped with a knife, a tin cup, a gun, and a bottle gourd. Travis lost his case, but he gave notice of appeal, and Judge Burnet granted a second trial. During a recess for dinner, the conflict between the farmers was settled by Smith, who bought the cattle about which the ownership was in dispute.

The excitement thus being over, the young folks, who had gathered for the trial, proposed a dance. But since Mrs. Rose wanted to hear some preaching, having heard none in Texas in a year, a Mr. Woodruff was asked to sermonize. He had no Bible and was thus unable to oblige, but he volunteered to pray. To comfort the hostess, Travis promised to send a

[5]Mixon, Life and Letters of William Barret Travis. See also Travis, Diary, entry for April 17, 1834.

Bible to her if he could fine one in San Felipe. When Mr. Woodruff finished praying that those present would lead "pure lives," Williamson joined in the singing of "On Jordan's Stormy Banks" and "Come, Thou Fount of Every Blessing." Several days later he sent side combs to the little girls to pay for the use of their playhouse. Travis sent the children a Sunday school book, but he had to send word that not a single Bible was for sale in San Felipe.[6]

Williamson's legal talents were further occupied in those days with matters concerning the titles to the lands occupied by the fifty-two families that had settled in Milam's colony. Milam's grant had expired in 1832, and a Mexican, Juan Vincente Campos, had been made empresario of the territory. Williamson, in his capacity as Milam's agent, petitioned the state government at Coahuila that the settlers during Milam's administration be given possession of their lands. But the government held that since Milam's contract had expired the families in this territory could not be recognized as belonging to it.[7] Such a decision doubtless only added to Williamson's growing conviction that the Mexicans were a race of scoundrels.

In the midst of the court session in the fall of 1833, Williamson, as if he had nothing else to do, surprised everyone by announcing his candidacy for alcalde of the San Felipe district. Although at the time his relationship with Austin was strained, the founder's plain words, at the convention of 1833, scoring the alcaldes and emphasizing the necessity of judicial reform may have appealed to a sense of civic duty in Williamson, for Austin had characterized alcaldes in general as follows:

> The alcaldes, who are the highest judicial officers in Texas and have unlimited jurisdiction in all cases, are elected annually by the people, and those who are ignorant and corrupt and without responsibility are as liable to be chosen as the wise, the virtuous and the responsible. This remark is justified by the fact that the

[6]Mrs. Dilue Harris, "The Reminiscences of Mrs. Dilue Harris," *Quarterly of the Texas State Historical Association*, IV, 101 ff.

[7]Lois Garver, "Benjamin Rush Milam," *Southwestern Historical Quarterly*, XXXVIII, 178-179.

office is without emolument and is extremely burdensome, and will therefore seldom be sought by those best qualified to fill it.[8]

Something of Austin's meaning is apparent from letters written to him by various alcaldes and preserved in the Austin Papers. The writers' ignorance of English grammar and spelling as well their miscomprehension of the spirit of legal justice was as obvious to Austin as it is to anyone who reads those letters today. Indeed, so competent a man as Henry Smith, serving in an alcalde's capacity at Brazoria, reveals in his reminiscences the farce upon justice frequently characteristic of trials at the alcalde courts. Referring to a case in which "a few idle and dissolute vagabonds" had been accused of murder, Smith relates:

> . . . I summoned twelve good and respectable citizens as a jury of enquiry, in order that the testimony could be made out. the testimony was examined—the proofs plain, and the fact not denied. The jury retired and very soon served me with a truly polite note, complimented me highly for my assiduity and promptness in arresting and securing the prisoners, and concluded with a notice that they had then no further use for my official services — that I might consider the prisoners as arrested from my charge, and that they would deal with them as, in justice, their crimes merrited. I could not resist the multitude and of course was compelled to acquiesce. The jury very soon agreed in their verdict and as good men generally will do, yielded to the calls of mercy, as they were not willing to inflict death without a lawful warrant, they substituted the lash. The culprits were taken to the grave of the unfortunate who had been but recently burried, and there tied and whipped by the jury by turns, until an attending physitian said they had enough. They were then set across the River, faced to the east, and ordered to leave the country forthwith. they took up the line of march and I have not heard of them since.[9]

But Williamson, neither "ignorant" nor "corrupt," was vastly more competent than the run-of-the-mill candidate to announce for the office. Since the position was "without emolument," the inference is either that he desired to be of service or that he wished to checkmate the increasing tendency of the Mexican government to exercise close super-

[8]Barker (ed.), *Readings in Texas History*, 197.

[9]Smith, "Reminiscences of Henry Smith," *Quarterly of the Texas State Historical Association*, XIV, 33.

vision over the colony. One thing is certain: the campaign was a test in San Felipe of the popularity of the group who had been lately in open opposition to current Mexican policies in Texas; and the fact that Williamson's only opponent, Silas Dinsmore, won the San Felipe box by a plurality of thirty votes, despite the vigorous campaigning of Travis, was a straw in the wind forecasting that in the heated debates preceding the outbreak of the revolution in 1835, the "Tory spirit" of San Felipe would make the town a stronghold of pacificism.

In the race Travis labored mightily in behalf of his friend. He records that in the Spanish section of the town he induced eight voters to support Williamson, and he also bought drinks to win over some wavering Texans. As the campaign progressed, Travis bet William B. Aldridge ten dollars on Williamson, and later he wagered B. L. Burks a ten-dollar hat that Williamson would defeat Dinsmore by more than 150 votes. On December 11, the early election returns—except from the San Felipe box—were all favorable to Williamson. The rural vote later swept him into office by a majority sufficient to win Travis his hat, and on January 1, 1834, Williamson was installed in an office that today would be comparable to that of "a combined mayor and city-judge."[10]

Records of the correspondence, written or supervised by Williamson, between the administrative officers of San Felipe and the Mexican officials, show the variety of the activities with which the alcalde was concerned. He had to read and have published the statutes, edicts, and decrees issued both by the national and state governments and usually sent to him by the political chief at San Antonio; and he was required to acknowledge in detail the receipt of such documents, whether issuing from "the most excellent" governor, the "honorable congress" of the state, the "sovereign general" congress, or his "lordship" the political chief. Had a local alcalde received a letter from the emperor or president of the Mexican nation, the vocabularies of both the Spanish and English languages would have been in-

[10]Travis's participation in Williamson's campaign is described in his diary.

sufficient to furnish the ornate terms of address the alcalde would have been supposed to use in reply. The correspondence further included the forwarding by the alcalde to his political superior the various petitions of the local government and other reports on matters of community welfare.

Such a mixture of vital and irrelevant correspondence was sent to the local ayuntamiento in the same parcel that the casual alcalde or his secretary, drowsily reading copies of a treaty between "the Mexican government and Peru," or "a decree of the honorable congress relative to orders of the prelates and other religious," might have gone to sleep before coming at last to decrees concerned with "new organization" of the local ayuntamientos, to "the appointment of a commissioner of police" for the district, and to the treatment to be accorded "the wild Indians who may arrive in this village with horses and mules."[11] By the time Williamson was established in his office, he was personally so contemptuous of the Mexican authorities that in general he made only the motions of serving their interests. He exerted himself only when the welfare of the local district needed his attention or when he could be helpful to a neighboring jurisdiction, and this was precisely the attitude of Travis, who a little later was engaged as Williamson's secretary.

The alcalde's correspondence with Músquiz at San Antonio must have harrassed that punctilious, polite, and conscientious official. On March 31, tardily acknowledging the receipt of missives received several weeks earlier, Williamson excused his failure to reply sooner by asserting that he "lacked a translator or secretary," and this, he said, accounted for the previous correspondence which he had written to Músquiz "in English, which is my native tongue." Músquiz probably realized that the excuse was lame, for Williamson knew the Spanish language well: half his business as a lawyer was examining land titles written in Spanish, and in this very year he was to journey to Monclova, then the state capital, to converse with Mexican officials. But Músquiz merely replied, ". . . in as much as you now have

[11]R. M. Williamson to Ramón Músquiz, Statement of correspondence received from the chief of the Department . . . , June 2, 1834, in Bexar Archives, University of Texas.

a secretary, who will also serve as a translator . . . in the future, I hope you will fulfill the requirements of the law." The announced difficulty of Spanish expression was not so easily overcome, however, for later Travis also blandly recorded an inability to read the language.

Músquiz's letter of April 17, asking for better coöperation, had further requested an overdue list of foreigners arriving in the colony for the first three months of the year as well as a report of the strength of the local squadron of civil militia. Earlier, Williamson had sent a list of immigrants for the first two months. Now he waited until April 29 before he leisurely informed Músquiz that a statement about the foreigners would be sent "by special mail, or in any case by the next regular mail." At the time Williamson also declared he was unable to call together the ayuntamiento to consider several laws, which he had lately received, until May 28 because "they live at such a great distance from this Villa." Assuring the political chief, as usual, of his "distinguished consideration" and in the name of "God and liberty," Williamson completely ignored the request for information about the strength of the militia. About a week later, however, in a note of two sentences, written in English, he informed Músquiz: "The civilian battalion of this municipality has been disbanded. Therefore, I cannot remit the required report."[12]

By this time Músquiz probably realized that the local government at San Felipe could not be expected to render even the lip service it had formerly accorded; and in turn Williamson was beginning to surmise that bullets would be the only effective method of communicating with the Mexicans. Stephen F. Austin, bearing the petitions of the convention, had been imprisoned in Mexico City, following his arrest in Saltillo on January 3, 1834. When it learned the news, the ayuntamiento of San Felipe was thereafter concerned mainly with getting the founder of the colony out of jail.

Austin's imprisonment was the immediate result of a letter he had written from Mexico, in a mood of disappointment,

[12]*Ibid.*

to the ayuntamiento of San Antonio, urging that all the ayuntamientos of Texas be ready "to place themselves in communication with each other without a moment's delay" for the purpose of organizing a local government for Texas as a state of the Mexican federation. Particularly objectionable was Austin's sentence: "I am firmly persuaded what I recommend is the only means of saving us from anarchy and ruin." The officials at San Antonio, however, instead of acting favorably on Austin's advice, sent a copy of his letter to the state governer at Monclova, who forwarded it to Gomez Farías, the Mexican vice-president, with whom Austin had been conferring. When Farías read the letter, he was so incensed that he immediately ordered Austin's arrest.[13]

In April, 1834, Williamson, in collaboration with Travis, drafted a vigorous petition to the Mexican national congress requesting Austin's release. The memorial, dated the twenty-eighth, was the first of a series of six addressed to the government by Texas ayuntamientos in Austin's behalf. The second came from Matagorda on May 17. It may be significant in this respect to record that Williamson was officially to install the ayuntamiento of Matagorda in June.[14] Trips he made there preparatory to the official installation may have had something to do with those resolutions.

However that may be, the San Felipe requests, logical, eloquent, and written in a comparatively restrained style, indicate thorough familiarity by the drafters with all the circumstances related to Austin's arrest. The petition began:

> The accusation against him [Austin], if we are correctly informed, is based on his letter to the Ayuntamiento of Bexar, and bearing date the 2nd of October, 1833—and the accusation we understand to be *Treason*. Your memorialists have too high an opinion of the intelligence of the Mexican Judiciary to believe that any expression contained in that letter can be tortued [*sic*] into anything like Treason.

The compliment on the intelligence of the Mexican judiciary was for the writers an extreme concession, but it is the

[13]Barker, *Life of Stephen F. Austin*, 436.

[14]Williamson to Músquiz, June 10, 1834, in Bexar Archives, University of Texas Library.

only literary pleasantry in the document which conjectures shrewdly that the real reason for Austin's arrest was "a suspicion of the fidelity of the people of this province," and not the mere letter which Austin had written. This misgiving, spread by "the secret and unprincipled efforts" of the enemies of the colonists, the resolution asserts, may have gained credence in Mexico from "the occurences at Velasco, Anahuac, and Nacogdoches" which, the paper hastens to add, "were brought about by the arbitrary and unconstitutional acts of the Military."

At this point the document cleverly links the insurgent activities of 1832 with the cause of Santa Anna to which, it declares, the Texans rallied "with one accord." Concerning their approval of the rising Mexican general, the authors declared:

> The cause of Santa Anna was not only uncertain, but the great probability was that he could not sustain himself. The situation was such as to make every patriot weep. The fondest hopes of liberty appeared to have been blighted; and surveying the condition of the Republic, naught presented itself but one wide ocean of blood. The constitution had been torn in a thousand fragments, & scattered to all the winds of heaven; the sun of freedom appeared to have dawned for the last time upon unfortunate Mexico. . . .

As to Austin, personally, the writers declare that the ayuntamiento of San Felipe was not enthusiastic about defending Austin as an individual:

> He [Austin] opposed the people in their call of the convention. He opposed them in asking for a state government; and he was beaten for president of the convention purely on account of his known hostility to the measures . . . . Had his recommendations been pursued, the military would yet have been in Texas. . . . [He] was from the first settling of this colony the most scrupulously circumspect in regard to Mexican institutions, Mexican views, and Mexican rights . . . . He was elected as the delegate to Mexico, not from any unbounded confidence that he would zealously urge the people's claim to a state government, but in the hope that he would not dare desert the object of his mission, and that his supposed influence with the government would aid in procuring what they conceived to be but fair and reasonable requests.

Members of the convention, it is contended, were so doubtful of Austin's zeal that they appointed two other persons, later prevented from making the journey, to go with him to Mexico as "a check upon him."

But failure to sustain Austin in his present predicament, the paper points out, would be a desertion by the people of Texas of their own principles. Hence, it is argued that the fateful letter dispatched by Austin to San Antonio represented not his own views but those of the overwhelming majority "of FORTY THOUSAND citizens, zealous of their requests and suspicious of him." That Austin's letter was not "sanctioned by any one of the ayuntamientos throughout Texas" might appear strange, but, the memorial submits, after Austin left Texas, several events had transpired "to give a different direction . . . to the cause of the people." First of all their fears had been quieted by "the auspicious termination" of the civil war, and the people, as a consequence, hailed "with unalloyed satisfaction" the triumph of Santa Anna, and felt confident of "the dawn of a happier and more prosperous period." The news lately received in Texas of the repeal of the noxious eleventh article of the law of April 6, 1830, had been an evidence that their faith had been well founded. The implication was thus obvious that the legitimate wishes of the colonists with regard to statehood would also be respected.

Further evidences of the fact that Austin's letter did not "express his individual sentiments," the memorial says, were expressed in letters subsequently received in Texas, in which Austin retracted his expression of October 2. With such a reversal, the writers had little sympathy. They said:

> . . . Strange, inconsistent man [Austin] recommended to the people to "hold no more conventions, tolerate no more aspiring men, and to address the government only through the medium of the legitimate channels" [the ayuntamientos].

Having thus established that the San Felipe memorialists were not defending Austin from personal sympathy, the paper presents a dignified appeal for Austin's release from prison—an appeal not only calculated to impress upon the Mexican government the injustice of Austin's detainment but also designed to emphasize to the officials the essential character of the Anglo-American people. It follows:

If any wrong has been committed it has not been by Colonel Austin—If any treason has been intended the whole people of Texas alone are guilty. He represented in his letter their feelings and intentions at the time he was dispatched to Mexico: and if he erred or violated any law, or was wanting in proper respect, or attachment to the government, the people of Texas should alone be the sufferers.—But the people of Texas repel with indignation the charge of treason, and they deny that in either word or deed they ever contemplated any measure unwarranted by what they conceived their constitutional privilege. They indeed proposed to organize and they have always conceived that they had an undoubted right to do so. But for what would they organize? Not for the purpose of resistence to the government—Not to dismember themselves from the Mexican Republic; for if the question was put to the vote of the people their answer would be unanimous *nollumus mutari*. But that they might present themselves through their representative in the city of Mexico and add to the Republic a State calculated to be its pride and strength; and inhabited by a people, who, rocked in the cradle of liberty had been taught from lisping infancy that he who received the protection of a government was bound to aid in sustaining its soverignty and independence; and that he who meditated differently was a traitor to that country, and would be a villian among his fellow beings. The American character is not correctly understood abroad; they are not of a revolutionary disposition! No people are more ardently and more affectionately attached to liberty, order, and a faithful observance of law.—No people are more unrelenting and determined in their opposition to usurpation and oppression. Hold out to the people of Texas the Olive branch of peace; convince them that their wants are considered, and their rights protected in the counsels of the Nation, and the voice of complaint will be hushed; and they will rise as one man and swear to rally under no flag save that of the Mexican Nation, to know no government save that of their adopted country.

In conclusion, this Ayuntamiento for itself and the people of this jurisdiction, and speaking the sentiments of the whole united people, would respectfully request that Stephen F. Austin be discharged and permitted to return to his constituents. The grant of this request it is not conceived will interfere with the course of justice or be incompatible with the honor and character of the Mexican Nation; but will furnish to the people of Texas renewed evidence that the reign of depotism has ceased, and that all their just and reasonable requests will receive considerate attention from the ruling authorities of the country.[15]

[15]Printed document, signed April 28, 1834, in Bexar Archives. Also published in *Texas Republic* (Brazoria, Texas), July 5, 1834.

Lawyers Peter W. Grayson and Spencer H. Jack bore the memorial and similar petitions from six other ayuntamientos to Mexico, where Austin, although still to be a prisoner for months, was at least cheered to learn that he had not been forgotten by his colonists.[16] The petitions had little or no effect upon the Mexican government, but Williamson was not a man to let a cause die with a petition.

On July 4 he addressed the ayuntamiento in a ringing speech, the thesis of which was to deplore the failure of the Mexican government to grant Texas statehood. Incidentally, he included in the address a statement of his faith in simple democracy, and again he urged Austin's release.

Referring to the shelving of the petitions of the convention of 1833, Williamson said:

> Our Constitution has been rejected. Our application refused. We still continue our unnatural connexion with Coahuila. Our fondest hopes, our most cherished anticipations have been blighted. Our earnest entreaties have been disregarded. Our able, our eloquent and PATRIOTIC memorial has scarcely been read, and we have been told, that the grievances of which we complain, find no sympathising friend in the Government, would receive no redress, from the congress of the nation;—In a word, we have been told that the happiness, prosperity, security and safety of the people of Texas form no part of the policy of the government....
>
> Let us then speak plain to the government on this subject. Let us avow our own acts, by proclaiming *the truth*, that the people of Texas *once harmonized in the great end of a state government*. A respectful memorial on the subject from this Ayuntamiento, and from the different Ayuntamientos of Texas, to the government might be attended with great good to the citizens and the country. As citizens of Texas, and members of this body, *let us try it*.

The address further explained that the original petitions for statehood proceeded from conventions rather than from ayuntamiento officials because these men were elected for purposes other than political agitation. In a statement reflecting his confidence in the wisdom of the community, the young advocate of the "people's cause" continued:

> Are we wiser, more informed, more honest or more patriotic than the balance of the community, that we should take upon ourselves the privilege of advising or remonstrating with our

[16]Richardson, *Texas, the Lone Star State*, 109.

fellow citizens on the important point, whether or not the people of Texas should organize themselves into a State. We may depend upon it, the people have too much good sense, too much independence to be influenced by any thing of the sort emanating from us, as a political body; they have been accustomed to think, and to judge for themselves; and they are not to be persuaded that any inward excellence, or extraordinary infallibility, is peculiar to the name of Ayuntamiento. We cannot induce them to believe that, we as a political body, are more competent to judge of their wants, their rights and necessities, than their whole united talent.[17]

Aside from the San Felipe memorial on behalf of Austin, the only other document of historical importance signed by Williamson and Travis during their term of office in 1834 was also concerned with Austin, but in this instance their recommendation was, on the surface, a blow to a project lately initiated by the founder. In February Williamson and Travis recommended, at the behest of the ayuntamiento, that Sterling C. Robertson be reinstated as empresario of a prospective colony located on the western frontier of Austin's grant. This land had been recently awarded to Austin, following a series of complicated legal and administrative activities concerning it. Settlement rights originally had been given to Robert Leftwich, who, with Austin's help, got Mexican permission to transfer the contract to a Tennessee land company which later did little or nothing about settling the territory. In June, 1830, this company authorized Robertson to place two hundred families on its grant, but by then the Mexican law of April 6, 1830, previously discussed, prevented further Anglo-American colonization. When Robertson arrived in Texas in October of 1830 with a few families, he was forbidden by Mexican authority to carry out his plans. Later, after the Mexican government abrogated pertinent articles of the law of April 6, a French company began negotiations for the unsettled land. Such an award would have either delayed colonization or opened the way for wholesale land speculation, and to prevent such eventualities Austin applied for and received the grant. Robertson

[17]J. D. Williamson Papers. Also printed in the *Arkansas Gazette*, September 2, 1834, p. 2, col. 1.

thereupon protested vigorously, and an approval of his cause by the San Felipe ayuntamiento resulted.[18]

From this, it has been inferred that Williamson, by reinforcing the claim of Robertson, dealt shabbily with his old friend, and that possibly he acted with a view of having the territory left open to speculation. In the absence of any justifying statements by either Williamson or Travis, their reasons for signing the ayuntamiento petition are unknown; but it is a mistake to assume that Williamson was in any respect favorable to wholesale speculation in Texas lands. So far as his personal feelings were concerned, Williamson disliked Robertson. On March 10, Francis W. Johnson wrote a letter to Williamson from Tenoxtitlan indicating the spread of feeling in Robertson's favor—and of Williamson's probable reaction to it, Johnson and the alcalde being the cronies they were. Johnson wrote:

> I find the Robinson [Robertson] fever raging . . . [and] fear civil war the result of this damnable contagious poisen emitted throughout the land by Robinson and his satellites. Some measures must be taken to check this mad man.[19]

The fact that on June 16 Williamson hired Travis to defend the claims of the Alabama Company for its eleven-league grants, should Robertson file suit against the company, is further evidence that Williamson had little or no personal enthusiasm for Robertson.[20] The only reasonable conclusion as to why Williamson and Travis signed the favorable recommendation on Robertson's claim to the colony is that as officials they were obliged to approve a motion passed by the city council. The paper was signed before news of Austin's arrest reached San Felipe, and, at the time, Williamson probably felt disinclined to exert himself for Austin as an individual.

The idea that Williamson was interested in nullifying Austin's contract for the purpose of promoting land speculation is entirely unfounded, but the notion has been enter-

[18]Barker, *Life of Stephen F. Austin*, Chapter XI.

[19]F. W. Johnson to R. M. Williamson, March 10, 1834, in Barker (ed.), *Austin Papers*, II, 1047.

[20]Travis, Diary, entry for June 16, 1834.

tained for several reasons. In the first place some of Williamson's friends—Johnson, Dr. Robert Peebles, and Sam Williams, to name three—were definitely among the bigger speculators.[21] In 1832 Williamson himself had written to Dr. Asa Hoxey, an old friend of Alabama days, outlining the advantages of buying cheap eleven-league grants of Texas land from the Mexican government.[22] In the colonization law of Coahuila and Texas of March 24, 1825, previously related, a national enactment had incorporated a reservation entitling the federal authority at its discretion to sell Texas land to Mexicans, the individual grants not to exceed eleven leagues (48,708 acres) at prices ranging from $100 to $250 per league—about one-fifth to one-half cent an acre. As early as 1830 James Bowie had induced Mexican citizens to buy a total of fifteen or sixteen of these grants for him. The use of Mexicans as purchasing intermediaries later became such a common practice that Empresario Ben Milam complained that his colonization efforts "were in great danger of being defeated by claimants of eleven-league grants."[23]

As Milam's representative, Williamson could hardly have engaged in a practice so completely at variance with his own efforts as a colonization agent. His recommendations of the league purchases to Hoxey were for the purpose of inducing some of Williamson's former Alabama associates to emigrate to Texas. The letter to Hoxey was written in 1832, before the practice of speculation became a matter of serious concern to the empresarios. Williamson, as noted before, had always shown an inclination to buy and sell real estate, but there is a vast difference between bartering a few leagues of land and speculating in millions of acres. In fact, until the "bewildering series" of Mexican laws of 1834 and 1835 opened huge regions of Texas to conjectural land transactions, many of the best citizens of Texas had purchased eleven-league titles and "some held grants in their name for friends residing

[21]E. C. Barker, "Land Speculation as a Cause of the Texas Revolution," *Quarterly of the Texas State Historical Association*, X, 80.

[22]Letter, Asa Hoxey to R. M. Williamson, December 2, 1832, in *ibid.*, IX, 285-286.

[23]Barker, "Land Speculation," *ibid.*, X, 78.

in the United States." These were such common practices that no one thought of raising a hue and cry about them.

The series of laws passed in 1834-1835, however, brought forth speculation immense and unrestrained. As glaring examples, under a law of April 19, 1834, Williams, Peebles, and Johnson obtained a grant for 1,771,200 acres; and under the law of March 14, 1835, Williams and John Durst received title to 596,072 acres which they immediately resold in blocks of about 50,000 acres, located mainly in the present counties of Harrison, Red River, and Nacogdoches. In the confusion of many statutes, even the national government contemplated the purchase of Texas lands already sold by the state government.[24]

To obtain their prizes, Williams and his associates had dangled before the eyes of Governor Augustín Viesca a promise to raise a thousand armed men to repel Indian attacks. By 1835 the wasteful policy of the government became notorious, and when the governor called for armed resistance from the Texans to repel an attack of Santa Anna, the *Texas Republican* described his appeal as a call "to sustain him and vile congress that have bartered our public lands for a song." Austin, also, was strong in denunciation of the land sales.[25]

There is not a shred of evidence to show that Williamson was in any way connected with such gigantic land transfers. His own expression upon the subject on July 4, 1835, before a crowd in San Felipe, which included men who would have challenged an untruth instantly, minces no words about his attitude toward speculation:

> I have been your fellow citizen for years, and you cannot believe that I am influenced by speculation. On the honor of a man I assure you that I have all to lose and nothing to gain by the disturbances of our country; and I am in no way connected either with the speculation or the speculators![26]

[24]*Ibid.*, 80-83.

[25]*Ibid.*, 88.

[26]R. M. Williamson's address of July 4, 1835. Circular printed by F. C. Gray, Brazoria, in Gulick (ed.), *Lamar Papers*, I, 206 ff.

In 1834, when the public lands were being pillaged, Williamson was thinking about a subject far less profitable but much more exciting than selling land. By September the alcalde had come to the conclusion that the entire Mexican government, including the party of Santa Anna, was despicable. Previously, as his memorial in behalf of Austin indicated, he had clung to the hope that liberal principles, as announced by Santa Anna, might render cohesion between Texas and Mexico tenable; but on September 11, writing from San Antonio to Henry Smith, Williamson said:

> By today's mail we had important news from Monclova, the Capitol of Coahuila. It seems the state government upon the plan and principles of the constitution [of 1824] is completely dissolved. A military despot is governor, whose ignorance is alone equalled by his arrogance. There will be no congress this present year in Monclova and every constitutional officer of the state, so far as I have been informed, has been deposed by the insurgents.

The characterization of Santa Anna as "a despot . . . whose ignorance is alone equalled by his arrogance" shows clearly that Williamson had renounced all loyalty to Mexico. His formerly asserted faith in the liberalism of Santa Anna having vanished, the only role he could now consistently advocate for Texas was complete separation.

In a letter to Smith, Williamson warned of a plan by Santa Anna to overthrow the civil authority at San Antonio; this plan Williamson said he hoped would be resisted by force. In concluding, Williamson announced that he planned a trip to Monclova on the next day.[27]

This was to be one of his last peaceful journeys for several years. The storm clouds were flying.

[27]Letter, R. M. Williamson to Henry Smith, September 11, 1834, printed in John Henry Brown, *Life and Times of Henry Smith*, 29.

CHAPTER VI

Voice of the War Party

From the beginnings of the colonization movement, separation of Texas from Mexico and the ultimate fusion of the territory with the United States were inevitable. Differences in Anglo-American and Mexican character made permanent unity impossible. Had there been mutual understanding and tolerance, and especially had the Mexicans encouraged the Texans in developing their resources and in establishing acceptable institutions of religion, justice, and education, the troubles between them might have been composed without bloodshed.[1] But, although the Texans were not blameless, official government conduct toward them was in the greater part stupid, arbitrary, and, sometimes, even brutal. Moreover, the constantly changing nature of the federal administrations made it difficult for the Texans to understand what government they were obligated to support. From 1829 to 1835, when the shooting started, Mexico spawned internally four major revolutions and was the scene of numerous state and local insurrections.[2] Restrictive laws imposed by these shifting central powers, together with a callous disregard of the Texan petitions, filled the colonists with foreboding as to the integrity of the Mexican nation.

Nevertheless, Texans in general exercised remarkable restraint. Those favoring outright independence by force from Mexico—the "War Party" men—were overwhelmingly outnumbered in the first months of 1835. Even as late as November, when the Texas Consultation decided to set forth the causes "which have impelled us to take up arms, and the objects for which we fight," the delegates were unable to

[1]Barker (ed.), *Readings in Texas History*, 182.

[2]*Ibid.*, 180.

decide among themselves whether they were fighting for independence or for the Mexican Constitution of 1824.[3]

What finally led to the beginning of hostilities, in the fall of 1835, was the sober realization by Texan leaders, as Williamson had concluded a year previously, that Mexican liberalism, as espoused by General Antonio López de Santa Anna, for whom Williamson and the insurgents of 1832 had boldly declared, was not liberalism at all; on the contrary, it was merely a professed doctrine calculated to gain support for Santa Anna, who soon successfully made himself a dictator. Eventual recognition by the Texans of the character of Santa Anna was, as Dr. Barker has observed, "the last unbearable straw upon the proverbial camel's back."[4]

Born in Jalapa, in the state of Vera Cruz, in 1794, Santa Anna was a small-statured Mexican of relatively pure Spanish descent. His father had hopes that the boy might become an honest merchant, but Santa Anna's instincts were more suitable to a refined thug than to "a counter-jumper." After joining the Mexican army as a cadet, he rose rapidly. His first military action of any consequence was in the Battle of the Medina at San Antonio in 1813. In this melee, Mexican regulars engaged in a bloody conflict with a force of American adventurers and Indians from the "Neutral Ground," located between the jurisdiction of Mexico and the United States. In the engagement, the federal troops ambushed a force of about 850 Americans, who were overpowered after several hours of fighting. The Mexicans captured 112 prisoners and promptly stood them before firing squads. They also shot most of a group of 215 prisoners whom they captured soon afterwards in San Antonio. From this battle, Santa Anna formed a poor opinion of the fighting qualities of the Americans. He also concluded that the massacre of prisoners was a proper procedure.[5]

Santa Anna's liberalism was patently a fake. He was

[3]E. C. Barker, "The Texan Declaration of Causes for Taking Up Arms against Mexico," *Quarterly of the Texas State Historical Association*, XV, 176-177.

[4]Barker (ed.), *Readings in Texas History*, 181.

[5]Wilfrid Hardy Callcott, *Santa Anna*, 3-17.

essentially a sadistic little opportunist with a cat's subtle mentality for self-gratification. Styling himself "the Napolean of the West," he entertained illusions of grandeur.

By the end of 1834, when Williamson relinquished his position as alcalde, the political situation was fast growing alarming. In Coahuila the citizens of Saltillo had declared for Santa Anna, but Monclova remained loyal to the discredited liberal party which originally projected Santa Anna into power. As previously related, officials at Monclova, hoping to raise sufficient funds to defend the city against possible invasion from Saltillo, had authorized the sale of thousands of acres of land in Texas to land speculators. In consequence, the Texans ignored the governor's frantic appeals for armed aid. Commandant of the Eastern Interior Provinces, General Martín Perfecto Cós, a Santa Anna man, declared the proposed land sales a violation of the federal colonization law and sent a detachment of troops marching against Monclova. As a result, the legislature adjourned in panic, and the governor was arrested by the invaders.[6]

Nearer home, affairs were becoming explosive. Santa Anna's lack of gratitude for the Turtle Bayou Resolutions was manifested in January by the appearance at Anahuac of Captain Antonio Tenorio with a detachment of Mexican troops and a collector to re-establish the customhouse. At Brazoria, where tempers were easily strained, a deputy collector was installed.

No sooner had Captain Tenorio established himself in Anahuac than the troubles which led to the semi-revolt of 1832 were resumed. An Anahuac merchant, Andrew Briscoe, became indignant over what he thought was an unwarranted imposition upon the flow of commerce in the town. Once again practical jokes were played upon the Mexican soldiers, and soon Briscoe and a friend were placed in the guardhouse.

News of Briscoe's arrest arrived in San Felipe in June, almost simultaneously with the receipt by James B. Miller, the Texan political chief, of a letter from General Cós relating the news of the arrest of the state governor and the suspension of civil government at Monclova. Court being in

[6]Barker (ed.), *Readings in Texas History*, 177.

session, San Felipe at the time was crowded. A group of excited men seized General Cós's military courier and opened letters addressed to Captain Tenorio at Anahuac. A letter from General Cós assured Tenorio that heavy reinforcements were sailing to his aid; and a letter from Colonel Ugartechea, who had been appointed commandant of Texas, stated that Mexican troops of Santa Anna, lately victorious in Zacatecas, were at Saltillo preparing to march into Texas.

As a result of these disclosures, the more warlike citizens of San Felipe raised a clamor for armed resistance. A meeting, held immediately, adopted a resolution that the troops at Anahuac should be overpowered and ordered to leave the state. The fiery Travis, spurred by the memory of his own sufferings under Bradburn, promptly stirred himself to raise the troops necessary for the expulsion of Tenorio. Next day Williamson presided over a gathering which denounced Santa Anna for his violations of the national constitution of 1824. This meeting, Williamson observed, was not attended by a group of hotheads; on the contrary, it had as an audience some of the most respected and oldest citizens of the colony.[7] In their judgment war was inevitable, and they thought it should be prepared for immediately. Williamson naturally felt himself vindicated by these conclusions, for at last the doctrines of the war party were gaining numerous and powerful adherents. Consequently he began the composition of what was to become his famous address of July 4, 1835—a speech that was to stir the hearts of his listeners "like a trumpet peal." Williamson's making the speech was one of his outstanding acts that prompted that distinguished old Texan, Colonel John S. Ford, to write, long afterwards, that "Williamson did more than any one man to nerve our people to strike for liberty."[8]

While Williamson was composing his oration, Travis, on June 29, with a force of twenty-five hotspurs and a small cannon, thundered into Anahuac, demanding the surrender

[7]*Ibid.*, 178.

[8]John S. Ford to O. M. Roberts, March 20, 1897, in Sleeper, "Three-Legged Willie."

of Tenorio. The next day the Mexican captain gave up and agreed to take his men out of Texas.[9]

In writing his speech Williamson assumed only one line of reasoning which may be termed defensive. He realized that many conscientious citizens of the colonies were under the impression that the chief source of opposition to Santa Anna was occasioned by the fact that his government had invalidated the acts of the state legislature which had permitted large-scale land speculations. As a consequence Williamson several times mentioned his disdain of the speculators and endeavored to show that speculation was a false issue dragged in to obscure the concerns of the hour.

When Travis returned to San Felipe, both he and Williamson found that the peace party members had roused from their lethargy. Taking counsel of their fears, the leaders hastily disavowed the actions of the war party. On the day before Travis led his armed insurgents into Anahuac, peace party followers at Columbia piously denounced the meeting over which Williamson had presided at San Felipe on June 22. The Columbians not only condemned the actions of individuals which might involve Texas in a war with Mexico, but also, in a bit of specious rationalization, declared that, since Santa Anna was revising the constitution, adherence to the constitution of 1824 would be rebellion. A little later, other meetings condemned Travis for his assault upon Anahuac.[10]

There can be no doubt that these activities slowed the pace of the would-be rebels. Miller apologized for the meeting of June 22 at San Felipe; and Travis, asserting that his activities at Anahuac were prompted by motives of patriotism, asked the public to withhold judgment upon him until he could publish a defense of his actions. Williamson, however, was undaunted by squeamish protests. On July 4, in San Felipe he delivered the fighting speech which ranks with Travis's impassioned appeal from the Alamo as one of the genuinely heroic utterances of the times. While many of the colonists indulged in the wishful thinking that Santa Anna

[9]Barker (ed.), *Readings in Texas History*, 178.

[10]Richardson, *Texas, the Lone Star State*, 116.

intended them no harm, Williamson, in a ringing voice, advocated the immediate seizure of San Antonio by force and warned the populace that they could almost hear the bugles of their enemies. He bluntly branded Santa Anna as a dictator, a sworn enemy of a republican form of government. Most of the speech is quoted here, for it so incensed the Mexican officials that they committed actions which made the revolution inevitable:

I have no desire to appear before you, expressing my individual opinions, and I speak to you, not only of my own sentiments and feelings, but those of a meeting respectable alike for its numbers, and the individuals composing it. What I shall say, I religiously believe, and what that meeting did was induced solely from disinterested and patriotic motives . . . . Fellow-citizens—you are in the midst of a revolution that threatens your destruction, and without knowing it, you stand on a precipice that crumbles beneath you and which every moment threatens to precipitate you in the abiss below.—You are lulled to sleep in the belief that speculation alone has created the present excitement. But be entreated no longer to indulge in this dangerous belief, but to examine for yourselves the true situation of affairs.—Examine for yourselves the late movements of the General Government. Look into their ulterior designs, as avowed in congress, & you will perceive that so far from speculation having anything to do with the present subject that the troops of the general Government are on their march to Texas, for the purpose of compelling you to either leave the country or submit to an Imperial Government, with strong military stations in your Country to awe and keep you in subjection.

Your republican form of Government is broken down. Your state authorities have by the military been driven from the exercise of their constitutional duties, and detain in custody the Governor of your State, and of your choice. Not only in Coahuila and Texas has this arbitrary and despotic course been pursued, but other states of the Federation mourn the loss of their constitution and their liberties, and at this moment the proud and gallant & republican state of Zacatecas mourns the loss of two thousand citizens, slain in battle by the troops of Gen. Santa Anna, and the survivors now endure the galling chains of military rule.—Durango and other states have also fallen beneath the rule of military power, and every state and province of the Mexican Republic (excepting Texas) have submitted to the Dictator.

How this state of things came about, I will endeavor faithfully to explain to you, and if I wilfully mistake a single fact, may I forever after be branded with infamy among you. To understand, you must first know that the form of Government is virtually altered, and that another form is about to be established in its stead, and at this time Gen. Santa Anna instead of being your President has been invested by the General Congress, with the absolute powers of the Dictator. Elected President by the Republican Party, he no sooner took his seat, than he threw off the veil of disguise, and to the amazement and consternation of the Republican Party, he exhibited himself the friend and supporter of the Aristocrats and defender of the Clergy. His first step was to call into power and place into office the Old Aristocrats, the sworn enemies of a Republican form of Government, and to drive from his councils those who elected him, and who had proven themselves the true and devoted friends of the Constitution.

Among those, are the ever true and gallant and devoted Republicans Gen. Mexia and Governor Zavalla. The party now in power, is formed by the junction of the Aristocracy and Clergy with the remains of the Old Spaniards. Their policy and their interests and the accomplishment of their most ardent wishes are founded in the destruction of the Federal System. On this depends their existence as a party, the firm establishment of their power, and their continuance as privileged class in opposition to the fundamental principles of a liberal system founded on equality of rights; already has that party in Congress, through their committee, declared "*That the constitution requires a radical reform that the only article which remains inviolable is the one which declares for intolerance of religious feeling and established privilege classes in a State, which, founds its principles on the inviolable and noble basis of equality*" and after making the declaration, that the constitution should be altered, the same Congress declares that "*It has the right of altering the Constitution at its pleasure without pursuing the formalities required by that instrument*" and in continuance of the plan of operations General Santa Anna is invested with the powers of a dictator and at this moment has all the absolute power of a despot and only now requires a diadem on his brow to obliterate the name of Liberty from the Mexican Code—

To all these invasions of the sovereignty of the States the people would in all probability have submitted had not the aristocracy made the last final blow at their liberties and lighted the flame of civil [war]; the civic Militia had at all times previously proven the sure and safe bulwark of the liberties of the people, and the attempt of Guerrero and Bustamente, to destroy the constitution had been manfully and successfully resisted by them. Against this body the congress struck a deadly blow and passed a law disbanding them, and permitting only one gun to be retained in the hand of every five hundred men in the country, and requiring the states to surrender all the surplus arms to the general government.

To this decree, many of the States submitted, but others resisted it, knowing that to deliver up their arms, was to deliver themselves over to an aristocracy, whose object was plainly Monarchy.

Among the States resisting were Zacatecas, Durango, Chihuahua, Chiapas, and Coahuila and Texas. The legislature of Coahuila and Texas, in addressing the General Government in regard to the change of Government and creation of a Dictator says;—"*For these reasons the State of Coahuila and Texas legitimately represented by its legislature, PROTEST in the most solemn manner that having confederated by virtue of the Fundamental compact, and under the basis which in it is established, does not acknowledge nor will not acknowledge the measures and provisions which emanate from the General Congress* .... The General Government which should put its attention to the revolutions of the South, prepares an expedition of troops against a pacific state, such as is Zacatecas, that has given so many days of Glory to the Nation, by brideling arbitrary power and abuses.—The commander General of the Internal States of the East, intervening in the Interior administration of the State of Coahuila and Texas, in the most scandalous manner even to the dictating of orders to prevent laws, made by the Legislature, being complied with, moving the troops from the places which they guard on the frontier, and where they are necessary to protect the inhabitants from the barbarous Indians, and bringing them toward this capital in order without doubt to suppress the supreme authorities. The General Government to whom this body has applied to curtail these abuses, and advances of the Military authority, preserve a profound silence in the delicate affair, so that every thing indicates the dangerous road we are traveling in, and which, should there not be every degree of reflection, prudence, and mildness of procedure, we shall be again involved in all the disasters of a civil war and the misfortunes consequent upon it even more afflicting and terrifying, than any which have preceded."

To compel obedience and reduce those states to submission, Santa Anna on the 18th day of April last marched from the city of Mexico at the head of *six thousand men*. His first attack was on the gallant, patriotic and Republican state of Zacatecas whose citizens he defeated in battle, and making prisoner the Governor, and dispersing the Congress, garrisoned the whole country with strong garrisons; the same fate is nearly sustained by Durango, and from being a free and sovereign state, she is reduced under the power of the Dictator to a military garrison. While this state of things were going on in Zacatecas and Durango, General Cós was ordered to put down the authorities of Coahuila and Texas. The governor sent an order to all the Departments of the state for the Militia to turn out to sustain the state authorities, but not receiving sufficient aid, he attempted to escape with the public archives to Texas, in order there to re-establish the government and where he expected to be sustained by a people who have ever been free and who he confidently expected would rally to sustain the constitution they had sworn to support and the public officers they had elected. In his flight however he was arrested by the military order under the order of General Cós, and has been sent a prisoner to Monterrey. Not only has he been arrested but also some of the members of congress; the others having fled for safety to the mountains. The militia of Coahuila have been disbanded and have surrendered up their arms to the Government and that whole country is now a military garrison. All the states have succumbed to the power of the Military and as Texas is the only spot unconquered, Santa Anna is marching his troops here to compel a submission to the new Government. And the people have to determine whether they also will yield to the power of the Dictator. Give up their arms—suffer their country to be garrisoned with strong military posts, and live under the rule and sway of the military. They must do this or they must prepare for war — they must submit to the military government or defend their province and their rights with the sword and the bayonet, and they must do this without delay for the enemy is fast advancing on our country.

Fellow Citizens, let me again assure you that this is the true state of affairs. These are the reasons that actuate the General Government—The sale of the four hundred leagues of land has nothing to do with the subject. You are justly indignant at that sale, so also am I, so also is the meeting which I represent; but that can and ought to have no weight with the public mind at this time. It is too inconsiderable to be noticed when compared to the importance of our country, our property, our liberty and lives, which are all involved in the present contest between the states and the military—Two spies from Colonel Ugartechea, stationed at San Antonio were arrested in San Felipe, and in their possession the official correspondence of Ugartechea and General Cós was found. General Cós writes to the Commandant at Anahuac that the two companies of New Leon, and the Morales Battallion would sail immediately for Texas, and that they would be followed by another strong force, which he had solicited the government for, and which he had no doubt would be obtained. Col. Ugartechea says that the business of Texas will be soon regulated, as the government has ordered a large division composed of the troops that went against Zacatecas, to Texas and which are now at Saltillo, that force is three thousand four hundred men.

For what, Fellow Citizens, are they coming, in the name of GOD say not speculation; they are coming to compel you into obedience to the new form of Government; to compel you to give up your arms, to compel you to have your country garrisoned; to compel you to liberate your slaves; to compel you to swear to support and sustain the government of the Dictator; to compel you to submit to the imperial rule of the aristocracy, to pay tythes and adoration to the clergy—For these purposes, Fellow Citizens, they are coming, and for this purpose a party of soldiers it is said have already landed at Copeno. Under the excitement created by all this information many of the people of the jurisdicion of Austin, during court week, assembled to consider of the situation of the country, and of the adoption of means for its protection. A declaration to support the General and State Constitution and the officers of the state was unanimously agreed to, and also it was resolved to release the governor and drive the military from San Antonio.

Much pains has been taken to persuade you that this meeting was gotten up by speculators, and that no necessity existed for it. But, Fellow Citizens, believe no such slanders, pay regard to no such falsehoods. At the first meeting held in which it was resolved that the country was in danger, and that the governor should be released, James B. Miller, the Political Chief was Chairman; and in his official character, he called on the people of his department to turn out for the purpose. At the second meeting were many of your oldest fellow citizens, who can have no views of speculation but who all unanimously, upon investigation, declared the country was in danger and that no time should be lost in preparing for war, the Alcalde and Ayuntamiento of Austin were of the same opinion, and ordered a turn out of the people to protect the country. There were at the meeting many persons from the jurisdiction of Mina and Matagorda, all of whom believed that no time was to be lost in preparing for war. The meeting at San Felipe had no desire to dictate to the balance of the community or to involve it in war; the only reason why the meeting at San Felipe first acted was because at that place the news of danger was first received, and the danger appeared too imminent to admit of delay. Every matter of importance has to be brought about by the action of a few. The whole people never have moved at once in a body. It is only by meeting in different places that the sense of the country can be ascertained.—The meeting at San Felipe commenced the matter and I hope that meetings will be held in every part of the Province, to determine what shall be done. But that meeting resolved that San Antonio should be taken, and for these reasons. They considered that the question of war was settled. That forces were coming against Texas, and in a very short time all Texas would have to turn out and fight—that opinion we still entertain, and still think San Antonio should be taken. The citizens of that place have at this time . . . come among us requesting of us assistance to drive the military from that place in order that they may unite with us in the common cause of protecting the country. By taking that place we would procure one hundred and sixty stand of musquets, many cannon and much ammunition, and also about eight hundred head of horses, belonging to the government, and which we indispensably require for the protection of the country. But, Fellow Citizens of Texas, other weighty and important reasons exist why that place should be taken; should you permit San Antonio to remain in the hands of the enemy your country is lost. Five hundred troops can so fortify San Antonio as to resist the united attack of all Texas. In that situation they have only to send out their parties of men and harrass and destroy the country, without ever coming to a pitched battle; they will so annoy and harrass the country by continued depredations and alarms, that wearied out, dispirited and disheartened, the people will gladly retreat beyond the Sabine. When you least expect it they will descend upon you and call you from your fields to Battle and before you can rally, they will kill and burn and destroy. In the depths of winter they will call you by their depredations to the field, and a thousand attacks and a thousand false alarms will destroy your patience and your property and make your country not worth contending for.—But if possible even worse than all this you permit an enemy to be there stationed that will send the Indians continually upon you.

Inhabitants of the Frontier—your situation will be deplorable; instigated and protected by the Mexicans, the Indians will be your constant enemies; they will be the continued ravagers of your country and destroyers of yourselves. If you drive them from your neighborhood they will seek refuge and protection under the troops of San Antonio, and will retire only to return with renewed violence and destruction. You will hear around your habitations the Indian yell, mingling with the Mexican cry, and the shrieking of your murdered wives, rousing the slumbers of the cradle, from the midst of your burning buildings, will tell you, when too late, of the error of your policy in permitting San Antonio to be garrisoned by Mexican troops. Fellow Citizens, depend upon it your policy is wrong and the danger great. If you would save the country and protect the frontier, San Antonio must be taken; already has Anahuac fallen, already has the spies of the country been arrested and the correspondence examined—already have you proceeded too far to retreat—already are the troops of the Dictator on the march against you, and you have to fight, surrender or run away. There will be no necessity for your garrisoning San Antonio, once drive off the military, and the inhabitants of that department will protect and defend the place. Fellow Citizens—by taking St. Antonio you will also secure the person of Don Ramon Musquiz the Vice Governor, who by the constitution is now your Governor, he has expressed his willingness to act provided the Colonists will sustain him, but he dares not attempt it so long as San Antonio is in possession of the enemy. What can you or will you do, unless you bring him into the colonies and reestablish the Government. At this time your Courts of Justice are closed, you have no head to direct you, and you are in a state of Anarchy and confusion. You can only remedy this by procuring the Vice Governor and re-establishing the Government.—Unless you do this in less than one month every thing will be in disorder and you will have no security for your persons and property, except the strength of your arms.

Three fourths of the people of Texas are new comers and have as yet received no titles to their lands, the last legislature passed a law decreeing that every person in Texas should receive their land, but before the commissioners were appointed, the Governor was arrested.—

In what manner are these citizens to get titles to their lands. The intention and policy of the present ruling authorities of the nation is to destroy the system of colonizing and so soon as the military become possessed of Texas, that soon will the last league of land have been given to North Americans, instead of receiving the titles they will be declared foreigners and driven from the country; there is but one possible way of avoiding this result and that is by taking San Antonio, bringing the Vice Governor to his place in order that the commissioners may be appointed to put the people in possession of their lands.

Citizens of Texas, you who have not yet received your titles must be up and *doing*—the taking of San Antonio is important to you inasmuch as no Governor can be had until it is taken, and until you have a governor you can obtain no land—and depend upon it, if you would secure your land, you must do it ere the military become masters of the country.

Fellow Citizens of Texas.—Our interest, is common and no possible reason can exist for difference of opinion. We may differ as to the mode to be pursued but one sentiment can pervade every breast; which is the safety and protection of the country—Let us by all means harmonize and act in concert, for it is only in union that we are strong, only united can we succeed—Let us no longer sleep in our posts; let us resolve to prepare for War—and resolve to defend our country against the danger that threatens it—A sacrifice has to be made—Let us sacrifice a portion at once—In order to secure the remainder—already we can almost hear the bugles of our enemies—already have some of them landed on our coast and you must prepare to fight. Liberty or Death should be our determination and let us one and all unite to protect our country from all invasion—and not lay down our arms so long as a soldier is seen in our limits—[11]

Profoundly as this address stirred those inclined toward belligerence in Texas—it was printed in Brazoria and had a wide circulation—its effect upon the peace party and the Mexican authorities led to actions which destroyed all hopes of a tranquil settlement of the matters in dispute. The non-

[11]R. M. Williamson's address of July 4, 1835. Circular printed by F. C. Gray, Brazoria, in Gulick (ed.), *Lamar Papers*, I, 206 ff.

belligerents fell into a paroxysm of apologetic protestations; meeting at San Felipe on July 14 and 15, they adopted pledges of loyalty to Mexico. Miller, probably yielding to pressure, wrote an apologetic letter to General Cós; and a conference of committees from San Felipe, Mina, and Columbia sent Edward Gritten and D. C. Barrett to Matamoros with letters to General Cós assuring him of widespread indignation throughout the colonies over such activities as Travis and Williamson had engaged in.[12] On July 25, Dr. James H. C. Miller, an extreme pacifist, wrote a letter, to be forwarded to Colonel Ugartechea, suggesting the arrest of Williamson and his friends as a means of forestalling further resistance to Mexican authority. The writer, who may be said to have been a bit sneaking, held forth as follows:

> . . . All here is in a train for peace, the war and speculating parties are entirely put down and are preparing to leave the country. They should now be demanded of their respective chiefs—a few at a time—first Johnson, Williamson, Travis, and Williams—and perhaps that is enough. Captain Martin, once revolutionary, is now, Thank God, where he should be, in favor of peace and his duty, and by his influence, in a good degree, has peace been restrained. But now they should be demanded—the moment is auspicious the people are up. Say so and oblidge one who will never forget his true allegiance to the supreme authorities of the nation and who knows that till they are dealt with, Texas will never be at quiet. Travis is in a peck of troubles. Dr. Miller disclaims his act in taking Anahuac and he feels the breach.
>
> Lorenzo de Zavala is now in Columbia attempting to arouse &c. Have him called for and he also will be delivered up. Williamson, Johnson, and Baker are now on a visit to him and no doubt conspiring against the Government.
>
> Fail not to move in this matter and that *quickly*, as now is the time.[13]

By July 30, according to a letter written by John W. Smith, Ugartechea had issued orders for the arrest of Williams, Williamson, Johnson, Travis, Zavala, and Baker. The Mexican officer informed Smith that only the delivery of

[12]Richardson, *Texas, the Lone Star State*, 116.

[13]J. H. C. Miller to John W. Smith, July 25, 1835, in Domestic Correspondence, State Archives, Austin, Texas.

these men would prevent troops from marching into the colony to take them by force.[14]

By his actions, Ugartechea was merely anticipating what was to be expected of him by his superiors. After forwarding Miller's letter to General Cós, who had probably already read Williamson's address, the colonel was soon ordered not merely to demand the arrest of the leaders of the recent agitations but also to use military force to carry out the order. Indeed, Cós was so indignant that he refused to discuss affairs with Gritten and Barrett until he could be assured that the agitators had been jailed.[15]

A report to the citizens of Mina by Barrett, who had attempted to engage the general in conversation, leaves no doubt of the attitude of Cós toward Williamson and other war party leaders. Barrett asserted that most imperative of all Cós's demands was the surrender to Mexico of Lorenzo de Zavala, the liberal former Mexican governor and onetime friend of Santa Anna. Next on the required list was "W. B. Travis, esq, and next Robt. M. Williamson." Also included were Baker, Williams, and Johnson "together with the individuals concerned in 'abusing' the government messengers and 'violating' their dispatches."[16]

During the latter part of July, however, Williamson was oblivious to the cloud hanging over his head. His arrest might well have meant his execution; it could not have meant less than long imprisonment or banishment from the colony; but a few days after delivering his speech, Williamson rode off to a war unrelated to the Mexicans. The Tehuacana Indians were on the rampage. Having committed a series of depredations against the colonists, they were being engaged by a small and greatly outnumbered force under the command of Robert M. Coleman. The Indians succeeded in surrounding Coleman's troops at Parker's Fort, close to the present site of Groesbeck. Upon learning of the situation, the San Felipeans organized three companies, one captained

[14]John W. Smith to Andrew Ponton, July (?), 1835, in Gulick (ed.), *Lamar Papers*, I, 220-221.

[15]Richardson, *Texas, the Lone Star State*, 117.

[16]D. C. Barrett to Citizens of Mina, August 23, 1835, in Barker (ed.), *Austin Papers*, III, 105-107.

by Williamson, to send to Coleman's rescue. When the reinforcements joined Coleman, the Indians retreated. They were pursued and finally defeated at Tehuacana Springs, and the Texans chased scattered Indian groups up the Trinity as far as the vicinity of the present city of Dallas. Only when this campaign was finished did Williamson learn of the furor his July 4 speech had stirred up. Since, for obvious reasons, he could not return to San Felipe, he took up residence at Mina, later to be known as Bastrop.[17]

The citizens of Mina immediately evidenced their esteem of him by electing him to be one of their delegates to a consultation which was being generally requested throughout the colonies. Williamson, however, was to have few peaceful days in Mina. As captain of a company of mounted riflemen, he had hardly finished the fighting with the Indians when it became necessary to deal with the Mexicans. Early in September, a force of Mexican cavalry had arrived near Gonzales for the purpose of seizing a six-pound cannon which the Texans had been using to intimidate the Indians. Answering urgent appeals from Gonzales for reinforcements, Williamson's company was on hand when a troop of about 180 Mexican cavalrymen arrived on the west bank of the Guadalupe River with the intent of crossing into the village. The Texans, having removed the ferry boats, stood menacingly on the east bank; for two days Mexican and Texas forces faced each other across the river. With affairs thus in suspense, Williamson and a few others drew up the cannon in plain sight of the Mexicans and emblazoned upon a sign above it, in huge and glaring letters, the defiant words: COME AND TAKE IT. This challenge, possibly coined by Williamson, became the fighting sentence woven a little later into the first Texas revolutionary battle flag. When the Mexicans heard the whang of Texan bullets splattering in the dust about them, they retreated about six miles on the road to San Antonio.

On October 1, Colonel John A. Moore, who had been elected commander of all volunteer forces gathered at Gonzales, called a war council which decided it would be a shame to disappoint all the stout fellows who had gathered for the

[17]Sleeper, Three-Legged Willie.

defense of the town by disbanding without a fight. Next day, consequently, the Gonzales volunteers crossed the river, and flying a flag displaying a drawing of the disputed cannon, a lone star, and the words of their fighting challenge, they advanced to the Mexican positions and fired the opening rounds of the war. After a few volleys, the Mexicans fled back to San Antonio.[18]

An honorable discharge for Williamson as captain of the mounted rifle company was signed by Colonel Moore in Mina on September 13.[19] Williamson's discharge, however, did not mean that his services to the army terminated. On October 17 a letter signed by Barrett and B. Manlove, delegates from Mina to a state consultation which had failed to draw a quorum on October 16, states that the citizens of Mina had sent their delegates instructions to meet at Washington rather than at San Felipe, and a postcript adds, "The other delegates *now in the Colonial Army* have been notified. . . ."[20]

Since Williamson was one of the other delegates, it is obvious that he had not severed his connection with the army; he had merely given up his command as a captain of the mounted militia company. After September 13, Williamson, widely acquainted and popular with all save the most radical members of the peace party, was called upon to exercise his well-known talents as a speaker, writer, and recruiting officer in securing support from the people for the army in the field. This aid was necessary, since the army at Gonzales was existing on its own resources. That army leaders were depending on Williamson to secure supplies for them is evidenced by a letter to "Dear Willy" written on November 18 by Johnson, Williamson's old commander at Anahuac, who then was serving as an officer under Austin, while the Texas army was debating whether to besiege San Antonio.

Assuming that Williamson was then at the consultation

[18]Old Soldier, "First Breaking Out of the Texas Revolution at Gonzales," *Texas Almanac for 1861*, p. 60.

[19]Comptroller's Military Service Records, No. 271, State Archives, Austin, Texas.

[20]Barrett and Manlove to the General Consultation at San Felipe, October 17, 1835, in Consultation Papers, State Archives, Austin, Texas.

in San Felipe, Johnson presented his old friend with a realistic description of the plight of the Texas forces. Colonel Ugartechea, Johnson said, had been reinforced, despite "the vigilance" of the Texans, who had experienced considerable "desertions" in their lines. These desertions, Johnson explained, had been remedied in part by incoming recruits, but the army was being held together solely by the "patriotism of the men and the unremitting exertions of the officers." All would fail, Johnson thought, unless "prompt, definitive, and efficient meaures" were taken by the convention, for the town of San Antonio and its garrison were strongly fortified. Moreover the Mexicans were increasing the strength of their position hourly. "We can do nothing without battering Cannon ball, etc.," Johnson declared. Further, he said the pieces of artillery which the army had were too small and that the supply of balls were "but few." The officers were trying to remedy "the evil by collecting all the copper and bells about the old mission and casting it into balls for the pieces we have here."

To Williamson personally, Johnson plead: "For God's sake have the battering piece forwarded with ball, etc. Tent cloth and other things are in great requisition, and it is the only thing that will keep the present force together." And he added, "The keeping of this force together is all important to the success of Texas."[21]

Johnson's poignant request did not fall on deaf ears. Although the consultation had adjourned four days before Johnson wrote his plea, Williamson turned the letter over to the council of twelve which was then directing governmental affairs. Williamson had been accustomed to rendering aid to the Texas army. In 1840, the Republic of Texas returned to him the sum of forty-five dollars which he had spent for beef in July, 1835, with "a Mr. Frost then living near Parker's Fort . . . for a detachment of troops in the service of Texas."[22] Insignificant as the sum may seem, Williamson's funds in 1835 were none too plentiful.

[21]Johnson to Williamson, November 18, 1835, in Army Papers, 1835, State Archives, Austin, Texas.

[22]Comptroller's Military Service Records, No. 9640. State Archives, Austin, Texas.

CHAPTER VII

Drafter of War Causes

In September, 1835, while affairs were thus approaching a climax, and a nervous tension was rising throughout the colonies, Stephen F. Austin, haggard from long imprisonment, opportunely came home. His counsel was soon required on many matters, none more urgent than the feasibility of holding a consultation to determine the Texan course of action toward Mexico. Such a meeting had been urged as early as July 4 by the committee of safety at Mina, but the call was more emphatically voiced a week later at Columbia, where war party members were in control of the ayuntamiento. A San Felipe meeting had also favored the proposal. Additional demands for the convention were put forward by committees of correspondence, similar to those in the North American colonies during the Revolutionary War, lately sprung up over the colonies. These committees were headed by a central committee held over from the convention of 1833. A meeting at Columbia on August 15 requested this group to send out a call for a consultation of all Texas. The response was a letter urging delegates to hold a gathering to form plans either for securing peace—if possible—or for preparing the people for war.[1] Despite all the apparent pressure, however, the consultation's champions were members of the outnumbered war party. Neither the appearance of the Mexican force at Gonzales, nor the additional news that General Cós was on his way to San Antonio with reinforcements, nor the fact that many prominent men were proscribed by the Mexican government was sufficient to rally the colonists into unified opposition to the federal government. The peace party and those undecided as to the proper course of action awaited the advice of Austin.[2] In

[1]Richardson, *Texas, the Lone Star State*, 117 ff.

[2]Barker, *Life of Stephen F. Austin*, 480.

this crisis, therefore, the founder's decision was of supreme importance. Had he favored pacification, the revolution, despite the abilities inherent in such men as Travis, Johnson, Wharton, and Williamson, would have been little more than an abortive insurgence.

Most conscientious and patient of all the Texans in fulfilling his obligations to Mexico, Austin by 1835 had his fill of the Mexican government. He realized that war was inevitable, and he emphatically approved the idea of the consultation. By thus sanctioning a proposal of the war party, he added enormously to the prestige of those who had long advocated resistance to Mexican authority. Austin's decision, however, was the result of a conviction that at last had become fundamental with him. By September, he wrote that "the formation of a government (perhaps a nation) is to be sketched out," and in October he added, "No more doubts—no submission. I hope to see Texas forever free from Mexican domination of any kind . . . that is the point we shall end at—and it is the one I am aiming at." Austin not only urged the election of delegates to the consultation, but also he wrote out his ideas of what the consultation should do.[3]

Affairs were approaching an explosion on September 21, when General Cós, commanding a small force, landed at Copano, and a force of Texans rapidly gathered to prevent his junction with Ugartechea. A battle at Copano was prevented only because many of the armed colonists were sent to Gonzales to prevent the Mexicans from impressing the cannon. After the skirmishing there, reinforcements continued to pour into Gonzales, and Austin, early in October, was invited by a committee of officers to join the army there. After accepting the invitation, he was soon elected commander-in-chief.[4] Thus once again he became a friendly associate of Williamson's.

So many of the men chosen to attend the consultation scheduled to meet at San Felipe on October 16 were in the army that the delegates who gathered there on that date

[3] *Ibid.*, 483.

[4] Richardson, *Texas, the Lone Star State*, 122.

did not constitute a quorum. A note to General Austin written by Williamson on October 14 shows that Williamson, as a delegate, was on his way from the army to the meeting. Williamson stated: "The gentlemen you confided to my charge are thus far on their way to San Felipe and in good spirits."[5] From this one sees that Austin once again was "confiding" in Williamson and that the two old San Felipeans, after recent years of estrangement, had become friendly again. Although they still were not agreed upon specific methods of settling the issues, they were now united in a common cause. Indeed, Austin richly deserved Williamson's cordiality, for on October 12 his army started a march for San Antonio, and twelve days later it was encamped before the city.[6]

When the long awaited consultation finally began on November 1, Williamson took his seat at the opening roll call. Many of the ablest men of the colonies were in attendance, including Sam Houston from Nacogdoches; John A. Wharton, the war party stalwart, from Columbia; Captain Wyly Martin, of Anahuac renown, representing San Felipe; Thomas Barnett, the former San Felipe alcalde, also a San Felipe delegate; Lorenzo de Zavala, the exiled Mexican statesman, representing Harrisburg; and Barrett, a peace party leader, who shared with Williamson the distinction of being a delegate from Mina.

The consultation settled down to serious work on November 3, the first day a quorum was present. Following a motion of Sam Houston to elect officers, Dr. Branch T. Archer was chosen president. His inaugural address, based on suggestions sent to him by Austin, presented three major measures for immediate consideration: (1) a declaration of the causes for which the Texans were fighting, (2) the propriety of establishing a provisional government to prevent Texas from falling into "the labyrinth of Anarchy," and (3) the organization and maintenance of a military force adequate to deal with the Mexican invaders.

[5]R. M. Williamson to C. B. Stewart, October 15, 1835, in Barker (ed.), *Austin Papers*, III, 185.

[6]Richardson, *Texas, the Lone Star State*, 122.

Among other matters to be considered, Dr. Archer said, were certain lands in Texas now being claimed by "several warlike and powerful tribes of Indians"; procedure for awarding land titles to new arrivals now aiding the Texas army in battle; adjustment of the fraudulent land sales carried out by the late government of Coahuila and Texas; and the establishment of mails and an express department. In an eloquent flight, Archer said:

> Let me remind you that the eyes of the world are upon you . . . let us give evidence that we are the true descendants of that band of heroes, who sustained an eight years' war against tyranny and gave liberty to a new world. Let our achievements be such that our mother country, when she reads the bright page that records them, shall proudly and joyfully exclaim, "These are my sons!"[7]

In concluding, Archer declared that his own view of the cause for which the Texans were fighting was to establish "the corner stone of liberty in the great Mexican Republic." To draft a statement of the official views of the consultation, he appointed a committee of twelve, one from each district. He named Wharton the chairman, and Williamson one of the committee members. Upon beginning the assignment, the group soon discovered they could not agree among themselves whether Texas was fighting to be independent or to defend the Mexican Constitution of 1824, and presently they asked the house for instructions.

The consultation as a whole, consequently, spent November 4 in debate. Williamson and Wharton made long and vigorous speeches in favor of outright independence, but Daniel Parker of Nacogdoches staunchly advocated adhesion to the constitution. Martin Parmer of Tenaha spoke in support of Williamson and Wharton and was followed by J. D. Clements of Gonzales, who defended the constitution. On the next day Wharton made another plea for independence, whereupon Williamson's fellow townsman, Barrett, lengthily upheld the constitution and was given leave to submit in writing further views upon the subject. Supporting Williamson and Wharton, J. W. Robinson of Nacogdoches

[7]See "Journals of the Consultation," in Gammel (ed.), *Laws of Texas*, I, 511.

made a resounding speech in behalf of independence which drew a reply championing the constitution from J. B. Wood of Liberty.

Sam Houston, desiring to end the seesaw discussion, offered a motion that the committee be instructed to "draft a declaration in favor of the constitution of 1824," but he soon withdrew his motion in deference to Wharton. The second day's discussion closed with an address from the president, who was called from the chair to present his opinions. No records of his talk remain, but students of the convention believe that he favored adherence to the constitution.

On November 6 a spirit of impatience pervaded the assembly. Williamson was refused his request to read his plan for the establishment of a provisional government. Wharton was barely granted permission to make additional comments; and when he concluded, he was lectured by a delegate who read passages from a law book to prove that Wharton's proposals were treasonable. Undaunted, Williamson once again requested permission to read his plan, and this time he was allowed to speak. What he said is unrecorded, but at the conclusion of his reading, the consultation voted on the question as phrased by Sam Houston, "All in favor of a provisional government, upon the principles of the constitution of 1824, will say aye." The result was thirty-three ayes and fourteen noes. When the question was put in another form, "All in favor of a declaration of indepence will say aye," only fifteen ayes were mustered against thirty-three noes.

The consultation's vote, obviously, was a setback to Williamson and the other members of the war party, but it decisively revealed the will of the assembly. Wharton's committee, therefore, resumed its deliberations, having for its consideration at least four plans, those of Parker, Barrett, Austin, and Williamson. Thus Williamson was the only member of the war party who is known to have submitted a plan.

Parker's proposals have not been preserved, but they are thought to have been not materially different from the proposals of Barrett and Austin. Austin favored a provisional government, with separation from Coahuila, but he advocated the retention of the existing laws of Coahuila and Texas until more leisurely times could afford deliberations for the adoption of new laws. He favored pledging the faith of the state in order to obtain means for prosecuting the war "in defense of the constitution." Land claims of Indians, he maintained, should be guaranteed in order to keep them pacified while the Mexicans were threatening, and he further favored the annulment of the fraudulent land grants of 1833. Advocation of these measures, together with the establishment of a courier service, and the organization of a militia and a regular army, Austin thought, was as far as the consultation should go.

Barrett's proposals were lengthier, but, on the whole, they harmonized with Austin's. They were not without influence in shaping the final declaration.

As to Williamson's ideas—he had two papers, incorporating substantially the same points—Dr. Barker, whose researches upon the consultation constitute the chief source of the information presented here, says: "Williamson's draft is interesting as the blunt statement of a man who tried to tone down the expression of his real feelings to meet the wishes of a squeamish majority."

Williamson's document began with the generalization that Texans as "Anglo-Americans" were "a free born and reflecting people" who believed that "all government originates with and resides in the *people*." It stated that upon entering the territory of Mexico, the colonists took up residence under a constitution which guaranteed a people's government, and it asserted that "without [the Texans'] privity of Consent the only form of Government known and acknowledged by them has been changed." Because of this, Williamson declared, "eight thousand" men were mobilized in support of the Mexican Constitution of 1824. They were fighting for "Constitutional Liberty" against the "consolidated" forces of the Mexicans. As a consequence, the Texans were "separate from and independent of" the existing Mexican government.

Williamson's document, as Dr. Barker has shrewdly observed, declared Texas independent of the existing Mexican state, but it did not declare for any other form of Mexican government.

A fourth document, in the same handwriting as the document containing Williamson's proposals described above, attached three paragraphs to the original Williamson submissions. These additions asserted the overthrow of the form of government acknowledged by the Texans; stated that Texas, as a consequence, was no longer bound "to adhere" to a people who had changed that form of government; and expressed confidence that the Texan cause would be sustained by the generosity of civilized nations.

The committee worked through November 6, and the next day Wharton presented the assembly with its finished handiwork. Following is the result of its deliberations:

DECLARATION OF THE PEOPLE OF TEXAS IN GENERAL CONVENTION ASSEMBLED

Whereas, General Antonio Lopez de Santa Anna, and other military chieftains, have, by force of arms, overthrown the federal institutions of Mexico, and dissolved the social compact which existed between Texas and the other members of the Mexican confederacy; now the good people of Texas, availing themselves of their natural rights

SOLEMNLY DECLARE,

1st. That they have taken up arms in defence of their rights and liberties, which were threatened by the encroachments of military despots, and in defence of the republican principles of the federal constitution of Mexico, of eighteen and twenty-four.

2d. That Texas is no longer morally or civilly bound by the compact of union; yet, stimulated by the generosity and sympathy common to a free people, they offer their support and assistance to such of the members of the Mexican confederacy as will take up arms against military despotism.

3d. That they do not acknowledge that the present authorities of the nominal Mexican republic have the right to govern within the limits of Texas.

4th. That they will not cease to carry on war against the said authorities whilst their troops are within the limits of Texas.

5th. That they hold it to be their right during the disorganization of the federal system, and the reign of despotism, to withdraw from the union, to establish an independent government, or to adopt such measures as they may deem best calculated to protect their rights and liberties, but that they will continue faithful to the Mexican government so long as that nation is governed by the constitution and laws that were formed for the government of the political association.

6th. That Texas is responsible for the expenses of her armies now in the field.

7th. That the public faith of Texas is pledged for the payment of any debts contracted by her agents.

8th. That she will reward, by donations in lands, all who volunteer their services in her present struggle, and receive them as citizens.

These declarations we solemnly avow to the world, and call God to witness their truth and sincerity, and invoke defeat and disgrace upon our heads, should we prove guilty of duplicity.[8]

Three of these articles were taken from Williamson's drafts—one from his original submission and two from his more lengthy proposal. Two articles were authored by Barrett, and the three final paragraphs were inspired by Archer's inaugural address. The convention spent most of November 6 discussing the proposed declaration and, in the end, adopted it. On November 8, the house passed Sam Houston's resolution that all members of the convention sign it—indicating that it passed by a narrower margin than the journal of the consultation indicates. The convention ordered the printing of one thousand copies of the document.

As a whole, the finished declaration is so phrased that the war party, although unsuccessful in its efforts to have outright independence incorporated as one of the articles, could be well satisfied with the efforts of its champions. They certainly gave it "a brusquer tone than their numerical strength in the consultation warranted."[9] When Austin read it, he thought it tended fully as much to independence as to adhesion to the Constitution of 1824. He feared Santa Anna might take advantage of it to give the war a national, social character—thus alienating liberal Mexican groups who might sympathize with a revolution aimed only at frustrating the efforts of Santa Anna.[10]

Following the adoption of the declaration, Williamson had an important role in the various other activities of the as-

[8]*Ibid.*, 522.

[9]Barker, "Texan Declaration of Causes for Taking up Arms Against Mexico," *Quarterly of the Texas State Historical Association*, XV, 173 ff.

[10]*Ibid.*, 184.

sembly. He urged that the declaration be translated into Spanish and that copies be furnished to the states of the Mexican Republic, and he was made a member of a committee to consider military matters referred to the consultation by Austin. Although not appointed a member of a committee of twelve to "draw up and submit a plan or system of provisional government for all Texas," he was elected to a committee of five to revise portions of the submissions of the planning committee, when, upon being presented, the proposals drew fire from the assembly. After spirited house debate, the plan of the provisional government finally adopted contained twenty-one articles listing the general powers of the governing body and twelve articles regulating the Texan military forces. Powers of administration were lodged in a provisional governor and a lieutenant-governor, both to be elected by the consultation, and a council of twelve, to consist of one member from each district. Each member of this council was to be chosen by a vote of the delegates from his district.[11]

The transitional "constitution," thus adopted, replaced Spanish jurisprudence with English common law and established the right of trial by jury. It suspended the authority of "all commissioners, empresarios, surveyors, or persons in any wise connected with the location of lands," and it required that all public records be turned over to commissioners appointed by the consultation for safekeeping. Williamson was appointed a commissioner for the department of Bexar.

When the council elected officers, it chose one of Williamson's friends, Henry Smith of Brazoria, for governor over Austin by vote of thirty-one to twenty-two. The delegates from Mina—Williamson, Barrett, and J. S. Lester—chose Barrett to be Mina's representative on the council of twelve.[12]

When the new government was barely two weeks old, Wyatt Hanks, of Bevil, submitted a letter signed "by a large number of citizens" commending the election of Williamson as commander of a corps of rangers, urgently needed, and

[11]See "Journals of the Consultation," in Gammel (ed.), *Laws of Texas*, I, 523 ff.

[12]*Ibid.*, 534.

then about to be organized. Accordingly, on November 28, Williamson was chosen by the council of twelve, by a vote of six to five over James Kerr, to be the first major of the Texas Rangers.[13]

Williamson assumed his duties immediately. Within a week he submitted a letter to Barrett for the approval of the council on the subject of Indian depredations.[14] By surveying the activities of the redskins and busying himself with the organization of the ranger corps, Williamson was preparing for his role in the full-blown revolution which the climactic year of 1836 was to usher in.

As 1835 faded, the Texan cause was braced by an incredible triumph wrought by Williamson's old client, Ben Milam. Late in November, Edward Burleson had succeeded General Austin as commander of the Texas army, Austin having been commissioned by the council to go to the United States to solicit aid for the Texan cause.[15] A period of indecision upon the part of Burleson and other army leaders as to whether to attack San Antonio or to retire into winter quarters was seemingly resolved by a decision of a war council on December 3 to abandon the siege. This dismal eventuality was prevented by Milam, who, although only recently arrived, regarded the disbanding of the army as disastrous. He drew a line, it is said, across the ground, and shouted to the bewildered troops, "Who will follow old Ben Milam?"[16]

After three hundred men volunteered for the adventure, Milam stormed San Antonio and in less than three weeks inflicted a crushing defeat upon a Mexican army of thirteen hundred men, commanded by General Cós. The Mexicans surrendered, and Cós agreed to withdraw his army from Texas.[17] Killed in the fighting was the great-hearted Milam, whose memory one of his soldiers later thus enshrined:

[13]"Journal of the Proceedings of the General Council, in *ibid.*, 601.

[14]*Ibid.*, 610.

[15]Richardson, *Texas, the Lone Star State*, 122.

[16]Garver, "Benjamin Rush Milam," *Southwestern Historical Quarterly*, XXXVIII, 193.

[17]*Ibid.*, 199.

It was four to one, not gun for gun, but never a curse cared we,
Three hundred faithful and fearless men who had sworn to make Texas free.
It was mighty odds, by all the gods, this brood of the Mexique dam,
But it was not much for heroes such as followed old Ben Milam!

With rifle-crack and sabre-hack we drove them back in the street;
From house to house in the red carouse we hastened their flying feet;
And ever that shout kept pealing out with the swift and sure death-blow:
"Oh, who will follow old Ben Milam into San Antonio?"

Behind the walls from the hurtling balls Cós cowered and swore in his beard,
While we slashed and slew from dawn til dew, and Bexar, how we cheered!
But ere failed each ruse, and the white flag of truce on the failing day was thrown,
Our fearless soul had gone to the goal in the land of the Great Unknown.

Death brought the darksome boon too soon to this truest one of the true,
Or men of the fated Alamo, Milam had died with you!
So when their names that now are Fame's—the scorner of braggart Sham—
In song be praised, let a rouse be raised for the name of Ben Milam![18]

At the time, Milam's victory was a splendid Christmas gift to Texas.

[18] *Ibid.*, 197-198.

CHAPTER VIII

Major of the Texas Rangers

The decree establishing the Texas Rangers provided for a force of 150 men, but an activating ordinance later divided the corps into three companies of 56 men each. They were to be commanded by a major, and each company was to have a captain, a first lieutenant, and a second lieutenant as commissioned officers. Individual rangers were to furnish their own food, clothing, horses, ammunition, and other supplies. At all times they were to be armed and supplied with one hundred rounds of "powder and ball." For their services, they were to be paid $1.25 per day. This ordinance was passed on the day the decree creating the regular army was adopted. Provisions for the army established that the major of the rangers was to be subject to the orders of the army commander-in-chief.[1] Thus, in effect, the rangers were an adjunct to the army, created separately to afford the colonists protection against the Indians while the army was dealing with the Mexicans.

Despite the zeal of Major Williamson, the rangers never attained full strength. Their immediate organization was delayed not only by a scarcity of available recruits but also by dissatisfaction on the part of the men because the companies were not allowed to elect their own officers.[2] The grumbling of the rangers was a phase of a carping spirit spreading rapidly through all Texas.

On February 14, the council's advisory committee directed Williamson to move his men to the frontier to guard against Indian attacks.[3] The order signified that a second ranger

[1]Ralph W. Steen, "Analysis of the Work of the General Council, Provisional Government of Texas, 1835-1836," *Southwestern Historical Quarterly*, XLI, 335.

[2]*Ibid.*

[3]*Ibid.*, 336.

company had been organized, for one of Williamson's companies, under the command of Captain James Tumlinson, had been patrolling the headwaters of Brushy Creek, thirty miles northwest of the present site of Austin.[4]

This company, as related by Noah Smithwick, who had re-entered Texas and thrown in his services with the rangers as an enlisted man under Captain Tumlinson, was surprised early in January by the unexpected appearance at their camp of a young white woman, "her clothes hanging in shreds about her torn and bleeding body." She stumbled upon the rangers at their suppertime and sobbingly informed them that she, her husband, her brother, and her two small children, while travelling to their home in Guadalupe, had been attacked by a band of Comanches. The men were killed, and she and the children were captured. The Indians bound them on mules, but the smallest of the children, a baby, cried so continuously that one of the Indians snatched it and dashed out its brains against a tree.

Confident the woman would not attempt to escape without her remaining child, the Indians did not bother to bind her during the night. While they slumbered, she carefully wrapped the boy, and stole away, leaving him "to the mercy of the brutal barbarians." She went straight to the river, hiding her tracks in the cold waters. Smithwick continues the narrative thus:

> Once she thought she heard her child call, and her heart stood still with fear that the Indians would be awakened and miss her. She momentarily expected to hear a yell of alarm, and, not daring to leave the shelter of the bottom timber, she meandered the winding stream, sometimes wading in the shallow water along the edge, and again working her way through the brush and briers, tearing her clothing and lacerating her flesh, never pausing in painful journey till late in the afternoon, when she came upon the first sign of civilization in some gentle cows feeding in the river bottom.
>
> Perceiving that they were milk cows, she felt that she must be near a white settlement, but she dared not attempt to call assistance lest the Indians be in pursuit; so she secreted herself near the cows, which she surmised would soon be going home, and, waiting till they had finished their evening meal, followed them into the

[4]Smithwick, *Evolution of a State*, 118.

station, having spent nearly twenty-four hours in traveling a distance of only ten miles on open ground.

Fortunate, beyond hope, in finding the rangers there, she implored us to save her child, describing the mule he rode, the band of Indians and the direction they were traveling.

Hastily despatching our supper, we were soon in the saddle, and with a trusty guide (Reuben Hornsby), traveled on till we judged that we must be near the trail, and fearful of crossing it in the darkness, we halted and waited for daylight. As soon as it was light enough, our scouts were out and soon found the trail, fresh and well defined as if the marauders were exercising neither haste nor caution in their retreat, having no doubt spent a good portion of the previous day in a fruitless search for their escaped prisoner. They did not seem to be at all alarmed as to the consequence of her escape, and it was about 10 o'clock in the morning when we came upon them, just preparing to break camp. Taken completely by surprise, they broke for the shelter of a cedar brake, leaving everything except such weapons as they hastily snatched as they started. I was riding a fleet horse, which, becoming excited, carried me right in among the fleeing savages, one of whom jumped behind a tree and fired on me with a musket, fortunately missing his aim. Unable to control my horse, I jumped off him and gave chase to my assailant on foot, knowing his gun was empty. I fired on him and had the satisfaction of seeing him fall. My blood was up and, leaving him for dead, I ran on, loading my rifle as I ran, hoping to bring down another. A limb knocked my hat off, and one of my comrades, catching a glimpse of me flying bareheaded through the brake on foot, mistook me for a Comanche and raised his gun to check my flight; but another ranger dashed the gun aside in time to save me. The brave whom I shot lay flat on the ground and loaded his gun, which he discharged at Captain Tumlinson, narrowly missing him and killing his horse; when Conrad Rohrer ran up and snatching the gun from the Indian's hands, dealt him a blow on the head with it, crushing his skull.

The other Indians made good their escape into the cedar brake, where it was worse than useless to follow them; but, we got all their horses and other plunder, and, to crown our success, we achieved the main object of the expedition, which was the rescue of the little boy, though the heedlessness of one of our men came near robbing us of our prize in a shocking manner. The Indians, careful of the preservation of their little captive—they intended to make a good Comanche of him—had wrapped him up warmly in a buffalo robe and tied him on his mule preparatory to resuming their journey. When we rushed upon them they had no time to remove him, and the mule, being startled by our charge, started to run, when one of our men, not seeing the rider was a child, gave chase and, putting his gun against the back of the boy, pulled the trigger. Fortunately the gun missed fire. He tried again with like result. The third time his finger was on the trigger when one of the other boys, perceiving with horror the tragedy about to be enacted, knocked the gun up, it firing clear, sending a ball whistling over the head of the rescued child. Providence seemed to have interposed to save him.[5]

While Tumlinson's company was being occupied in this manner with the Comanches, Major Williamson was struggling to complete the organization of the additional ranger companies so urgently needed for the protection of other frontier outposts. Colonel William F. Gray, of Virginia, journeying down to San Felipe after having met Austin and the Texas commissioners in New Orleans, crosssed Williamson's trail on February 17. In his diary Gray, a shrewd observer, noted that "Major Rob. M. Williamson, of the Rangers, seems to be an intrepid Indian fighter. Has a wooden leg." Always on the outlook for a good horse, the major offered Gray half a league of land in Milam's colony for his horse, but Gray, not knowing what "confidence" to place in Williamson or his titles, declined the trade.[6]

Good horses, especially to a ranger, were always at a premium. The Indians also kept their eyes sharpened for opportunities to acquire fast mounts. The major's idea of the best Indian scrap he ever had was a fight brought on by the intention of a group of Indians to steal some horses from a small ranger force composed of Williamson and five of his men. As the story goes, Williamson's party had been alternately pursued and dodged by a few stealthy Indians for several days. Knowing the Indians were in the habit of attacking a camp just before dawn, the rangers adopted a strategy to end their troubles. When night came, they built a huge campfire, and each man wrapped his blanket around a log of wood roughly approximating the size of a man. They then concealed themselves a short distance away. As anticipated, before dawn the Indians stealthily approached the camp. They saw in the glow of the fire what appeared to be six well-wrapped, sleeping men. Without snapping a twig, the Indians crawled forward; and when they were but a few

[5] *Ibid.*, 119-122.

[6] William F. Gray, *From Virginia to Texas, 1835*, pp. 113-114.

feet away from the fire, they sprang to their feet. With a terrible yell, they plunged their daggers into the logs. The impact of the knives probably caused the more quick-witted of the savages to conclude the rangers had very tough hides; but they were not permitted to philosophize, for before they could straighten up, the rifles of the rangers, spitting red into the night, killed every one of them. Williamson had been in many Indian fights, but he said he considered this the most satisfactory of all.[7]

That a force of rangers, or any group of fighting effectives, could not long be spared from the war against the Mexicans soon was made obvious in the spring of 1836 by events which completely nullified Milam's victory at San Antonio. The success which had touched off such high hopes was marred largely by typical American wrangling.

Governor Henry Smith and the council started off auspiciously, but by the new year, a rift developed between them. Smith quarrelled violently with the council and eventually called some of the members "knaves and fools." After the capture of San Antonio, the council had favored an invasion of Matamoros by Texas forces under F. W. Johnson, but Smith and Sam Houston, who had lately been chosen by the council to be commander-in-chief of the Texas army, opposed it. The governor, in a rage, read to the council a report accusing Johnson, who had started a march to Matamoros, of stripping the garrison at San Antonio of all its supplies. Smith demanded that the council coöperate with him or adjourn until March.[8]

The council, undaunted, deposed the governor and installed Lieutenant Governor J. W. Robinson as chief executive. Smith refused to surrender the government archives and continued to receive mail addressed to the governor. The council, under Robinson, could not muster a quorum after January 17. In effect, until a convention called for March 1 assembled, this internal friction had the result of destroying the Texas government.

[7]Fanny Chambers G. Iglehart in San Antonio *Express* (San Antonio, Texas), April 2, 1911. Mrs. Iglehart was the daughter of Thomas Jefferson Chambers, an intimate of R. M. Williamson in San Felipe.

[8]Richardson, *Texas, the Lone Star State*, 125.

Meanwhile Johnson, having been given the go-ahead signal early in January by the council, had not gone very far toward Matamoros when he decided to abandon the idea of the invasion. The council then appointed James W. Fannin, Jr., to lead the Texan forces. But Johnson soon reversed his decision, and his commission was reapproved by the council. Thus the expedition had two commanders. About this time Governor Smith interposed by sending Houston to Goliad with the orders that Houston was to lead the advance on Matamoros.[9] But when Houston appeared before Johnson's men near Refugio, the Texas soldiers refused to accept him as their commander-in-chief. Houston, nevertheless, persuaded most of the men to abandon the idea of an invasion. As a consequence, Johnson was left a force of about 150 men, most of whom, on March 1, were killed in the vicinity of San Patricio by a cavalry force advancing into Texas under the command of General José Urrea. Johnson and a few others escaped.[10]

Meanwhile, Fannin with a force of about four hundred volunteers from the United States was encamped at Refugio. A few weeks before the massacre of Johnson's forces, Santa Anna, with a large detachment of the force of six thousand men he planned to use in the invasion of Texas, appeared at Laredo. By February 3, the dictator's advance guard reached San Antonio, where Travis and James Bowie had a small force ready to defend the city. Fannin, confused by the conflicting orders of the council and alarmed by the reports of Johnson's defeat and the advance of the Mexican armies, fumbled uncertainly as to the proper move to make. Owing to transportation difficulties, he was prevented from reinforcing Travis; because of undisciplined troops he was unable to take advantage of a brilliant stratagem by which a spy in his service had divided Urrea's forces. Adding to Fannin's confusion, about the middle of March, he was ordered by General Houston to retreat to Guadalupe Victoria. Upon receiving the order, Fannin was unable to march immediately because more than a third of his force had been sent

[9] *Ibid.*, 126.

[10] *Ibid.*, 127.

out to aid in the evacuation of settlers near Refugio. This detachment was soon routed and either killed or captured by Urrea. Finally, on March 19, with his main force, Fannin began his retreat. That afternoon he was attacked by Urrea's army.

The Texans repulsed the initial attack, but next day Fannin surrendered his men to a superior force of Mexicans. At Goliad, a week later, by Santa Anna's orders, 350 North Americans in Fannin's command were shot to death.

Already at San Antonio, a similar tragedy had been enacted. There, after the withdrawal of the forces of Johnson and Grant early in January, J. C. Neill remained in command of a force of about one hundred poorly equipped men. On January 17, Houston ordered James Bowie to proceed from Goliad with a small force to reinforce Neill. A few days later Governor Smith ordered Travis to go to the relief of San Antonio, and Travis set out with thirty men—all he could raise—to fulfill the order. Additional reinforcements, mostly from the United States, slowly gathered there so that by mid-February the San Antonio garrison had about 150 fighters.

Then internal strife once again blighted Texas prospects. When Colonel Neill left to visit his family, some of the volunteers chose Bowie as their leader; others followed the orders of Travis. Houston, upon sending Bowie to the relief of the garrison, had enclosed orders to Neill to abandon San Antonio, but these orders were contemptuously ignored. "We consider death preferable to disgrace, which would be the result of giving up a post so dearly won," Travis wrote in a dauntless mood. When Santa Anna's advance forces reached San Antonio on February 23, the Texans confined themselves within the walls of the Alamo and prepared to withstand the siege.[11]

Meanwhile Major Williamson and his rangers were busy fulfilling, as far as they could, the council's order of February 14 "to fortify strategic points so as to more surely protect the frontier from Indian attacks."[12] The news of Travis's

[11] *Ibid.*, 128-129.

[12] Steen, "Analysis of the Work of the General Council," *Southwestern Historical Quarterly*, XLI, 336.

plight reached Williamson "by express" at Gonzales, where the major immediately issued a proclamation to his "Fellow Citizens of Texas." There can be no question but that Williamson would have gone to Travis's relief with his rangers had he not been ordered specifically to patrol the frontier. Williamson's rangers did all they could, however, for the doomed men in the Alamo. "We are drying beef for them; we are hunting and also grinding corn," Williamson told the citizens, whom he sought to arouse thus:

> By express from . . . [torn] date of the 23rd Inst information which I could . . . [torn] that Two Thousand Mexicans under the command of Seizma have arrived and are in possession of the public square of Bejar—The American Troops under the command of Col. Travis and Bowie (150 men in number) have been compelled to confine themselves to the Walls of the Alamo where they are at present. . . . [torn] If there is one in the land [that will go] forward for his country's cause now is the acceptable moment. Now let him forward: for every man is a host.—Let us rally to their aid! Let us defend our frontier—Let us save our women and children secured from the rapacity of Mexican Soldiery—Texans only Arouse! Up in a moment aid . . . [torn].[13]

Williamson's circular as well as the tragic appeals written under gunfire inside the Alamo by Travis were of no avail. On March 6, Travis, who is said to have written the "most heroic document of American history" in his famous appeal for aid to people of Texas and "all the Americans in the World," fell shot through the forehead as he commanded the north battery of the Alamo fortress. For fourteen days, 150 men had held off Santa Anna's force of some 4,000 Mexicans, but on March 6 the Mexicans overpowered all resistance. A series of assaults, during which the invaders had been picked off like flies by the deadly Texan rifles, finally enabled the enemy to climb the walls. When the fierce hand-to-hand fighting ceased, piles of Mexicans lay dead about the body of David Crockett, who had come to San Antonio with a few of his Tennessee lads. Dead also was James Bowie, who during a part of the siege had been

[13] R. M. Williamson to Fellow Citizens of Texas, February 5, 1836, in Consultation Papers, State Archives, Austin, Texas.

"roaring drunk,"[14] and who had also been ill enough to be confined to his bed on the fatal day. Despite this, when he was killed, dead Mexicans lay about his bed. Not a single Texan was spared. Half an hour after the fighting stopped, Santa Anna, desiring to see the remains of his more famous enemies, found the body of Travis beside the gun carriage where he fell. Inside the small fort were the bodies of Crockett, Bowie, and many others no less brave. In the afternoon the Mexicans burned them all in a common funeral.[15]

When the news of the fall of the Alamo and, a little later, of the massacre at Goliad spread through the colonies, a spirit of panic swept Texas like wildfire.[16]

Even before the fall of the Alamo the rangers had been called in from their outposts. Williamson's circular appealing for aid to Travis was written in Gonzales, where General Houston, fresh from a convention which had superseded the council and which had renewed his commission as commander-in-chief of the Texas army, arrived on March 11. Houston intended to lead the forces which had been assembled there to the west bank of the Cibola River to unite with Fannin. But upon arrival at Gonzales he heard rumors of the fall of the Alamo. The cagey Houston, although pretending to doubt the reports, believed them implicitly. He immediately dispatched orders to Fannin, commanding him to fall back to Victoria.

Two days later Houston sent out a small party of scouts, including the famous Erastus "Deaf" Smith, with orders to approach near enough to San Antonio to learn the truth about the Alamo. These men had ridden only twenty miles when they met Mrs. Almaran Dickerson, wife of a captain who had been slain there, hastening to Gonzales. From her they learned not only the fate of Travis and his men, but also the fact that a Mexican division under General Joaquín Ramirez y Sesma was already marching eastward. When the

[14]Letters of W. B. Travis and John J. Baugh, in Amelia Williams, "A Critical Study of the Siege of the Alamo," *Southwestern Historical Quarterly*, XXXVI, 281-283.

[15]*Ibid.*, XXXVII, 40.

[16]E. C. Barker, "The San Jacinto Campaign," *Quarterly of the Texas State Historical Association*, IV, 245.

scouts brought Mrs. Dickerson to Gonzales, her reports sent the settlers there and probably some of the soldiers in the army, which numbered 375 men, fleeing eastward in terror.

Immediately, Houston decided to evacuate Gonzales; but before the Texans left, they applied to it what is now called the "scorched-earth" policy. Houston gave a few of his baggage wagons to the citizens to assist them in carrying away their most vital possessions. Two pieces of cannon were thrown into the river. By midnight, with the flames of the town lighting the way, Houston's army began its retreat toward the Colorado River.[17]

By this time, Major Williamson, who had been at Gonzales when Houston arrived there, had been sent to Bastrop (Mina), to await the assembly of all the ranger forces there, for at Bastrop settlers from adjacent frontier communities were assembling preparatory to a general exodus from the war areas.[18] Protecting the retreat of the civilian populace and serving as scouts and spies for the army were henceforth to be the major activities of the rangers.

Accordingly, early in March, Captain Tumlinson's company rode into Bastrop, where Williamson took personal command of the unit. Tumlinson and a number of other rangers left to remove their families to safety. The roads were filled with fleeing refugees, whose numbers increased greatly when Houston began this retreat.[19]

Most of them were poorly prepared for a hasty evacuation, and to prevent their being surprised by advancing Mexican troops, Major Williamson gave Ranger Smithwick a command of eight men with orders that they should post a "picket guard" beyond Plum Creek on the San Antonio road. Smithwick's detachment had barely started when a courier from Williamson overtook them with orders that all except two men should return immediately to Bastrop. News of the fall of the Alamo and of Houston's retreat had reached Williamson.

This information appalled even the hardened scouts.

[17] *Ibid.*, 241-243.

[18] Smithwick, *Evolution of a State*, 125.

[19] *Ibid.*, 123.

Smithwick read the orders to them and asked, "Well, boys, who's going to stay with me?"

They looked blank. Someone said, "I'm not going to stay here to be murdered."

A sixteen-year old boy, Jim Edmundson, evidently one of those careless young fellows who might have ridden with anyone's patrol to "jest at the dawn with death," spoke up.

"By gummie, Cap," he said, "I ain't afraid to stay with you anywhere."

As the other rangers rode back to Bastrop, Smithwick and young Edmundson rode forward to their destination. After two days of constant patrolling—during which time they were as wary of Indians as of Mexicans, but found no signs of either—the two rangers started back to Bastrop.

Evidence of the haste with which the settlers had left was found at houses along the way. At Cedar Creek, Smithwick and Edmundson saw "chickens and eggs [enough] to make a preacher's mouth water."[20]

Meanwhile Bastrop was being deserted as fast as the colonists could get across the river. Almost fifty years later one of the refugees recalled a very important favor rendered to him at the time by Major Williamson:

> We came in great haste to Bastrop, fearing we might find Mexicans already there. We found Col. Williamson, or "Three-Legged Willie," as he was called, with a small company of men, stationed there for its protection. I remember my shoes were worn almost entirely out when we reached Bastrop, and Col. Williamson presented me with a pair of good boots, which were indeed acceptable. We crossed the river and collected our cattle at Judge Smithy's place. . . .[21]

The nervous dread that hung over this party was shared by all the refugees. As cattle were being rounded up, a youth, Hugh Childress, developed an over-active imagination.

"Let's hurry," he shouted, "for I smell the Mexicans now!"[22]

[20]*Ibid.*, 124-125.

[21]John H. Jenkins, Sr., in Bastrop *Advertiser* (Bastrop, Texas), November 8, 1884.

[22]*Ibid.*

When Smithwick and Edmundson returned to Bastrop, everyone except Williamson and a company of nineteen men had gone. Upon the arrival of these scouts, Major Williamson and his men sank all the remaining boats near the town and started down the east side of the river. When they had gone about ten miles, they met a courier from Houston, who ordered them to remain at Bastrop for the purpose of transporting across the river as many cattle as possible.[23] This was doubtless the first order Williamson had received from Houston since the retreat of the army from Gonzales. Accordingly, the rangers retraced their steps. Back at Bastrop, the boats being sunk and the river being "up swimming," Major Williamson ordered Smithwick and three other men to go up to Webber's place to sail a small boat, known to have been recently constructed there, down the river to the ranger encampment. At Webber's, Smithwick and Ganey "Choctaw Tom" Crosby manned the boat and started down the river with it, while their companions led their horses along the banks. The "dugout" was hard to navigate, but two days later Smithwick piloted it into Bastrop, with a pretty good canoe, found up the river, attached.

As there was no chance to get any cattle across, the rangers made themselves comfortable in a camp opposite the deserted town. They believed that the Mexicans would not come by Bastrop; so, keeping only a sentinel posted at the ford, they watched the new spring color the landscape, ate the provisions left behind by the fleeing townsmen, and leisurely whiled their time awaiting further orders from General Houston. But this idyllic interlude lasted only a few days, for one morning, looking across the river, they saw a Mexican army, about six hundred strong, in possession of the town. The boat which the rangers had brought down the river had been captured.

Thus it was that Williamson, who had done so much to bring on the revolution, got his first glimpse of one of Santa Anna's avenging armies. But at this introduction, with only twenty-two men at his disposal, the major had only one choice: a hasty retreat. Smithwick says: "We didn't

[23]Smithwick, *Evolution of a State*, 125-126.

stand on the order of our going, but went at once. . . ." The fact is that the rangers retreated in such haste they left their sentry, an old man named Jimmie Curtice, behind. As they were galloping away, Smithwick thought of him. He rushed over to the major and said, "You ain't going to leave Uncle Jimmie on guard, are you, Major?"

"Good God, no!" shouted Williamson, "Ride back and tell the old man to come on!"

Smithwick galloped back to find Uncle Jimmie sitting against a tree, with a bottle of whiskey beside him, "as happy and unconscious of danger as a turtle on a log."

"Uncle Jimmie," Smithwick shouted, "mount and ride for your life! The Mexicans are on the other side, and our men are gone!"

"The hell they are," said the old man, calmly. "Light and take a drink."

"There's no time for drinking," said the impatient Smithwick. "The Mexicans may swim the river and be after us any minute—let's be off."

"Then," said Uncle Jimmie, "let's drink to their confusion."

Smithwick, deciding that the quickest way to start the old man was to oblige him, got off and took a drink. When at length they leisurely mounted, Uncle Jimmie said, "Well, we can say one thing; we were the last men to leave."[24]

While Williamson and his rangers were thus departing from Bastrop, the cause of Texas had fallen low indeed. Houston's forces, after leaving Gonzales, had reached Burnham's crossing on the Colorado on March 17. By this time they had been reinforced, and their strength, Houston reported, was about six hundred men. After remaining two days at Burnham's, they crossed the river and descended to a site near the present town of Columbus. Here they remained in camp for about a week expecting to do battle daily, for on March 21 General Sesma with about 725 Mexicans arrived on the west bank of the Colorado about two miles above the Texans and pitched camp.[25]

[24]*Ibid.*, 127.

[25]Barker, "San Jacinto Campaign," *Quarterly of the Texas State Historical Association*, IV, 243-244.

The two armies remained in their positions, almost within shouting distance of each other, for five days. Houston's forces, growing daily, had swelled to a number between twelve hundred and fourteen hundred men. Everyone expected the Texans to cross the river and drive the Mexicans from the country, for Houston had several times declared his intention of fighting on the Colorado. But on March 26, the inscrutable mind of "The Raven" had somehow reversed itself, and later in the afternoon he gave the orders that began the retreat toward the Brazos.

The disappointment with which the army received Houston's decision was sharp. By this time the news of Fannin's rout was being circulated through the colonies with an alarm approaching hysteria; and when it was seen that the army of Texas was falling back from the Colorado, the confusion of the colonists mounted into panic compounded. Reinforcements marching to join the army turned about and fled with their families toward the Sabine and the protection of the United States. Troops already with Houston deserted by the hundreds. When he reached San Felipe on March 28, he had only half the force that was with him on the Colorado. At San Felipe, Houston again confounded his critics by turning north, instead of going south into the established settlements. At this point Mosley Baker and Wyly Martin, Williamson's old associates in the Anahuac campaign, had all they wanted of Houston's tactics. They refused to follow him farther. But Houston persisted in his course in the direction of Groce's about twenty miles up the river.

Upon leaving San Felipe, Houston's army was caught in a furious rainstorm which continued for three dark, terribly discouraging days. The army's wagons bogged down; the marching men were knee-deep in mud. During this period they moved only eighteen miles. Opposite Groce's on March 31, Houston went into camp and remained there for nearly two weeks.

His camp site was in the Brazos bottoms near the margin of a large pond and a deep ravine. The rains continued almost daily. To add to the discomfort, an epidemic of measles broke out in the army, and "nearly every tenth" man was stricken. Houston, however, doggedly concerned himself with perfecting a better organization of his troops, forming a new regiment, and creating a medical staff.[26] While in this camp, the Texans learned of the arrival of Santa Anna at San Felipe, and soon they could hear the Mexican artillery firing upon the Texas company which had remained there under Captain Mosley Baker when Houston turned north. In the camp the soldiers were becoming increasingly doubtful of Houston's pugnacity, a feeling shared by President David G. Burnet, who, on April 7, wrote the following terse note to the commander-in-chief:

> Sir: The enemy are laughing you to scorn. You must fight them. You must retreat no farther. The country expects you to fight. The salvation of the country depends upon your doing so.[27]

While all this was happening, Major Williamson had established contact with Houston and was covering with his own retreating rangers the flight of the settlers left exposed by Houston's continuous retreat. The desolation of the country through which the rangers passed, according to Smithwick, beggared description:

> Houses were standing open, the beds unmade, the breakfast things still on the table, pans of milk moulding in the dairies. There were cribs full of corn, smoke houses full of bacon, yards full of chickens that ran after us for food, nests of eggs in every fence corner, young corn and garden truck rejoicing in the rain, cattle cropping the luxuriant grass, hogs, fat and lazy, wallowing in the mud, all abandoned. Forlorn dogs roamed around the deserted homes, their doleful howls adding to the general sense of desolation. Hungry cats ran mewing to meet us, rubbing their sides against our legs in token of welcome. Wagons were so scarce that it was impossible to remove household goods; many of the women and children even had to walk. Some had no conveyance but trucks, the screeching of which added to the horror of the situation. One young lady said she walked with a bucket in hand to keep the trucks on which her mother and their little camping outfit rode from taking fire.
>
> And, as if the arch fiend had broken loose, there were men—or devils, rather—bent on plunder, galloping up behind the fugitives, telling them the Mexicans were just behind, thus causing the hapless victims to abandon what few valuables they had tried to save. There were broken down wagons and household goods scattered

[26] *Ibid.*, 245-246.

[27] *Ibid.*, 330.

all along the road. Stores with quite valuable stocks of goods stood open, the goods on the shelves, no attempt having been made to remove them.[28]

Travelling eastward across the country toward the Brazos, the rangers assisted fleeing civilians in every manner possible, and Williamson availed himself of the opportunity to recruit for General Houston's army any able-bodied man who could be persuaded to fire a rifle.

After a day or so of travelling with the refugees, Williamson, desiring to establish contact with Houston, rode on ahead of his rangers in company with Uncle Jimmie Curtice, Ganey Crosby, and a few other reliables. He left in command Lieutenant George M. Petty, whom he had previously recommended to the council for a commission, and who, according to Smithwick, was a man destitute of experience.[29]

As the rangers rode into Brenham, they found a notice from Williamson, sticking on a tree and informing them of the massacre of Fannin's men. It terrified even these bronzed, lank veterans who had faced violent death many times. In Smithwick's squad was an old man named John Williams, who had been through several revolutions in which "he had developed a holy terror of the Spanish methods of warfare." Williams tore up his commission, fearing that if it were found upon him it would condemn him to certain death. Smithwick "cursed him for a coward."[30]

By this time Major Williamson was encamped at Washington-on-the-Brazos, where he busied himself in enlisting recruits for Houston and sending out spying patrols for the purpose of dispatching information about the Mexicans on down to the general at Groce's. On April 7, Williamson wrote to Houston two letters which reveal the nature of the ranger chieftain's activities. The first shows that in choosing recruits Williamson would overlook larceny and insubordination in a man if he be "alarmed" into fighting.

The major wrote thus:

I send enclosed to you by Major Barr the list of recruits I have made for service in the command. Three [?] of these men are to

[28]Smithwick, *Evolution of a State*, 128-129.
[29]*Ibid.*
[30]*Ibid.*, 130.

Washington April 7th 1836

To Genl Houston

Since writing this morning by Majr. Barr. I recollect that I omitted stating to you that one of my spies Daniel Gray returned last night. He gives information of a chase given him by a party of mounted men in number eight, supposed by him to be Mexicans— I think he is mistaken. five men are still out in the same direction and were mounted and have had time to report— I take them to be a party of your spies that have given chase— in a few hours we will know the truth.

yours obly

R. M. Williamson
Majr

PS write me immediately you receipt of this— a Mr Henry told me you wished me to come down— I have no acquaintance with Henry and think you would have written me to that effect if necessary

Williamson

R. M. Williamson to Sam Houston, April 7, 1836

be relied upon as men that will do their duty. The other (Murphy) has been under guard for several days by my order. I still send him under guard to you in charge of Major B. His confession *under sentence of death* makes him guilty of Petty Larceny—though the sentence was passed upon him for disobedience of positive order from [me] commanding at this place. The sentence has been respited—and I beg you to release him and make a soldier of him. I believe he will do his duty as such for he is much alarmed.

A Mr. Henry tells me you desired me to ride down and see you—I am not acquainted with Mr. Henry, but if things go today and tomorrow I will visit you at headquarters—Spies are still out. No reports.[31]

By afternoon Williamson had reconsidered his promise to ride down to visit the general at headquarters. The statement in that morning's letter, "I am not acquainted with Mr. Henry," implies that Williamson may have been a trifle miffed with Houston for expressing so informally a desire for a meeting. In a postscript to a letter written later in the day Williamson bluntly demanded of Houston a written request for a visit, if he desired one. The second letter further relates an incident concerning the spying activities of Williamson's rangers.

Since writing this morning by Major Barr, I recollect that I omitted stating to you that one of my spies Daniel Gray returned last night. He gives information of a chase given him by a party of mounted men in number eight, supposed by him to be Mexicans. I think he is mistaken, five men are still out in the same direction and well mounted and have had time to report—I take them to be a party of your spies that have given chase—in a few hours we will know the truth. . . .

Write me immediately your receipt of this—a Mr. Henry told me you wished me to come down and see you. I have no acquaintance with Henry and think you would have written me to that effect, if necessary.[32]

But Williamson's confusions as to Houston's wishes were soon ended, for shortly after April 13, when Houston finally transported his forces across the swollen Brazos by steam-tug, the major and his rangers had joined the main army. Santa Anna, meanwhile, unable to cross at San Felipe, had

[31]R. M. Williamson to Sam Houston, April 7, 1836, in Army Papers, State Archives, Austin, Texas.

[32]*Ibid.*

gone south to Fort Bend and crossed the river there, so that he was in front of the Texans when they turned south. Houston, after crossing the Brazos, proceeded to Donoho's, a few miles east of Groce's, where he was joined by companies under Wyly Martin and Mosley Baker. By this time the Texans had received the famous Twin Sisters, a pair of six-pound cannon, donated by the citizens of Cincinnati, Ohio.[33]

Thus reinforced, the Texans began their march southward towards a split in the road beyond McCurley's where the thoroughfare forked—one way leading east to Nacogdoches and the other extending south to Harrisburg. While still at Donoho's, the army was soaked by a heavy rain, and the march was delayed until late in the forenoon. Once under way, the soldiers slogged over a "level, boggy prairie," their wagons often sinking to the axles. Several times General Houston dismounted to give his teamsters a lift. Everyone was tense, for it was being freely talked that if Houston should order a turn—as nearly everyone feared—towards Nacogdoches, he would be deposed without further ado as commander-in-chief. But when the divide, near the residence of one Mr. Roberts, was reached, Roberts, standing at his gate, pointed to the advance guard the road to the right and informed the men it would take them to Harrisburg "as straight as a compass." Instantly a cry was raised, "To the right, boys, to the right!" Thus, without orders, the Texans started down the road that led them ultimately to San Jacinto.

Major Williamson definitely was with the army at this time. Dr. Labadie, who four years before had spoken sharply to Bradburn in company with Williamson and who was now a member of Houston's medical staff, related that about six miles down the road to Harrisburg, he saw "Three-legged Willie" galloping up to General Houston, who ordered Williamson to "go with all possible speed to the Red Land Company, with directions that they should join the army, as it had now changed its course to Harrisburg."[34]

[33]Barker, "San Jacinto Campaign," *Quarterly of the Texas State Historical Association*, IV, 250.

[34]*Ibid.*, 312-313.

On the forenoon of April 18 the army arrived at a place opposite the site of what had been Harrisburg. The town had been lately burned by Santa Anna's forces. Houston camped there overnight, and on the next morning he put an end to speculations about his willingness to fight. In an address to the army he announced that the soldiers would shortly engage the enemy. "Victory is certain!" he thundered; "Remember the Alamo! Remember Goliad!"[35]

After leaving his baggage train and a force of nearly two hundred sick and ineffectives under guard at the camp, Houston marched the army down the left bank of Buffalo Bayou and pressed on across Vince's Bridge, below the mouth of Sim's Bayou, towards San Jacinto. The march continued until midnight, when the fatigued soldiers were allowed a few hours of rest. At daybreak the columns were set in motion again. They were halted for breakfast when scouts rode up with the information that the advance guard of the enemy was returning from New Washington. The Texans then marched hurriedly to Lynch's Ferry, where they plainly saw the approach of the enemy's advance guard. Then they dropped back about a half-mile to establish themselves in a live oak grove on the bank of the bayou.

In the army's front, extending towards Vince's Bayou was a prairie, about two miles wide, beyond which, to the south, was marsh land. On the east rolled the San Jacinto River, and at the army's back was Buffalo Bayou. Such was the position of the Texan army on the eve of San Jacinto as the Mexicans marched on to the prairie in front of them, from the direction of New Washington, and pitched their camp near the marshes at the southern edge of the field. The Texans had 783 men; the Mexicans about the same number.[36]

In the afternoon Santa Anna ordered out a six-pound cannon under the protection of a force of cavalry and fired a shot into the Texan camp. When the Twin Sisters promptly roared in reply, the Mexicans hastily withdrew their cannon

[35]Marquis James, *The Raven*, 244.

[36]Barker, "San Jacinto Campaign," *Quarterly of the Texas State Historical Association*, IV, 256, 258.

to the protection of a near-by cluster of trees. A little later Colonel Sidney Sherman with a small cavalry detachment rode out in an attempt to capture the enemy gun. After a lively skirmish in which the Texans lost two men and a few horses, the attempt was given up. In this engagement, Private Mirabeau B. Lamar, a cousin of Williamson's who had joined the army on its march to San Jacinto, so pleased Houston by his bravery that he was made commander of the cavalry regiment. That was all of the fighting for the day.[37]

The dawn of April 21 broke red with the beauty of a spring morning as the two armies nervously awaited the battle. At nine o'clock General Cós with a force of five hundred troops marched over Vince's bridge to reinforce Santa Anna. Houston, fearful of further reinforcements, immediately sent out a party led by Deaf Smith to destroy the bridge.

At noon John A. Wharton, the war party leader, went from group to group exhorting the fighters. Mosley Baker made a stirring speech to his company. General Houston could not mistake the eagerness of the troops. "All right," he grumbled, "fight and be damned!"[38] Early in the afternoon Houston called a brief council of war. There was sharp disagreement among the officers as to the proper move. Houston was silent as the council wrangled, but soon he dismissed it. He had decided to fight.[39]

About three o'clock the general arranged the army for an attack by extending a line of infantry for about a thousand yards. On each wing he placed one of the Twin Sisters. On the extreme right, Lamar commanded a force of sixty horsemen, among whom was Williamson. At four o'clock all was in readiness. Houston, on a big white stallion, rode up and down the lines. An improvised four-piece band played a brief bit of a popular love song, "Will You Come to the Bower I Have Shaded for You?" At the general's nod, the command, "Forward!" rang out.

Natural projections in front of the Mexican camp con-

[37]James, *The Raven*, 247.

[38]Barker, "San Jacinto Campaign," *Quarterly of the Texas State Historical Association*, IV, 316.

[39]*Ibid.*, 258.

cealed the Texans stalking the tall grass until they were two hundred yards from the foe. Suddenly, a few enemy bugles blared wildly. Nearly all of the Mexican soldiers were sleeping or leisurely loafing, their rifles stacked at a distance. A few of them opened fire, and some of the Texans returned it. Houston was upon them in an instant. "Hold your fire!" he shouted; "God damn you, hold your fire!"

Scattered shooting from the Mexicans continued, and Houston's horse fell from under him. He borrowed one from a cavalryman, and the line surged on until it was within throwing distance of the Mexican barricade. Then the Twin Sisters fired a volley that shattered a section of the flimsy breastworks. The Texan infantry fired with deadly effect. "Remember the Alamo! Remember Goliad!" they cried hoarsely, as they flung themselves upon the startled Mexicans.

The fury of the volunteers was terrible. Many of them did not reload, but with bowie knives and muskets they stabbed and struck their foes to death. Enemy soldiers not in the vicinity of the barricade fled like scared rabbits, and the Texans followed them, stabbing and clubbing some of them to death. Other Mexicans dived into the waters where they drowned. The battle proper lasted less than half an hour, but the pursuit went on far into the night until the rout was complete. Six hundred and thirty Mexicans were killed, 208 were wounded, and 730 were ultimately captured. Less than forty escaped. Texan casualties were exactly thirty—six killed and twenty-four wounded.

In the first volley at the barricade, General Manuel Fernández Castrillon, attempting to rally his men, was slain. Santa Anna, roused from his siesta, rushed out to see the terrible panic of his troops. He jumped on a black horse and galloped wildly from the field. A Mexican infantry officer rallied a few men under the cover of near-by trees, but a sharpshooter picked him off, and the soldiers fled. General Juan N. Almonte managed to gather up about four hundred men and march them hastily out of the range of fire. The Texas cavalry drove a hundred Mexican horsemen down a vertical embankment at Vince's Bayou, now bridgeless, where they drowned.

The Texans fought so wildly that the professional Houston, riding about the camp, make the remark, "A hundred steady men could wipe us out." On the prairie he spotted something that startled him. With his field glass he saw a grey column marching "with the swing of veterans toward the battlefield." These were Almonte's men, and they were coming in to surrender in a body. Soon realizing this, Houston breathed a sigh of relief. He was on his third horse, and he was wounded. His right leg had been shattered above the ankle in the firing at the range. As darkness closed upon the scene of battle that shaped the destiny of Texas, the general fainted.[40] The Texans, delirious with joy, whooped it up all night. Next day Santa Anna was captured and soon signed an armistice, providing for cessation of hostilities. On May 14 he signed a treaty providing for the withdrawal of all Mexican forces beyond the Rio Grande. In a secret treaty Santa Anna agreed to work for a Mexican acknowledgment of Texas independence.[41]

A certificate signed by Charles Mason, secretary of war of the Republic of Texas, on May 26, 1838, gave Williamson "640 acres of donation land, in accordance with an act of congress passed on December 21, 1837, for having fought at San Jacinto."[42] But the main body of the ranger force was not so fortunate. Noah Smithwick was thirsty "for gore," and on April 21 the rangers were galloping towards San Jacinto, "the ferry at Washington having, by Major Williamson's order, been kept open" for them. Much to Smithwick's chagrin, however, when the rangers rode on to the battlefield, they found "dead Mexicans laying in piles." Overhead the buzzards were wheeling.[43]

[40]James, *The Raven*, 250-252.

[41]Barker, "San Jacinto Campaign," *Quarterly of the Texas State Historical Association*, IV, 259.

[42]Record of Bounty Certificates, General Land Office.

[43]Smithwick, *Evolution of a State*, 131.

CHAPTER IX

Life on the Circuit

On March 16, 1836, while the revolution was in full swing, fifty-nine delegates meeting in a blacksmith shop in Washington-on-the-Brazos drafted a declaration of independence from Mexico and adopted a constitution for the Republic of Texas. The engagement at San Jacinto, one of the decisive battles of American history, launched Texas on a national career that extended for a decade.

Williamson's reward for his services in making possible the new sovereignty was his election on December 22, 1836, by the Congress, under the terms of the constitution, to the position of judge of the third judicial district of the commonwealth. As such, he was also an associate justice of the supreme court, for the constitution read:

> The supreme court shall consist of a chief justice and associate judges; the district judges shall compose the associate judges, a majority of whom, with the chief justice shall constitute a quorum.[1]

Although in modern times the position of associate justice of the supreme court would be ranked higher than that of district judge, in the days of the Republic the role of district judge was the more important of the two positions. During Williamson's tenure of office, the supreme court rarely convened. The judges had arduous duties on their circuits, and there were relatively few cases on appeal. Indeed from the day his salary started on December 22, 1836, until January 22, 1839, when he resigned, Williamson was almost constantly occupied in the performance of his legal duties in the district courts.

In the days of the Texas Republic, the legal fraternity was a brotherhood in fact as well as in name. During court sessions, lawyers took along coffee pots, water gourds, tin cups,

[1]Gammel (ed.), *Laws of Texas*, I, 1074.

lariats, and blankets—all necessary accoutrements. In some counties the population was so sparse that nightfall often overtook the travelling barristers far from a lodging house or inn. When this happened, they chose, if possible, a place affording grass and water and "camped out." After staking their horses, they built a fire, brewed coffee, and cooked what food they had. When dinner was over, "they sat around the campfire, joked, told anecdotes, discussed topics of the day, sang a song or two, and thus pleasantly whiled away the time till they grew sleepy, when they rolled themselves in their blankets, with saddle and saddle bags for pillow, and with easy conscience passed into the land of dreams."[2]

It requires but little imagination to fancy that the lawyers must have enjoyed travelling on Williamson's circuit. His expert banjo-playing, his gift for singing, and his ability as a storyteller all made him an ideal travelling companion. He was friendly, laughed readily, and, being a born actor, he sometimes conducted "revival" meetings in which he combined "all the essential elements in himself."[3] He was always on the lookout for an opportunity to spin a yarn whether at the expense of others or himself. Not expecting to be taken seriously, he originated many of the droll tales concerning himself that were thereafter repeated by lawyers from circuit to circuit until they became legendary. Some of these stories still occasionally make the rounds at meetings of the Texas Bar Association.

During the Republic such stories were so plentiful that they made the judge, despite a continuous flow of newcomers into the nation, one of the best known men in Texas. In 1849, for example, the editor of the *Texas Banner* (Huntsville) in announcing Williamson's candidacy for Congress, digressed in a political article he was writing to relate an anecdote concerning Williamson as a judge. The editor wrote:

> We have heard many anecdotes told of three-legged Willie. One occurs to us at this time. . . . A man was arraigned for murder—twelve of his countrymen brought in a verdict of "guilty"—the

[2]N. D. Wood, "Reminiscences of Texas and Texans Fifty Years Ago," *Quarterly of the Texas State Historical Association*, V, 119.

[3]Smithwick, *Evolution of a State*, 63.

penalty was death. It devolved upon Three-Legged Willie, who was sitting upon the case, to pronounce the sentence of the law upon the wretched man who had forfeited his life. The Judge is a man of strong impulses—of generous and noble feelings. His heart sickened at the thought of pronouncing the sentence of death upon the unhappy man who sat before him. Though unused to the melting mood, the man got the better of the judge, and the big tears were seen rolling down his cheeks. The prisoner was asked if he had ought to say why the sentence of death should not be pronounced upon him. The man essayed to speak, but it was evident that he had lost the power of speech—he was quaking with fear—his hair stood on end—a livid death-like paleness came over his face, and his eyeballs literally started from their sockets in view of the appalling sentence which was about to be pronounced upon him. The judge gazed upon him for a moment and beckoned the sheriff to approach. "Mr. Sheriff," said he, "I think you had better take him out and hang him. He has lost all consciousness and sensibility and his neck can be be broke without his knowing it, or feeling it."[4]

An instance of Williamson's personal fearlessness was shown by a tale relating his performance after the sentencing of a prisoner for a particularly heinous offense. Williamson in pronouncing sentence had used scathing language. The prisoner said, "Judge, you can sit on the bench and use strong language toward me because I am unarmed and in shackles."

Williamson adjourned court for a few minutes and moved down from his bench. He had the prisoner released, and looking him in the eyes said tersely, "Shoot."

The prisoner did not move.[5]

Thomas Jefferson Chambers, the old Texan whom the Brazorians hanged in effigy following the first Anahuac disturbance, knew many tales of Williamson which he related to his daughter, Mrs. Fanny Iglehart. Mrs. Iglehart has set forth an account of a joke played on Williamson by several lawyers:

Willie had a fine pipe which had been presented him. Once, when holding court at Caldwell, Burleson County, the call for breakfast was made and he laid his pipe on the mantlepiece. Returning, he missed his pipe. There were several lawyers in the

[4]*Texas Banner* (Huntsville, Texas), July 22, 1849.

[5]Unsigned document in J. D. Williamson Papers.

room, who were attending court. He related to the lawyers an incident that happened to him when a boy. He said:

"I went to mill every Saturday and once I picked up a spur in the road and at once concluded to make personal property of it. I got down and buckled the spur on my naked heel and this made my nag, Old Susan, move off like a colt. I delivered my corn at the mill and then went fishing, first on one side of the stream and then on the other, and had trouble in getting a bite. In crossing on some logs, I split my big toe open on the spur, but went on and put the spur in the crown of my hat. Going back to the mill for my meal, the miller came out and said: 'Well, Bobby, you have a fine string of fish, but you will get a scolding for staying so late,' accompanying his speech with a vigorous patting on the head. The rowel of the spur made deep and painful indentations upon my cranium. I then took off my hat and handed the miller the spur, saying: 'Here you take the spur. I've about had enough of it.'"

At this juncture, one of the lawyers came forward, saying, smilingly: "Here, Willie, here is your pipe; this story is well worth your pipe."[6]

Mrs. Iglehart further relates a story which illustrates that the dignity Williamson assumed during sessions of court contrasted sharply with the informality of his conduct in lively society:

He was holding court in Washington, on the Brazos. Several of his friends, with whom the judge had often been on lively spells of exhilaration, not knowing that he was holding court in reality, he was so prone to make mock courts, with his wild companions, came into a genuine court session. One of the number called out to him: "Hello, judge, what have you got up now?" The judge promptly fined him for contempt of court, but the man was not to be convinced of the reality of the court, so he called out again: "Well, Willie, what's all this damned foolishness about?" Again he was fined and continued to be until the fines ran up to $50, when he had to be taken aside and told the real situation.[7]

Judge James E. Shepherd of Bonham, one of Williamson's legal intimates, related the following story of a trial of a man for stealing horses:

A man was brought before him [Williamson] who had stolen some horses. As there was no penitentiary, the punishment for stealing stock was a whipping. He was sentenced and the Sheriff executed the sentence, but the man's lawyer did not know that

[6]Fanny Chambers G. Iglehart in San Antonio *Express*, April 2, 1911.
[7]*Ibid.*

the Sheriff had already done so. The lawyer for the man wrote out many pages of manuscript urging a new trial. When the man was made aware of their efforts, he spoke out loudly to the court saying: "Never you mind, jedge, I have got enough: don't want any more new trials in mine, thank you."[8]

Hardships of travel, especially during bad weather, sometimes delayed the regular sessions of court. Records of the courts of Harris County, probably typical, contain many such notations as "Judge Absent," and "No Court." The Richmond *Telescope* of April 27, 1839—a few months after Williamson's resignation—complained that the time for holding court had passed. It pointed out that the judge had failed to appear and wanted to know why. Communications, the paper said, were excellent. It editorialized that "crimes flourish without courts."

In the spring sessions, however, "communications" were by no means always "excellent." The travelling lawyers had to ride through torrential rains, ford swollen streams, and take lodgings with any settler whose dwelling might afford them shelter from a storm. In many a log cabin the associate justices of the Texas supreme court accepted the humble hospitality of the owners, shared whatever food they offered, and slept on the floor. On one rain-swept night, Williamson sought refuge in a crowded cabin where an old grandmother was holding her grandchild on her lap. She was evidently unaware of the great station of her guest, for her remarks as the storm flared violently indicate that Williamson's appearance was not indicative of piousness or prominence. Judge Shepherd relates the story as follows:

> . . . In the night a terrific storm came up, accompanied by vivid flashes of lightning in an altogether too promiscuous way. A rude shock startled the family, who were all sitting quietly around a blazing log fire. The grandmother was holding her twelfth grandchild on her knee when a vivid electric flash found its way into the room down the chimney, tearing it to the last foundation stone. Three-Legged Willie was so sure the flashing lightning had knocked a hole in him that he examined himself from foot to head to locate the point of injury. His hands finally rested upon his brow and failing to find a hole, his attention was diverted to the old lady in the corner, who, still not comprehending the lightning's havoc and

[8]*Ibid.*

smelling the fumes of sulphur, screamed in an excited manner: "Children, didn't I tell you not to be fooling with your father's powder-horn?"

Willie replied: "Madam, this is no powder-horn; it is lightning."

Her answer was: "And not a righteous soul in the house."[9]

On another occasion, after a big rain when Williamson was in a hurry to reach town to begin court, he was retarded by a balky mule. Mrs. Hally Bryan Perry says she was told that Williamson pushed the mule hard, but it would not budge. Finally Williamson decided to set forth on foot, but the mule, being astride the path, left only a narrow footing to pass around. Thereupon Williamson drew himself to his full height and delivered an impromptu charge to the stubborn creature.

"As I go by," he shouted, "if you kick me, I'll twist your neck, if the court knows its mind, *and the court does know its mind!*"[10]

The Republic's courthouses, with but few exceptions, were extremely crude. Certain twentieth century Texas courthouses leave something to be desired in architectural elegance, but the most aesthetically unsatisfactory hall of justice in the state today would have been considered a masterpiece of the gods in Williamson's time. In some instances buildings for holding court were unavailable. The first district session convened in Columbus was held under a stately live oak tree with Williamson as presiding judge.[11] On the other hand, the hall in which the first court was held in Nacogdoches, Williamson again being the judge, had been erected "upwards of a hundred years."[12] Outside of Nacogdoches and San Antonio, however, courthouses, where such buildings existed, were poorly erected log cabins—drably primitive and thoroughly unsatisfactory for record-keeping.

The jails, if the bastille at Harrisburg was a fair example, emitted an "effluvia . . . so potent as to sicken the stoutest stomach." On this subject, Ashbel Smith, foreman of the

[9]*Ibid.*

[10]Mrs. Hally Bryan Perry to D. W. R., Interview, April, 1941.

[11]Galveston *Daily News*, February 17, 1911.

[12]Records in Nacogdoches Archives. Originals and ninety volumes of transcripts in Texas State Archives.

grand jury for the county of Harrisburg in the spring term of court in 1839, bore eloquent testimony. The building contained only two cells, separated by a narrow "anti-room." These were frequently crowded by six or more "human beings." Smith's denunciation of the status of the jail, in his capacity as grand jury foreman, appeared in the *Telegraph and Texas Register* as follows:

> [The] juvenile delinquent is prepared and trained for crime and high misdemeanors, by a forced intercourse with the hardened and shameless villain. Persons of the other sex who, unfortunately for the credit of our nature, are compelled to be held in durance we understand are confined in the narrow anti-room communicating with the cells. In addition to the mortification of their delicacy by being exposed continually to the view of the inmates of the cells, their eyes as well as their ears are saluted continually with all that is obscene, course, rude, indelicate and shocking to the modesty of the other sex.
>
> A jail such as ours, is not only injurious to the inmates, but is very liable to become a source of malignant disease to persons residing in its vicinity. The effluvia now environing the jail for some feet around are so potent as to sicken the stoutest stomach. And the grand jurors urge that the unfortunate in Texas, by confinement in such a noxious abode, should not suffer more severe punishment than is awarded to crime elsewhere.
>
> The night tubs of the jail are emptied only once in seven days. During this period their foul and putrifying contents stand in the cells of the prisoners. The jail officials inform the grand jury that the emptying of these pots is attended with much trouble and great expense, that it can be done only by night from the public situation of the jail. That all the police officers are required to be present to guard the prisoners on such occasions. They ought assuredly to be removed every morning—which might easily be done, were the jail in a less exposed situation.
>
> The present building cannot be made wholesome and healthful, yet cells ought to be white-washed, and more attention paid to cleanliness generally.
>
> Also, we recommend the erection of a larger, better contrived, and more commodious building, and that several important advantages would be gained by locating it in an airy situation more remote from the dense population of the city.[13]

But the spirit of civic welfare as thus reflected by Smith, despite the zeal of the citizenry to fight for their inherited

[13] *Telegraph and Texas Register* (Houston, Texas), June 5, 1839.

institutions, was more evident in oratory than in practice. Unused to jury service, some people found such duty a vexation and a bother. At the term of the Colorado County District Court of April, 1837, so many of the original venire were absent that Judge Williamson fined the missing jurors twenty dollars each and ordered them to appear at the next term of court to show why final judgment should not be passed against them.[14] At the opening of the term of court at Nacogdoches in September, 1837, only twenty of the original panel were in attendance. Accordingly, Judge Williamson ordered the sheriff to summon sixteen additional "talismen." During this session of two weeks, the judge, for one reason or another, excused for the whole term or a shorter period eight jurors who were in attendance.[15]

Although the personal example of Judge Williamson was exemplary, the conduct of some of the judges was decidedly not of a quality calculated to impress upon the citizenry an abiding respect for legal procedures. In the Congress of 1841, Williamson was a member of the judiciary committee of the House of Representatives which had to consider charges of grave misconduct lodged against Judge John M. Hansford of the Seventh Judicial District.

Articles of impeachment exhibited against Hansford charged that he "wrongfully, willfully, and unjustly did go on the bench in a state of drunkeness and inebriation." Specifically, it was charged that, in the Harrison County district court session of July, 1839, Hansford was "in a state of inebriation" when he empanelled a jury to try Charles M. Jackson on a charge of murder. His honor was evidently roaring drunk throughout the trial, for the impeachment charged that later "still laboring under the effect of intoxication," he adjourned the court until the next morning, ordering the jury empanelled "with nothing but bread and water until the final decision of the case." Hansford "then left the place of holding said court under circumstances to warrant the suspicion of improper motives." He

[14]Galveston *Daily News*, August 27, 1906.

[15]Proceedings of District Court begun and held in Nacogdoches on the first Monday of September, 1837, Nacogdoches Archives.

wrote back ordering the sheriff to adjourn court and to clamp the prisoner, who previously had been out on bail, in irons. The feelings of the jury can be easily imagined.

Other charges against the judge were that he ordered arbitrary, unjust, and oppressive imprisonment, and levied unwarranted and excessive fines. But Hansford's prize exhibition must have been at the town of Greensbrough in Harrison County in March, 1841. There during a trial he was, according to a charge, so "drunk and intoxicated" that he vomited "once or twice" in plain view of the assembled spectators. This, the impeachment asserts, caused "considerable merriment and laughter amongst the crowd" who evidenced their mood with "remarks of contempt and witticism" and by casting "stones and pebbles" at the person of the judge.[16]

Even with judges of better habits presiding, some of the penalties imposed under the laws seem to have been barbarous and cruel, although doubtless they were approved by custom. The evidence indicates that Williamson was one of the most humane jurists of the age. Williamson's fellow-justice, J. W. Robinson, however, seems to have felt few merciful impulses. In the trial of W. J. Bibbs, charged with grand larceny at Columbus, in Colorado County, in a special session in May of 1838, the prisoner pled guilty. Judge Robinson sentenced him to receive thirty-nine lashes on his bare back and to be branded on his right hand with the letter T.[17]

But despite the shortcomings of the law, the jurists, and the citizenry, and notwithstanding the difficulties involved in the development of the new and primitive nation whose sparse inhabitants were sprawled over the vastness of Texas, the first justices of the Republic made praiseworthy beginnings in establishing regular courts. True to the pioneer tradition, the settlers of Texas were extremely individualistic, and the task of bringing them under the discipline of an orderly legal system was not an easy one. The appearance of Judge Williamson and his travelling barristers in many

[16]Harriet Smither (ed.), *Journals of the Sixth Congress*, I, 205.

[17]Galveston *Daily News*, August 27, 1906; February 17, 1911.

counties marked the advent of the first court ever to be held under the procedures of Anglo-Saxon law in those counties.

To effect the beginnings of district court sessions, quick-wittedness and courage were qualities as essential to a judge as a knowledge of law. Since Williamson was endowed with these requisites, he was exactly the type of man for such business. His presence of mind at the first session of the district court in Shelby County in 1837 resulted in an utterance which would have entitled him to a place in history of Texas jurisprudence if he had never held another court. In one terse, perfectly-phrased retort Williamson symbolically signalled the triumph of modern civilization over the orientation of the backwoods and thus heralded the superiority of legal procedures over primitive practices, old in the days of Abraham.

On the night before the first district court was to be held at Shelbyville, in newly organized Shelby County, a mass meeting of the citizenry decided that the idea of submitting to the Republic's courts would be distasteful. Shelby is a border county on the Sabine River; and at its eastern limit, it was then the boundary line, by the treaty of 1819, between the possessions of Spain and the United States. Although it was part of the Spanish territory adjoining Louisiana, various governments of Texas prior to the days of the Republic exercised little sovereignty over the area. Consequently it was a fugitive's paradise. Through gentry fleeing justice both from the United States and from Texas found it a haven of lawlessness.

Unaware of the decision of the mass meeting, Judge Williamson and his entourage arrived the following morning and selected a site for holding the court. The sheriff then duly announced the opening of court, with the judge sitting behind a dry goods box. Soon a tall, unkept ruffian strode forward and informed the judge that an assembly of citizens of the county had resolved that the court should not be held. Without so much as a flicker of an eyelash, Judge Williamson calmly said that holding a mass meeting to decide whether to permit a district court session was a most unusual happening. Looking mildly at the man, Williamson asked:

THE CONSTITUTION IN TEXAS

"What legal authority can you give for such a procedure?"

Quickly drawing a bowie knife from his belt and slamming it on the box before Williamson, the spokesman for the frontier snarled, "This, sir, is the law of Shelby County!"

In a flash Williamson whipped out a long-barreled pistol. "If that is the law of Shelby County," he thundered, "this is the constitution which overrides all law!"

Placing the pistol beside the dagger, he turned to the sheriff. "Mr. Sheriff," he ordered, "you will please call the grand jury." The representative of "the people" slunk out of the courtroom, and the session proceeded.[18]

From reports of his victory in this battle of wits, Williamson's reputation skyrocketed, with all the embellishment which accompanies the versions of many narrators. Here, for example, is a version of the incident by H. L. Byloe:

> I find it recorded of one Judge Williamson of Texas, familiarly called "Three-legged Willie," who was one of the very early judges of that state, that in his court one day a lawyer by the name of Charlton stated a point of law, whereupon the court refused to be convinced by the counsellor's statement. "Your law, sir!" said the Judge. "Give us the book and page, sir."
>
> Charlton: "This is my law, sir," pulling out a pistol, "and this, sir, is my book," drawing a bowie knife, "and that, sir, is the page," pointing the pistol toward the court.
>
> The court: "Your law is not good, sir. The proper authority is Colt on revolvers."
>
> At that he brought a six-shooter instantly to bear on the head of the counsellor, who dodged the point of the argument and turned toward the jury.[19]

To some, such talk meant that Williamson was a rough-and-tumble jurist whose shooting irons were always handy at his sessions. Marquis James has somewhere picked up such a version. Of Williamson's courts, he writes:

> On his first tour of jurisdiction Three-legged Willie was welcomed with the information that the inhabitants desired none of Sam Houston's courts there. Judge Williamson unpacked his saddle

[18]J. D. Williamson to A. D. Sanford, July 14, 1941. Williamson based his recital on information related to him by his kinsmen and by friends of Robert M. Williamson.

[19]Account enclosed in letter, J. D. Williamson to D. W. R., July 26, 1940.

bags, and establishing himself behind a table, placed a rifle at one elbow and a pistol at the other. His honor had a way of snorting when he spoke. "Hear ye, hear ye, court for the third district is either now in session, or, by God, somebody's going to get killed!"[20]

James's tale definitely belongs to fantasy, for Williamson's courtroom demeanor was the quintessence of dignity and earnestness, and there is no record that he ever snorted. Yet, of Williamson's "dual personality," Smithwick says: "He would leave a courtroom over which he had just presided with all the dignity of a lord chief justice and within an hour be patting Juba for some nimble footed scapegrace to dance."[21]

Indeed, his accessibility outside the courtroom sometimes got him in precarious situations, particularly when his friends fell to quarreling. On one such occasion, it is reported, that he had to adopt a manner of expression more violent than any he ever used in court to save a man's life. J. M. Morphis relates the incident as follows:

> Once on a time Colonel Mayfield, Bart Sims, a large powerful old Texan, and Judge R. M. Williamson, were in Swisher's hotel together, when the Colonel taking umbrage at some remark of "old Bart," so called by his acquaintances, drew his pistol and was about shooting him to prevent which, Sims snatched up "Three-Legged Willie," as the judge was sometimes called, and holding him between himself and Col. Mayfield, exclaimed "Shoot damn you, shoot!" The Judge not liking his position, but unable to change it alternately exercised his powers of eloquence and denunciation.
>
> First he earnestly appealed to the parties, saying, "Gentlemen, this matter can be settled amiably; there is no necessity for any bloodshed. For God's sake, Col. Mayfield, don't shoot."
>
> Then, as Mayfield pointed his pistol at Sims, he said, "Mayfield, make a center shot; for damn you, I will kill you, sure, if my life is spared! Bart, damn your soul, let me down." From this appeal or threat, or somehow else, Col. Mayfield's ire cooled down, and he didn't shoot. But he afterwards swore that "Three-Legged Willie" saved old Bart's life on this occasion.[22]

[20]James, *The Raven*, 271.

[21]Smithwick, *Evolution of a State*, 63.

[22]*Democratic Statesman* (Austin, Texas), March 1, 1874.

CHAPTER X

Justice of the Third District

Although legend and anecdote concerning the judge as an individual combine to make his judicial career colorful, behind all the diverting talk is a record, important to the history of Texas jurisprudence, of Williamson's actual accomplishment.

Williamson shone as a bright star in the legal sky in comparison with some of the judges in the days of the Republic who, as the *Texas Banner* asserted, "were not very eminent jurists." As a youth, trained by some of the ablest lawyers of Georgia, he had moved in the legal atmosphere of the Georgia capital. Since coming to Texas, he had been the intimate of Stephen F. Austin, who made the first laws of the colony. In San Felipe, Williamson had been prosecuting attorney and city attorney, practicing in the courts of the alcalde. Alcade himself in 1834, he had served as judge for his local district.

Thus he not only knew Texas law and practice, but also he had had a share in making organic laws. As previously related, he served on a committee in 1833 which drafted a proposed constitution for the state when separation from Coahuila was proposed, and he was a member of a committee of five to amend the articles which became in effect the constitution of the provisional government during the early days of the revolution. It is true that except for a year of practice in Georgia his practical background had been entirely gained in Texas, but it was a first-class background, derived from professional association with men who, like Williamson himself, had instigated the Republic. Thus, it was not an accident, nor in mere gratitude for his services as a soldier, that the First Congress of Texas elected him judge of the Third Judicial District and associate justice of the supreme court. He was, as everyone realized, qualified for the office by his previous training and experience.

As a judiciary officer, Williamson's salary was three thousand dollars per year, payable semi-annually.[1] Under the provisions of the constitution, judges of the supreme court were to hold office for a period of four years, and they were eligible for re-election. Compensation for their services was mandatory on the part of the state, but a judge's salary could not be diminished nor increased during his term of office. The organic law required that the Republic be divided into convenient judicial districts—not less than three nor more than eight—and that the national congress should, as soon as practical, introduce by statute the common law of England with such modifications as local circumstances might require.[2]

A congressional act of December 22, 1836, divided Texas into four national judicial districts and required that the judges be elected by joint vote of both houses of congress. Each was to begin his services in one of the counties located in his own district, but he was to serve the next session in another district. No judge was permitted to preside in the same district for two consecutive court periods, unless he was called upon to do so by a judge unable to attend. Sessions were to be held twice annually in each county.

As judge of the third district, Williamson's home territory consisted of Austin, Washington, Milam, Mina, Colorado, and Gonzales counties. The law prescribed the specific week and month in which the courts of each county of all districts were to be held, but it made no provision as to the order of judicial alternation upon the circuits.[3]

Since in some counties there were no courthouses and in others the halls of justice were extremely primitive and have, through fire or decay, long since vanished, only scattered and fragmentary records of the early courts remain. But despite the absence of such documents, fragmentary recording, newspaper reports, and articles in the *Southwestern Historical Quarterly* give a partial account of Williamson's court service.

[1]Act approved by the Congress of Texas, December 9, 1836. See Gammel (ed.), *Laws of Texas*, I, 1129.

[2]*Ibid.*, 1074.

[3]*Ibid.*, 1261.

The outline of his judicial activity for 1837 is fairly clear. Annual sessions did not begin until March, probably because the winter season made holding court out of doors or in poorly equipped log buildings a genuine hardship. Williamson began his duties by following the circuit in his own district. Each session was limited to six days. The court for the county of Austin was to begin annually on the first Mondays of March and September; for Washington, on the second Mondays of the same months; for Milam, on the third Mondays; and for Mina, on the fourth Mondays. On the first Mondays after the fourth Mondays of March and September, the Colorado sessions were to begin; and on the second Mondays after the fourth Mondays of these months, the sessions were to be held in Gonzales County.[4]

No records, as yet, have been discovered of the first session at which Williamson presided in Austin County on the first Monday in March; but an extract from his charge to the grand jury of Washington County, during the session which began on the second Monday, is printed in the *Telegraph and Texas Register*, of Houston, on May 16, 1837. The judge's special instructions concerning the cases at hand were not printed, probably because the newspaper considered the trials of minor importance. The great service rendered by the district judges in the first year of the Republic consisted more in the establishment of the courts as regular national institutions than in any legal precedents they may have established. As a consequence, the judge's charge to the grand jury was an exposition of the philosophy of justice and the process of democracy rather than an address dealing with the legal concerns of the hour. Williamson's speech was deliberately intended to be an instrument of adult education. Although it sounds a little oratorical, after the manner of the day, it is, on the whole, admirably objective, its only bias being against the Mexicans, whom the judge characterized as a "semi-civilized tribe." With this exception, it is hard to see how the charge could have been more dignified or grave. Those speaking glibly of the deficiencies of the early legal fathers may learn from this charge that the

[4]*Ibid.*, 1258-1259.

ability of a judge presiding behind a dry goods box was not necessarily limited by the crudeness of the courtroom fixtures. Williamson said:

Since the adoption of the constitution of this republic, a complete organization of the coordinate branches of government, created by instrument, has taken place.

A chief magistrate, under the style of the president of the republic, has been duly elected by the people, regularly inducted into office, and is now in exercise of the executive power.

A national congress have also assembled, and in the exercise of legislative power, have enacted many laws highly essential to the restoration of good order and morals; and tending to ensure upon a permanent basis the happiness of the people.

The judiciary have also been organized by the appointment of judges under the constitution, and an act of congress creating their jurisdiction.

To this branch is entrusted the administration of justice, individual and national; a sacred attribute, upon the stability, integrity and burden of which (it has been said) *depends* all personal security and private property. For the influence it has upon the interesting transactions of social life are more sensibly felt by the great mass of people than is that of any other branch of the government; it extends to all the affairs of private life, and operates alike both as a prop to and a check upon, the executive and legislative branches: protecting on the one hand the laws and constitution from encroachment, and restraining in a salutary and prudential manner, on the other, those branches when from "temptation, passion, or interest," they would sacrifice individual or national rights.

Entrusted therefore with the administration of Justice, in the 3rd judicial district of the republic, it becomes my duty, under the laws to charge you gentlemen of the grand jury with all matters for the body of this county, that you may know or that may be made known to you, touching or otherwise affecting the prosperity, security, happiness and general welfare of the republic and the individuals composing it. In a government like our own I assure you gentlemen that the duty of charging you is to me a very pleasant task indeed—and the more pleasant is it to me at this epoch in the history of our government.

A knowledge of the origin of the greater portion of the inhabitants composing the republic, combined with the character, and form of government we have adopted form the *true* and *real sources* of the pleasing sensation I enjoy!!!

It is true that many of us have resided many years in Texas while forming an integral portion of domain; over which the late United Mexican states claimed to have, and did exercise diction and control; yet we came to the country duly impressed with proper notions of good government and good order. To this circumstance therefore may alone be attributed that prevailing harmony which has ever existed among, and characterized us during our connection with Mexico. In the country of our nativity we saw with admiration and favor the republic of Mexico erected on the continent, presented to the world, and recognized by our fathers. Based as it was upon fundamental principles not materially variant from those of our native land, thither we repaired with "*our eyes open*," and cast our lots in the wilderness, surrounded by numerous tribes of hostile and savage Indians, with full assurance, and a firm belief in *the solemn promises*, and *plighted faith* of the government of our adoption, that it would *protect*, *sacred and inviolate*, "Our person and our property." We had reason to believe that in a nation consisting of eight millions of people, there would be found a moral influence sufficiently powerful to carry into successful operation the great ends for which they had associated, by a practical administration of the *theory* and acknowledged form of government. But in this, how much were we mistaken? It is a fact, a lamentable truth, that since the organization of the Mexican Government, under the federal constitution of 1824, *there never has been* a uniform interior administration of its leading principles in any part of the nation. Civil war and secession dogged the administration of every department and branch of the government; while conspiracy and revolt characterized the greater portion of the natives, until their constitution, fractured, worn out, and destroyed, went down, "bathed in blood of the best patriots of the country." Such was the condition of all Mexico, and thus circumstanced were the people of Texas in 1835, when the effects of the revolution were visited upon them.

For some time many hoped that the evil hour of war, actual war, a war of extermination (on the part of Mexico) might be averted by conciliatory measures. Recourse was had to those measures—memorial remonstrance, and *even entreaty* were all of them, in their turn, of no effect.

The demon of liberty was walking in the land as a wild fire, and the conflagration was wont to dry up the last fountain. Having its origin at the capitol, its ravages were carried to several of the interior states, and finally found its way to this favored land of our homes, of our families. Yes, an actual war of extermination was prosecuted to the door of our dwellings by this semi-civilized tribe. But thank heaven and its providence, and the gallant officers and soldiers in the service of a suffering country, they have been beaten back and I trust will never again return among us. To say nothing of the evils in detail, resulting from such a war, the injury, or the wrong suffered by the individual engaged in it, its general tendency to demoralize the people of all ages, is as obvious as it is natural.

To check excesses, to arrest the progress of iniquity by a vigorous and timely administration of the salutary laws of the country, is the great honor for which you are summoned. . . . I have endeavored to make myself impressive on this occasion, from a proper consideration of the present condition of the country with a *comparative knowledge* of what has been *for the last ten years.* But enough of this. Let the historian assert his right, and exercise his prerogative.[5]

From Washington the judge went to Milam and Mina counties, as provided by law. He was holding court on the first Monday in April at Columbus, in Colorado County. As reported, this "first district court ever convened in Columbus was held under one of the stately live oaks which make this city famous for its magnificent oaks and lovely, shaded streets." Absent jurors were fined twenty dollars each, and the sheriff was allowed fifty dollars for his services. These services could not have been much other than corralling jurors, but, as previously indicated, that was a troublesome job. No business being before the court, Williamson doubtless took the opportunity, before it adjourned *sine die*, to address the grand jury with a speech similar to his talk at Washington.[6] When the requirements of the law were fulfilled, Williamson then journeyed from Columbus to Gonzales County, where, about the middle of April, he completed his first circuit tour.

This concluded his judicial duties until September, but between sessions Williamson provided himself an abiding source of inspiration for his future labors. On April 21, he married Miss Mary Jane Edwards, daughter of Colonel Gustavus E. Edwards of Austin County. The marriage was a triumphant success, for Williamson was completely devoted to his wife. The couple immediately established a comfortable home in Washington County,[7] and the summer passed so happily that it was with reluctance that the judge began his travels on the circuit again in September.

His second tour was in the First Judicial District, the initial session beginning on Monday, September 4, at Nacogdoches. The "Old Stone Fort," where the session was held, had been a scene of Spanish and Mexican colonial

[5] *Telegraph and Texas Register*, May 16, 1837.

[6] Galveston *Daily News*, August 27, 1906.

[7] *Telegraph and Texas Register*, May 9, 1837.

administration of justice in Texas from time out of memory of the oldest resident; yet Williamson's session was the first ever held in the county in which a grand jury was employed. Before, according to General Thomas J. Rusk, who practiced as an attorney during the term, "a man's rights, his liberty, yea, his life itself depended upon the nod of an epantelled fool from whose decissions there was no appeal."

A study of the Nacogdoches term gives a fairly complete account of the flow of events in one of the most advanced of the early courts of the Republic. At the opening meeting, the sheriff "returned a venire of the original panel of jurors," and those answering the roll call were charged to be in attendance on Tuesday morning, at ten o'clock. One of the jurors, Jesse Watkins, requested relief of service. His reason must have been considered valid, for the judge excused him from further attendance.

On Tuesday morning only twenty of the original jury panel were on hand, and the judge ordered the sheriff to summon sixteen additional "talismen." When this was done, the clerk and the sheriff placed all the names in a hat and drew twelve slips for a grand jury. Of those selected, the judge appointed John Forbes to be foreman. He then appointed Attorney J. G. Hyde to the position of district attorney pro tem. Lawyer James Taylor, on representation that he was a practicing attorney, was admitted to practice in the court.

On Tuesday afternoon, when the first case was tried, the grand jury returned "a presentment" against William Cruise and Bernardo Pantaleon for an affray, charging that these men on September 4, 1837, unlawfully assembled together and arrayed in "a warlike manner in a certain street or highway to the terror and disturbance of divers good citizens did make an affray in contempt of the laws of our said Republic." The jury, trying William Cruise, found him not guilty. Probably he had been drunk.

The session on Wednesday morning was given over to ordering certain plaintiffs to give security for costs of court in sixty days. In addition, Williamson excused, on the ground of sickness, Clara, a slave—who was to have been a witness in the case of the Republic *vs.* Peggy, a slave—from attendance at the court for the day. In the afternoon, the grand jury returned bills of indictment against Joseph Ferguson for assault and battery with intent to murder and for sending out a challenge to a duel. After indicting Peggy, a slave, for receiving stolen money, the grand jury was excused for the day. On motion of the district attorney, Miloe Mower, D. M. Shropshire and Jacob Mast were discharged "from their recognizance."

The trial of Joseph Ferguson was held on Wednesday afternoon. The grand jury charge was that on March 3, 1837, Ferguson "by drawing the trigger of a certain pistol loaded with gunpowder and a leaden bullet against one Mathew Sims with intent to discharge the pistol and with intent to murder and kill the said Sims to great damage of him," had offended "the peace and dignity of the Republic." From the indictment it appears, however, that Ferguson did not kill Sims, but, instead, with the pistol, "did beat, ill use and ill treat the said Mathew Sims to the great danger of the life of him." To this charge Ferguson pled guilty and was fined five dollars and the costs of the trial. He was then plunged immediately into a trial on another charge—that of challenging Martin Lacy to a duel. The grand jury charged that on March 2, Ferguson, "being of terbulent and quarrelsome" disposition, had tended to "disquiet" one Martin Lacy by "wickedly, evilly, and maliciously" sending Lacy the following letter:

Sir,

I will let you know with a few words what you have to depend on to meet me like a gentleman with arms or stop using my name in any way or I hope to live till I should see you again in person and then we will settle the matter. I wish you to understand that I wish no secret advantage of you. I consider myself on an equal footing with every man in any way from a needle to a cannon.

Ferguson also pled guilty to writing this challenge, but the records fail to give the penalty pronounced for the offense.

Upon completion of Ferguson's second trial, a jury for the trial of the case of Republic *vs.* Peggy, the negro slave charged with receiving stolen money, was sworn in and empaneled. Arguments by counsel, not recorded, were heard, and the jury was instructed to seal its verdict. Pronouncement of the sentence was deferred until Saturday, but the jury's verdict was read. It pronounced Peggy guilty, and the witnesses in the cases were discharged.

A little incident marred the tranquillity of Thursday morning's session. Nothing is recorded of the details, but Attorney D. L. Kaufman was fined ten dollars "for contempt to the court." Kaufman, in 1841, was speaker of the House of Representatives in the Texas Congress when Williamson served as a congressman from Washington County. Kaufman was also later to be a representative from Texas in the Congress of the United States.

Friday was a relatively light day. John D. Pinson, Samuel Bose, and James Bradshaw, each charged with an affray, appeared and acknowledged themselves "indebted in the sum of $500," should they fail to make personal appearance at the next session of the court to be held in March of 1838.

On Saturday, as the first week ended, business was brisk. Thomas W. Walden, indicted by the grand jury for wounding and beating Philip Carroll, was found guilty and fined five dollars and costs. Alexander McIver pled not guilty to an indictment for stabbing, and his trial was postponed until the next session after the defendant acknowledged himself indebted in the sum of three thousand dollars, should he fail to appear at court. Thomas T. McIver and K. H. Douglas were his bondsmen. Bernard Pantaleon, who had been charged on Tuesday with an affray, was found guilty and fined twenty-five dollars and costs. The sentencing of Peggy, the slave, was deferred.

But this was the first business of the following Monday morning. Williamson's sentence was that she should refund the six hundred dollars she had received or pay in "lieu thereof double value of same," and that moreover she should receive "on her bare back on Friday next at three o'clock P.M. thirty-nine lashes." She was to be in custody of the sheriff until the decree was executed.

A motion by Peggy's defense attorney, Richard Scurry, for an arrest of judgment was overruled, but the lawyer was granted leave, at his request, to file an exception and was given until nine o'clock Tuesday morning to do so. Later Williamson, upon Scurry's motion, granted an extension of time for filing the exception until two o'clock, Tuesday. Scurry said the exception would be filed "then or never," and he moved for an appeal of the sentence to the supreme court. Whether Williamson permitted this is not recorded, but the chances are that he did. Statements he later made while in the Texas Congress are the basis for this inference.[8]

After the sentencing of Peggy, only a few cases of consequence were presented to the court until its adjournment on Thursday. A lawyer, Samuel Dexter, was permitted to take the oath of an attorney and counsellor-at-law. Relative to the petition for emancipation of James and Sylvey, "free people of color," in a suit against Radford Berry and wife, Williamson overruled a motion that the case be submitted to the court. He evidently reversed this decision, for the next day the jury empaneled for the trial failed to agree on a verdict, and the case was entered on the docket for the next term. In a suit involving the use of a slave belonging to Thomas McFarland, by Richard Sparks and A. E. C. Johnson, the jury found for the plaintiff. Sparks and Johnson were ordered to pay McFarland $1,475.

By this time D. L. Kaufman already had been restored to the judge's good graces, for he was appointed one of the curators *ad hoc* and an attorney in the case of William Loyd *vs.* José de Piedras, who was absent from the Republic. Joseph Ferguson, of the belligerent disposition, was released, along with four other men, from paying fines assessed against him at a special term of court which had been held on August 17. All business was finished on Wednesday, when the judge was presented with a written testimonial of the grand jury's appreciation of his work. In part, it reads:

> [The grand jury] cannot surrender . . . the trust with which they have been clothed without bearing ample testimony to the talents, ability, and independence which have characterized his honor Judge R. M. Williamson now presiding in this court; we have listened with great pleasure and profit to his able, learned, and patriotic charge and we acknowledge with cheerfulness that we were not only enlightened as to our duties but from the eloquence and integrity of purpose with which the charge of his Honor was delivered; an impetus was given to our determination to do our

[8]Harriet Smither (ed.), *Journals of the Sixth Congress*, II, 184.

duty to our country and the community in which we live regardless of favour or affection . . . . We have admired the independence, honesty and praise-worthy impartiality which have so signally marked his cause.

Coming from a community of stalwarts some of whom considered themselves the equal of any man "in every way from a needle to a cannon," the resolution can hardly be dismissed as an incidental pleasantry.

Williamson replied with admirable brevity and restraint:

I have heard with much feeling the sentiments of your last presentment. I came among you to administer justice under the positive law of the land. Thus flattered by the grand jury, I return my sincere thanks to them, to the members of the bar, and to each and every member of the court for the notice that has been taken of me as the presiding officer of the term.

On behalf of the bar, General Thomas J. Rusk, being chosen by the lawyers, made the concluding speech of the session to the grand jury. He said:

Gentlemen, it is one of the proudest days of my life, we have battled against the damages and difficulties of the wilderness, the savage, and our common enemy but all this a savage might do. It is in vain we fight, it is in vain we conquer, if we do not establish on this soil a Government of equal and just laws that will protect the rights and redress the wrongs as well of the greatest as the humblest individual who claims the protection of our common Government. I have seen the enemy sweeping on our Country in immence numbers carrying death and distraction in their train. I have seen them met in their mad career by a handfull of free men, and I have seen the tide of war reel back to its source and the bloody tyrant go into chains, an humble suppliant for the poor privileges of living beyond the day of his Glory. That Gentlemen of the Grand Jury was a proud day, but the feelings I then had do not compare with those I now feel; I now see for the first time it has ever been done in the Country the imposing spectacle of discharging a Grand Jury in this house which has stood here upwards of One hundred years. Gentlemen this scene makes up feelings which I could not express a short time since. In this place a man's rights, his liberty, yea his life itself depended upon the nod of an Epantelled fool from whose decissions there was no appeal; now I see an honest, firm, intelligent Judge in his seat, an able District Attorney at his post, and A grand Jury before me of honest freemen; In this situation Gentlemen I feel safe and contented. We must soon go hence and the places which now know us will know us no more forever; but we have seen go into operation in its various branches and departments that government in whose hands we may safely leave the rights of those who are to come after us.

On Thursday after approving the clerk's reading of the minutes, Williamson officially pronounced the session adjourned.[9] Then he journeyed to Jasper County for a week of court there, and on the last week of the month, he opened a session at San Augustine. There he tried a total of forty civil and fifteen criminal cases. He refused to consider a divorce case upon the ground that the act of Congress establishing district courts gave those courts authority only in controversies in which the amount in dollars was to be considered and not in civil cases arising *ex delicto* between parties.[10]

While the San Augustine session was under way, Richardson Scurry announced to the court the death of Samuel Dexter, whom Williamson had permitted to practice as an attorney during the session at Nacogdoches. Judge Williamson promptly adjourned court in the dead man's honor and appointed Lawyers Scurry, Hyde, Taylor, and Kaufman, all of whom were practicing on the circuit with him, to draft resolutions "expressive of the feelings of the court." Kaufman made funeral remarks at the graveside in Nacogdoches.[11]

After the court at San Augustine, Williamson went to Sabine County, and from there to Shelby County, where, as related before, he employed a pistol to symbolize the constitution. The Shelby County term began on "the third Monday after the fourth Monday of September." A session at Red River County on the following week completed Williamson's tour of the first district.

Williamson concluded his legal activities for the year in Houston, where on the first Monday in December a session of the supreme court was scheduled to meet. The Houston *Telegraph and Texas Register* in announcing the forthcoming

[9]District Court Proceedings, Nacogdoches, September 14, 1837, Nacogdoches Archives.

[10]Unsigned document, J. D. Williamson Papers.

[11]*Telegraph and Texas Register*, November 25, 1837.

meeting, declared, "already we are pleased to note the arrival among us of some honorable members of the court, and a number of counsel attending from a distance. When this court shall be organized, all the departments of the government, as prescribed in the constitution, executive, legislative, judicial, will be in full and successful operation." Williamson's name was mentioned as one of the "members and officers" of the court. Colonel William Fairfax Gray was announced as clerk, and "John W. Moore, Esq.," sheriff of Harrisburg, was named ex officio sheriff of the supreme tribunal.[12]

Little is known of Williamson's court activities in 1838. During the spring term he was following the circuit once again in the third district. A fragmentary note survives of a session in Fayette County which had been added to the third district by a congressional act, approved on May 24, 1837. H. C. Hudson was district attorney, and Jerome Alexander was clerk. The notes contain no records of trials.[13]

Williamson's fourth and final circuit tour is shrouded in silence. He doubtless made it, and doubtless also he attended the second annual session of the supreme court which a congressional act of May 24, 1838, set thereafter annually for the second Monday of January at the seat of the government.[14] It must have been during or immediately after the session of the high tribunal in 1839 that Williamson decided to resign from the bench.

The necessity of his having to struggle so hard to support his family had been removed, for potentially he had become a wealthy man. On January 14, 1839, the Texas Congress passed an act directing the board of land commissioners of Washington County to issue to Williamson ten certificates, each good for one league and one labor of land, in satisfaction of Williamson's claims against the government for his services as the agent of Ben Milam.[15]

[12]*Ibid.*

[13]Julia Lee Sinks, "Early Courts of Fayette County," *Quarterly of the Texas State Historical Association*, VII, 81.

[14]Gammel (ed.), *Laws of Texas*, I, 1502.

[15]*Northern Standard* (Clarksville, Texas), January 19, 1856.

By now the Williamsons had a son, named Hoxie Collingsworth, for Dr. Asa Hoxie and Chief Justice James Collingsworth, and another baby was expected.[16] Tired of being away from home continually, and feeling that he had done his full share in establishing the courts, Williamson, after due deliberation, wrote the following resignation in Houston, on January 22, to the secretary of state:

> The undersigned District Judge of the third judicial district of the Republic aforesaid, begs leave to suggest through your department his resignation. No other considerations than those of an individual character better calculated to facilitate national and individual justice could have induced me to pursue this course at the present important crisis. That I have labored faithfully to discharge the duties of the trust confided to me will appear from the records of the judiciary.
>
> That I will labor still upon the same basis of Individual and National Justice, I trust will soon be made apparent to the various departments of the nation. I would add that I cheerfully sustain the leading principles of the present administration as already declared upon.[17]

With these words, he closed a phase of his career in which he had served his country intelligently, honestly, and with great unselfishness.

[16] J. D. Williamson to D. W. R., January 27, 1945.

[17] Department of State Papers, Letter Book No. 2, p. 205. Archives, Texas State Library.

CHAPTER XI

Texas Lawmaker

Although twenty years of life remained to Williamson following his resignation from the court, the termination of his judicial service marked the end of his great days. After a transitional period of two years, Williamson entered upon a legislative career that extended for nearly a decade; but, intelligent and distinguished as was his service in the Texas Congress and later in the Senate of the state legislature, the climactic days for the judge were finished.

He had risked his life in battles with the Indians and the Mexicans; he had ridden through rain and cold upon the circuit; and he had eaten the wretched food of the pioneer inns. These may be rollicking experiences for the young, but after a man becomes middle-aged, such habits begin to be wearing. And Williamson, although one never thought of it in his presence, was, after all, a cripple. When he quit the bench, he was weary with the great fatigue of years of ceaseless exertion.

Only a few of the leaders who transformed Texas from a wilderness lived long enough to reap the rewards of their toil. Except in folklore, Texas was nearly as hard on men as on "women and oxen." Stephen F. Austin died on a pallet "on the floor of a two-room clap board shack" shortly after his forty-third birthday.[1] John A. Wharton, Williamson's war-party associate, died in 1838;[2] Chief Justice James Collingsworth, General Thomas J. Rusk, and Anson Jones all committed suicide.[3] These are a few of the examples that prompted one of Williamson's early biographers, writing

[1]Barker, *Life of Stephen F. Austin*, 524.

[2]Thrall, *Pictorial History of Texas*, 630.

[3]*Ibid.*, 635.

in the *Texas Almanac*, to generalize that "the fate of our distinguished men has been most deplorable."[4]

Thus, by comparison, Williamson with a long legislative career ahead of him, was more fortunate than most of his friends, despite recurring illnesses which became more aggravated as time passed. Actually, the ensuing decade for Williamson was the happiest period of his life. It was not solely because of failing health that he quit the bench; he desired to be at home with his wife and children more than was possible when he was travelling on the circuit.

In the interval between his service on the bench and the beginning of his work as a congressman, Williamson continued to practice law, but except for an occasional trip to a court session, he was in regular residence at his own home, then near "Swisher's Post Office, ninety miles from Austin," in Washington County.[5] The Williamsons were living on a farm, operated by slaves under Williamson's supervision.

Unfortunately, except for the facts that Mary Jane Williamson became the mother of six children and that Williamson was completely devoted to her, little remains of her story. That she was cherished and respected by Williamson's associates and friends is attested by a statement of Judge Charles L. Cleveland of Galveston, who knew the Williamsons and who regretfully wrote that in contrast to her husband, "whose colorful deeds were set forth by many," little has been recorded of Williamson's "noble wife" whose qualities merited being "graved on the scroll of her Maker by the recording angel." Mary Jane Williamson, he said, was destined to be known only as "a mother of men," but the home she created, Judge Cleveland contended, was worthy of more than casual notice. Her kindness made her residence "the home of the orphan," generosity being a quality of character she shared with her husband.[6]

In the early days of Austin's first colony, Mary Jane, as a child, had started to Texas by boat from New Orleans to

[4]"Robert M. Williamson," *Texas Almanac for 1861*, pp. 85-89.

[5]J. D. Williamson to D. W. R., January 25, 1945.

[6]MS. quoting Judge Charles L. Cleveland, Galveston, Texas. In J. D. Williamson Papers.

Galveston in company with her father and mother, but en route the mother died and was buried at sea. Her father, Gustavus Edwards, took the little girl back to Nashville and left her with relatives to be reared and educated. When Mary Jane finished school, she joined her father in Texas and was living in his home when she married. Edwards, a spiritualist in religion, had fought in the War of 1812. He was evidently a man of means, for he was able to give one of his granddaughters a slave to be her personal attendant when she left Texas after the death of Mary Jane in 1856.[7]

The only available birth date of the Williamson children is that of their fourth child, Willie Annexus, who was born at Gay's Hill in Washington County on January 13, 1845. It is obvious therefore that the first child, Hoxie Collingsworth, who died in infancy, must have been born in 1838, prior to Williamson's resignation from the court.

The second child was a girl, Julia Rebecca, who, after her mother's death, went to Alabama, where she married William T. Rice and became the mother of Thaddeus B. Rice, at present the historian of Greene County, Georgia. Julia was probably born before her father began his legislative career in 1840 or in 1841. The third child, Patrick Jack Williamson, named for the man over whose plight Williamson swore at Bradburn, and Willie Annexus, born in 1845, were added to the family while their father was a congressman. The fifth and sixth children, James Bennett and Susan Bruce, were both born probably before 1850. Perhaps Susan was born after Williamson had retired from public life in 1848.[8]

Doubtless to provide for the needs of his growing family, Williamson sold some of his enormous landholdings. During the interval from January 22, 1839, to November 2, 1840, when he first took his seat in the House of Representatives, he sold 3,325 acres in San Patricio County and 1,280 acres in Aransas County to Henry Smith for eight hundred dollars. During the session of the Fifth Congress, on January 20, 1841, Williamson sold his holdings in Robertson County,

[7]Thad B. Rice to Winnie Allen, November 7, 1933.

[8]"Williamson Family of Georgia and Texas," *Southern Historical Research Magazine*, April, 1936, p. 171.

secured by certificate No. 6 of the Republic's grant for his service as Milam's agent, to Bearden Stroud for $4,500. On December 2 of the same year he sold his holdings, secured by certificate No. 3—property in Bexar County—to Philip J. Weaver for $3,500. Thus from land sales alone, he received $9,000 in 1841.[9]

As a partisan of his cousin, Mirabeau B. Lamar, Williamson had been studying the political alignments being formed in the Republic even before his resignation from the bench. On February 25, 1838, during a period when he had "leisure in the country and much Sobriety therewith" he wrote that Lamar's election to the presidency as the successor to Sam Houston was a certainty. The seven counties containing the most populous area of the Republic, Williamson said he had been assured, would go overwhelmingly for Lamar, giving him more than half the votes of the Republic. The chances of Lamar's rumored opponents, Henry Smith and David G. Burnet, both "highly esteemed" by Williamson, were thought to be extremely slim. Williamson wished Smith would get out of the race because he had been a great patriot, and Williamson did not wish to see him defeated. As for Burnet, Williamson hoped to "have him satisfied with popular office hunting by a single-handed race" with Lamar. Williamson said he was sending these political assurances because he wished to cheer Lamar up, having heard that his cousin was "housed up in a dirty little room in the sickly and Lord-forsaken city of Houston."[10]

In June, 1838, Williamson again emphasized to Lamar the flattering prospects in his favor, come election day. Fresh from a "privateering cruise" during which he "touched at Tiger Point, Wild Cat Cove, Yorkshire, Travis, San Felipe, Bracyville and Bernardo," Williamson found, he said, an overwhelming majority of citizens at those places in favor of Lamar's candidacy. Opponent Peter W. Grayson, who reportedly had entered the race with the support of Houston's following, Williamson dismissed lightly with a state-

[9]Record of First Class Certificates, General Land Office.

[10]R. M. Williamson to M. B. Lamar, February 25, 1838, in Gulick (ed.), *Lamar Papers*, II, 37.

ment that revealed his own attitude at the time towards Houston: "Grayson is regarded as the administration candidate, and the people are tired of that and of such men as advocate its measures."[11]

Unless certain statements sent by Williamson in his letters of April 7, 1836, to Houston can be construed as evidencing a distaste for Houston's policies,[12] the reference to Grayson is the first known indication of Williamson's disapproval of Houston. The probability is that Williamson had not shared in popular disapproval of the general during the San Jacinto campaign, even though some of Williamson's closest friends, including Mosely Baker, Wyly Martin, and John H. Wharton, despised the big man from Tennessee. A statement written by Williamson in a dispute with Houston many years after Lamar's campaign indicates that Williamson was a Houston man during the general's first campaign for the presidency.[13] John S. Ford, who served in the senate of the state legislature with Williamson, says: "Judge Williamson was a friend of Gen. Sam Houston and a general supporter of his measures."[14] Williamson, however, could not properly be classed as an habitual supporter of any administration. He voted, as the records disclose, according to his judgment, without fear or favor.

During the existence of the Republic, Williamson served five terms in the national congress. From November 2, 1840, to February 5, 1851, he was in the House of Representatives of the Fifth Congress. In the Sixth Congress, he served from November 1, 1841, to February 5, 1842, and in the Seventh Congress, his term was from November 14 to December 4, 1842. He also attended a called session of the Seventh Congress from December 5, 1842, to January 16, 1843. In the Eighth Congress, Williamson was in the Senate from December 4, 1843, to January 4, 1844, when his seat was declared vacant because of a dispute over election returns;

[11]Williamson to Lamar, June 28, 1838, in *ibid.*, II, 176.

[12]Williamson to Sam Houston, April 7, 1836, in Army Papers, Texas State Archives.

[13]*Texas Ranger* (Washington, Texas), July 28, 1855.

[14]Galveston *Daily News*, July 16, 1893.

but he returned to the House of Representatives in the Ninth Congress, serving in the regular session from December 2, 1844, to February 3, 1845, and from June 16 to June 28 in a called session.

In the First Legislature of Texas as a state in the federal union, Williamson represented Milam and Washington counties in the Senate during the regular session from February 16 to March 13, 1846. His final term as a legislator was in the Senate of the Second Legislature in the regular session from December 13, 1847, to March 20, 1848.[15]

In 1849, only a shadow of the great orator he had been when his health was good, Williamson bowed from the political scene in defeat, losing a race for the Congress of the United States. This, however, was the only political defeat he ever suffered at the hands of the public.[16] Of Williamson's legislative career, as a whole, one of his earliest biographers says:

> While it is not claimed for him that he originated many great measures, yet as a conservative his influence was widely felt and acknowledged. He stood ever as a faithful and incorruptible sentinel over the rights and interests of the state. . . . He was inaccessible to the threats or the flatteries of the cormorants whose object it was to prey upon the public treasury or the public domain. Individuals who had bills of doubtful merit before congress or the legislature feared the sleepless eye and invective of Williamson more than all others.[17]

The record of Williamson's personal participation in the legislative enactments during his terms of office is too detailed to permit a complete account here. Such a rehearsal literally would amount to writing a history of the passage of the laws and statutes of the times. This treatment, therefore, will merely summarize the major activities of his congressional service, except for his work in the Sixth Congress, 1841-1842, when, it is claimed, "mad extravagance ruled the hour and the country seemed on the verge of destruction." Consequently his service in the Sixth Congress will be given

[15]Harriet Smither to D. W. R., January 11, 1945.

[16]"Robert M. Williamson," *Texas Almanac for 1861*, pp. 85-89.

[17]*Ibid.*

in detail, since in those "dark hours when peace and credit and even life itself had almost fled . . . Williamson did not despair of the Republic."[18]

Williamson's role in his first term—the Fifth Congress, which convened on November 2, 1840—was prosaic. Although new to the role of a legislator functioning under Anglo-Saxon law, Williamson, by his work in the ayuntamiento of San Felipe and in the Conventions of 1833 and 1835, was no neophyte in manipulating the democratic processes. In the Fifth Congress, he introduced a resolution that the Judiciary Committee be instructed to inquire into the expediency of altering and changing the return and trial terms of the district courts; but a report from Congressman Isaac Van Zandt, chairman of the Judiciary Committee, states that "after mature deliberation" the committee was of the opinion that the proposed change would "retard the ends of justice."[19]

As chairman of a select committee to which was referred a resolution proposing to disband the regular army and to provide a different plan for the protection of the frontiers, Williamson reported that "the citizen soldier who volunteers in the defense of his country, his home, and his rights will ever prove more active and efficient in the expulsion of an enemy than the tardy movements of a regular army that for the most part has no interest in the country aside from the reception of daily wages." On the whole, however, his service in the Fifth Congress was swallowed up in routine activity.[20]

In the Sixth Congress the proceedings were considerably modified by the arresting force of Williamson's personality. He took his seat at the session on Saturday, November 6, 1841, five days late; and upon the motion of his friend, "the astute and tidy little Congressman, William E. Jones," of Gonzales, Williamson was added to committees on the judiciary, post offices, and foreign relations and retrenchment. Soon afterwards he was made chairman of a select

[18] *Ibid.*

[19] Committee Reports, Files of Fifth Congress, Texas State Archives.

[20] *Ibid.*

committee to report on the annual message of President Lamar; and, upon the motion of Congressman Gustavus A. Parker of Fort Bend, he was added to the committee on naval affairs—a significant appointment as it turned out. Upon the motion his friend John B. "Big Foot" Jones from Galveston, Williamson was added also to the committee on the state of the republic. Thus he was a member of five important standing committees.[21]

The personnel of the House of Representatives at the time was international, cosmopolitan, and colorful: three representatives were from North Carolina; four from South Carolina; three from Kentucky; four from Virginia; one from Pennsylvania; eight from Tenneessee; one from Wales (Simeon L. "hell-roaring" Jones); one from Arkansas; one from Ohio; one from Austria; one from Ireland; one from Vermont; and ten from Georgia. In the group were eighteen farmers, eighteen lawyers, and four merchants. The oldest was fifty-four, and the youngest, twenty-five. Williamson was thirty-seven.[22]

On Monday, November 8, Williamson introduced his first bill. Ever the lawyer, he sought to direct and regulate the proceedings in reference to lands which had been forfeited or escheated.[23] As a member of the committee on the state of the republic, Williamson soon had to consider a petition of Pleasant Bious, "a free man of color," who had settled in Texas allegedly ignorant of the law forbidding free negroes to remain in the Republic. He had a wife and children who, being slaves, could not leave Texas with him. His petition requested that he might remain in Texas and be protected from those who "might use the power of the law because he was black." The committee on November 8 reacted favorably to Bious's petition and recommended passage of a resolution granting his request. A week later the house rejected the bill, but a motion to reconsider "the whole" was passed. When it was again presented to the house, Williamson was one of a minority of seventeen who voted for rejection.

[21]Smither (ed.), *Journals of the Sixth Congress*, II, 15, 23, 26.

[22]*Ibid.*, 450.

[23]*Ibid.*, 18.

Congressman John Caldwell of Bastrop County then offered an amendment which provided that "nothing in the act shall be so constructed as to permit said negro to live in any other part of the Republic than the county of Houston where he is now domiciled." Williamson promptly moved the indefinite postponement of the bill and the amendment, and his motion carried, eighteen to sixteen.[24] Williamson's role in the affair thus indicates his personal disapproval of any legislation which might weaken the standardized practices concerning slavery.

On the same day Williamson voted with the majority in defeating an act to regulate proceedings in civil law suits, but he was defeated in his opposition to the amendment of an act to prescribe the method of proceeding to obtain the benefit of the act of habeas corpus.[25]

Thus far Williamson's activities had been ordinary enough, but on Friday, November 19, the tempo of affairs quickened. Williamson, as a member of the committee on naval affairs, was one of a majority of a select committee which submitted a report declaring that President Lamar's act in ordering the Texas navy "to join and cooperate with naval forces of Yucatan against Mexico" was disregardful of a "plain legislative mandate." An act of the Fifth Congress had decreed that the Texas navy should be laid up "in ordinary." The president, therefore, was pronounced guilty of "violation of a law of the land." Since a minority of the committee gave notice of intention to file a "counter report,"[26] Williamson's support of the majority indicates that he had split with Lamar, whom he had supported so enthusiastically in 1840. In the course of the committee's attempt to enact legislation for the recall of the navy, Williamson's disapproval of his cousin's policy increased. Action on the matter was delayed for two weeks, so that it was December 6 before a joint resolution to recall the navy was before the house. Williamson supported the resolution, although, by moving to strike out the bill's preamble, he sought to refrain

[24] *Ibid.*, 37.

[25] *Ibid.*

[26] *Ibid.*, 49.

from criticizing Lamar personally. The preamble contained language which might be construed as censuring the executive.[27]

A little preliminary jousting, mainly concerned with the preamble, preceded the major debates. Congressman Louis P. Cooke, of Travis County, a staunch supporter of Lamar, tried to get the whole matter postponed indefinitely by contending that it had been up for consideration so long and would consume so much time in debate that it would cost the people four thousand dollars to pass it.[28]

This drew fire from Congressman Nicholas H. Darnell, of San Augustine County, who accused Cooke of having been instrumental in effecting the bill's delay. After Cooke replied that he had favored immediate action, Williamson intervened by observing that Cooke "had a short memory" because Cooke and another gentleman of the select committee's minority had caused the delay. Cooke replied that if Williamson in his "winding and sinuous way" would revert "to the recess of his memory" he would recollect that Cooke had been in favor of quick action.

The vigorous sniping continued through the next day, when both Williamson and Congressman Isaac Van Zandt, of Harrison and Panola counties, attempted to have the preamble deleted, but Congressman George T. Wood, of Liberty County, and Congressman Nicholas H. Darnell, of San Augustine County, the bill's author, were opposed. After Williamson stated that he had favored killing the preamble when the bill was in the committee, Cooke, sensing an opportunity to divide the committee, arose to express the conviction that those who favored the deletion were "shuffling in the ranks." They had, he charged, "hurled an envenomed shaft at the executive head of the nation" and then "recoiled to avoid the responsibility." Cooke said he despised such tactics and would permit no one "to ride over the reputation" of an out-going president, who if he had "favors still to dispense, might not be assailed in this manner." He piously said he despised the disposition to "slime

[27]*Ibid.*, 113.

[28]*Ibid.*, 111.

over the path of a new incumbent"—inferring that Williamson and his colleagues were toadying to Houston, who had been re-elected president.

At this Van Zandt leaped to his feet, shouting that, if Cooke were so anxious to defend Lamar on the floor of the house, Cooke should "treasure up his wrath" for a "day of wrath" to come. Van Zandt made further remarks in answer to the more pointed parts of Cooke's speech which the reporter, perhaps conveniently, "did not hear." Nevertheless, the move to strike out the preamble was defeated twenty-two to fifteen. Williamson then shrugged his shoulders and moved the engrossment of both the preamble and the resolutions.[29]

On the following day, Williamson made the opening speech in favor of bringing in the navy. His remarks show that the passing of the years had not changed his contempt for the Mexicans, and his words definitely indicated his disapproval of the financial conduct of Lamar's administration. The report of the speech in The *House Journal* follows:

> It is well known to the House, Sir, the part I have assumed upon the bill now before it. Upon a former occasion I moved to strike out the preamble; and upon this occasion I rise to sustain the preamble and resolutions. The grounds I shall assume are tenable, and based upon good sound policy. That these grounds are true, will scarcely be controverted on this floor. What are the facts that were before the committee—they are; Sir, that the President has made a lawless disposition of the Navy; a disposition inhibited by law. A people setting up for themselves, and without declaring themselves free, open a correspondence with the President, and with him alone. A correspondence is conducted with a people unknown to the Nations of the earth as sovereign. Who are these people? They are an integral part of Mexico. What is Mexico? An enemy of Texas. Negotiations are set on foot contrary to the policy of *Nations*. . . . Where was the emergency that warranted this course? Gentlemen will tell you that the right was guaranteed under the Constitution. Sir, no such right was given—no such provision exists in the Constitution. They say it was one of the wisest acts of the Administration! It was a concomitant of that act of usurpation—it was correspondent with the Santa Fe expedition. It reminds me of a lesson of my boyhood—commit one error, and it requires a hundred more to sustain it. Profligacy is a distinguishing character of the Administration. Tired of getting along as reason dictated, profligacy has characterized its career.

[29] *Ibid.*, 111-115.

There is an opposition of duty and feeling operating upon me, but duty should govern. Ever since the last Congress, innovation has marked the career of the Executive. . . . The House had the matter before it, and refused to act. It had been before the Senate, and been indefinitely postponed. Because Congress did not positively object to it, the President took it for granted that he might set it on foot. It might result in glory to the Nation, but even if it did, I would still oppose it. I will oppose all efforts to trample upon the Constitution. Our Treasury has been broken in upon, and its means squandered. Unlawful appropriatons have been made to carry out their wild schemes, by an Executive who gave no other reason than that it had been a favorite with him. But to the point under discussion. The President's sending out of the Navy was the regular consequence of the Santa Fe expedition, and gotten up to sustain it. Did the Executive not send to the nearest Mexican post, *ex dedimus potestatem,* Commissioners, who reported that all was quiet, and no prospect of invasion, and yet he has sent out the Navy. I will explain who the people of Yucatan are,—they are Mexicans, nothing else. And who are the Mexicans? A semi-civilized race—faithless whenever opportunity offers. I will ask Hon. Gentlemen if they have forgotten that a Fannin once treated [with Mexicans] . . . His Excellency's letter, while a member of the Cabinet, had opposed the negotiation of a treaty with Santa Anna, and placed a black mark upon it, and yet he had sent out the Navy to aid Mexicans—to aid Yucatan. . . . Gentlemen insist upon it, that it was good policy to send out the Navy, but Sir, is it good policy to violate the law and trample the Constitution under foot! If that position be correct, Hon. Gentlemen have the question, and I the odds to combat. . . . The Navy has been sent out contrary to law—but perhaps Gentlemen will insist that we are crippling the enemy by sending out our Navy to co-operate with Yucatan. Is there any evidence that Yucatan has a Navy, and anything to show the propriety of co-operation? After the memorable massacre of Fannin, there are still some who would repose confidence in Mexicans; after our repeated experience and the result of our last mission. His Excellency might term the people of Yucatan free, but they were still Mexicans. Never, while he was a Representative in this House, would he give his sanction to any treaty with them. Independent of this, the arrangement had been made in violation of a law of the land. Now, Mr. Speaker, perhaps under the provisions of that law, his Excellency would endeavor to screen himself from blame, but there is nothing to sustain him. . . . There was no probability of an invasion of the county, and there was nothing to warrant the course he had taken.[30]

First to reply to Williamson's arguments was his "little

[30]*Ibid.*, 119-121.

friend," W. L. Jones of Gonzales, who said he had been given to understand from Williamson's speech that everybody in favor of sending out the navy would be annihilated, and that Williamson's argument that the dispatch of the navy was a necessary consequence of the Santa Fe expedition was a "great stretch of fancy."

Cooke also spoke in Lamar's defense by pointing out that the people of Yucatan had been driven, like the Texans, to seek independence and that, in view of recent Mexican depredations in Texas, the president had acted wisely.

The debates continued for several days. Wood sustained the arguments of Jones and Cooke by virtually restating the arguments of Cooke, but Van Zandt rallied to the defense of Williamson by attacking the "profligacy" of Lamar's policy and terming the excuses for sending off the navy "false and palpable."[31] A part of Van Zandt's speech follows:

> The gentlemen spoke of the faithlessness of the Mexicans; he alluded to the fate of Fannin, and the probable fate of Jourdan had he not fought his way through the enemy. He said that all Mexicans were alike, and that they might treacherously deliver over the navy to the enemy. The gentlemen drew a picture of a wretched female, ragged and almost naked, with her children around her, wringing her hands in bitterness, on account of the money which had been drawn from her for taxes, and paid out to send the navy to Yucatan. He represented this female as calling upon the government, in varied and pathetic terms, to know what had become of her money; whether they had paid off the national debt, or what they had done with it. The gentlemen concluded by alluding to the outrage upon the Constitution . . . and declaring him (Lamar) Dictator.[32]

Congressman John W. Dancy of Fayette County replied to Van Zandt with an attack both on his statements and those previously made by Williamson. In rebuttal to Williamson, who was said to have asked "in triumph what is Mexico? and what is Yucatan?" Dancy stated there was a difference between "the Northern Mexicans who were ignorant Indians and those of Yucatan who had Caucassion [*sic*] blood in

[31] *Ibid.*, 131.

[32] *Ibid.*, 130-131.

their veins." The late Zavala, Dancy reminded his listeners, was a native of Yucatan and an ardent friend of liberty.

Referring to Van Zandt's speech, Dancy said:

> The gentleman from Harrison had pictured to this House a half-clad woman, with her almost naked children, exclaiming that she cannot pay taxes when the money is thus squandered in violation of the laws and Constitution of the country. I defy him to show that one cent more has been expended in sending the navy to sea than would have been spent in keeping it in ordinary.[33]

In the afternoon session Congressman James S. Mayfield, of Nacogdoches County, continued the attack upon the bill by deriding the attempts of England to compose the difference between Texas and Mexico.

At the conclusion of Mayfield's tirade, Congressman Darnell, the bill's author, rose to its defense. He denied the sovereignty of Yucatan and concluded by repudiating that state as an ally. He said: "God save me from such friends and allies. When I recur back to the fields of San Jacinto, I am informed that about two-thirds of the Mexicans whose bones lie bleaching on that field were from the state of Yucatan."[34]

Williamson also made another speech in defense of the bill before adjournment, but his remarks were not printed. The next day, however, he was the first to speak in its behalf.

He said that he took the floor again with regret.

"Sir," he began, "we have no king in the land—yes sir, we have, it is the law of the land. But sir, we have no equal if the law is to be trampled underfoot."

At this point Jesse Grimes of Montgomery—destined soon to become Williamson's arch-rival—interrupted the discourse by inquiring if there was anything before the house. The speaker informed him the joint resolution for the recall of the navy was under consideration. Grimes asked if the bill had been read.

"Does the gentleman from Montgomery wish to read?" roared Williamson. "Let it again be *thundered* in his ear."

After the reading, Williamson resumed. "Let it be stated,"

[33]*Ibid.*, 134.

[34]*Ibid.*, 152.

he said, "again and again, Mr. Speaker, that violence has been done to the only king in the country— the law. Violence has been done. . . ."

At this point, members of the opposition began to walk about, and the speaker interposed by reading the house rule which required members to retain their seats and be silent when another member was speaking.

Said Williamson: "You wrung it in the right time. I have been endeavoring to look you full in the face for some time but men over my size have been walking between us."[35]

Williamson then lectured the house upon the folly of violating the laws even though it might seem expedient to do so. His speech concluded:

Gentlemen have contended that it was policy to sent out the navy —yes, it was policy that the Executive should put the laws and constitution under foot. I have been taught when I was a boy that, honesty is policy. Sir, this is a policy that will break the social compact; policy, sir; yes, sir, policy. Nobody that has fought for the country, will sustain at once a policy. Have we not been summoned here by the people in accordance with the provisions of the social compact? Have not laws been made, and yet gentlmen contended that *policy* should govern.

Sir, policy is the course of the ex-Executive. Give the privilege of the same course to the Executive just appointed. Sir, we had better adjourn *sine die* at once than sustain such a course. I would sooner adjourn to the infernal regions than to do it. The country has been trampled under foot by the Executive. The Government was divided into Legislative, Executive, and Judicial; and yet gentlemen said that there was no assumption of power by the Executive in sending out the navy contrary to law. Sir, the navy will never return without an expense of fifty or sixty thousand dollars.—That is the whole truth about your navy. Yes, Sir, an individual in this nation has swept off this strong arm of defense. Gentlemen say that he is brave—patriotic, and that he loves his country; but who gave him the privilege to trample upon rights, plain, sacred, and inviolate? He was elected by an overwhelming majority of the people to the Presidency, but was he elected merely for his patriotism. Has not that gentleman in the public speeches he has made—the books he has written—and the songs he has composed, maintained that the Mexicans were faithless. But the Yucatecos, they were a *splendid* people, entirely disconsonant in character with the Mexicans. Now it is well known that, of the Mexicans, the northern Mexicans are much the nearest to civiliza-

[35] *Ibid.*, 154-155.

tion. Gentlemen say that it is a splendid alliance with Yucatan, with a navy equal to our own. Sir, I have called upon gentlemen for proof of this, but they have failed to give it. Gentlemen have spoken of the navy that Santa Anna was building in Baltimore. No such navy is in existence. There was no proof of it before the House, and I trust honorable gentlemen will not beg the question on mere assertion. Sir, the Constitution has been violated, and I want to know if this violation is to be excused in the Executive? I say, no!—that his very station is a reason why it should not be permitted. Let this be understood, that it is only necessary to be an Executive to trample on the Constitution. Is that the sense of this House? No! I say not. When the House, by their action, decides that it is, I will say that it is not sense—it is any thing that it might be called in contradistinction to sense.[36]

Congressman Andrew J. Fowler, from Lamar County, finished the debating with a similar speech in opposition to Lamar's policy; and when he sat down, the house signified, by a vote of thirty-two to five, its desires to vote on the question. On the vote on the resolution proper, the opposition to the move to recall the navy prevailed, twenty to eighteen. Thus narrowly was Lamar's face saved.[37]

Williamson's having moved to delete the preamble to the measure indicated that he had no grudge against Lamar as an individual. Further proof of this is evidenced by the fact that on December 17 he voted against the appointment of a committee to draft articles of impeachment against Lamar, Burnet, and John G. Chambers, secretary of the treasury.[38] Although Williamson's stand with regard to the navy indicated at least that he was no rubber stamp congressman, one wonders if sending out the tiny navy against Mexico was not the sort of impudent but breath-taking recklessness that had so characterized the erstwhile war party leaders and the "brave and noble Willie" who, ten years before, had charged into Anahuac with a group of lusty insurgents at his back. Unquestionably Congressman Williamson was older now. He had become a conservative.

The report of the committee on retrenchment, signed by Williamson, sounds like a document that a modern com-

[36]*Ibid.*, 155-156.

[37]*Ibid.*, 160.

[38]*Ibid.*, 176.

mittee of budget-balancing senators might submit to the United States Chamber of Commerce as a panacea for the country's fiscal ills—although doubtless many of the proposals were timely, considering the desperate financial plight of the struggling republic.

The retrenchment committee prefaced its bill to abolish certain offices with an eloquent argument in justification of "the delicate but necessary operation" of rigid economy. The Texas Republic, the report declares, exhibited to the world the spectacle "of a bankrupt government, and an impoverished people." It continued:

> Year after year our appropriations have doubled, trebled . . . quadrupled our anticipated income. . . . Shall we hesitate upon the brink of ruin . . . in our career of prodigality? The farce which we have been playing, of attempting to sustain a government on the scale of an empire, can no longer amuse the world . . . visionary schemes of national grandeur are entertained only by weak heads or selfish hearts. We have plunged with heedless steps into the mire of debt, until we are ready to be engulfed in that Serbonian bog from which extrication is impossible. . . . It becomes us to look upon the picture, dark and sad as it may be, with eyes that flinch not and hearts that quail not . . . the prunning knife must be wielded. . . .[39]

The committee's idea of "pruning" was made evident on Monday, November 22, when it proposed a bill to abolish the offices of auditor, commissioner of revenue, stock commissioner, attorney-general, commissary of subsistence, quartermaster, translator to the land office, and a host of minor officials.

The committee recommended that the salaries of government officials be fixed as follows: president, $4,000; vice-president, $1,000; secretaries of state, treasury, and war, and commissioner of General Land Office, each $1,200; comptroller, paymaster-general, and draughtsman of General Land Office, each $700; treasurer and chief clerks, each, $600; assistant clerks, each $500; armorer, $300; laborers, per month, each $18; chief justice of Supreme Court, per annum, $2,000; judges of District Courts, $1,750.

The economies thus advocated were so altered by amend-

[39] *Ibid.*, 59-62.

ments—both raising and lowering the salaries—during the course of the ensuing debates, that Williamson voted against the measure finally passed by the house.[40] On Wednesday, the house increased the salary of the president from $4,000 to $5,000. Next day the salaries of the district judges were increased from $1,750 to $2,500. In defense of this increase, Mayfield said that reducing the salaries of the judges would "drive out men of talent" and leave the people "at the mercy of . . . stupidity, ignorance, and sottishness." Pay of congressmen was fixed at three dollars per day with an individual allowance of three dollars for every twenty-five miles of travel to and from the seat of government.[41]

On the other hand, Williamson was one of a minority of six to support a measure for funding and redeeming the public debt, which was about one million dollars. Under this and other burdens the Texas dollar in 1842 was worth twelve and one-half cents in comparison with the specie of the United States.[42]

The act was not passed, however, because the interest on the debt, proposed under the measure, was considered too high. The opposition claimed that payment of annual interest of $160,000 "in actual cash" was "almost as much as our entire national income." Such a payment was considered a gross extravagance, and Williamson and the other proponents found themselves being lectured upon the necessity of economy. Congressman Porter compared its champions with the extravagant Mrs. Grundy, thus:

> An honest countryman had, by industry and economy, accumulated a considerable property, and his wife, elated with their increased prosperity, was lavish in extravagant expenditures, and had cultivated the acquaintance of what is called fashionable society. Their property decreased, and the countryman, seeing ruin's inevitable approach, often tried to suggest retrenchments and salutary economy. On these occasions, his wife would cry out—well, what will Mrs. Grundy say? This he bore for a long time, until, outdone with the desperation, he exclaimed—damn Mrs. Grundy! Such appeals, Mr. Speaker, always make me think with the coun-

[40] *Ibid.*, 70.

[41] *Ibid.*, 69.

[42] *Ibid.*, 286.

tryman—damn Mrs. Grundy! If we legislate for our own good, we have enough and I am fearful more than we can do.[43]

But regardless of Porter's little pleasantry, Williamson was consistently an advocate of what he considered to be proper economy. As a member of the committee on finance, he supported a bill to recall the loan commissioners who had been attempting for six years to borrow five million dollars from the United States. The committee declared that prospects of this loan had already led the government into extravagance that resulted in increasing the public debt by one million dollars.[44]

In addition to watching the public treasury with a guardian's eye, Williamson was constantly on the alert to defend the congressional prerogative from undue encroachment by the executive. His opposition to the naval expedition to Yucatan had stemmed somewhat from his dislike of Lamar's disregard of a congressional decree. He similarly opposed Houston when the general appeared to be acting arbitrarily. Houston had barely begun his second term when he sent in a request to the house to see the papers which had prompted the approval of a joint measure providing for relief of Elizah Bennett and Jarrett Menefee. Van Zandt moved that the clerk be directed to furnish the papers. But Williamson, doubtless not whispering, declared "the president had no right to look behind the record which was presented to him." He said he hoped the secretary who brought Houston's letter of request to the house might be "allowed to go without it."

Williamson's view was sustained by Mayfield and Forbes. Upon being informed that the papers requested by Houston were in the senate, Van Zandt withdrew his motion to accommodate Houston, and Forbes offered a resolution that the president's request was in derogation of the authority of the house. Mayfield avowed if the principle of Houston's request were sustained, "it would be worth while hereafter to ascertain before passing bills whether they would be agreeable to the president."[45]

[43] *Ibid.*, 310.
[44] *Ibid.*, 87.
[45] *Ibid.*, 271-272.

Houston again drew Williamson's condemnation when he vetoed a bill for the relief of Captain Thomas N. B. Greer and his company of Boggy and Trinity rangers. In turning down Greer's petition, Houston said that the rangers in their campaign under Colonel J. H. Moore in 1835 had taken much valuable property and had retained it. Such reasoning drew quick fire from the former major of the rangers. Houston himself, Williamson declared heatedly, had allowed his soldiers at San Jacinto to retain the booty they captured.

"I hope the bill will be passed over his head unanimously!" shouted Williamson. It almost was. Houston's veto was overridden by a vote of thirty-one to one.[46]

Considerable insight into Williamson's personal code is evidenced by his stand upon relatively minor bills offered during the session. With regard to a bill providing for the erection of a penitentiary, Williamson said he thought it a bad plan to imprison women at all. He cited the case of the "notorious Murrell whose wife pursued a criminal course to get with him after his arrest."[47] With regard to the charges against Judge Hansford, Williamson recorded himself as being in favor of the impeachment, but he said he wished to be excused from being on the committee which was to conduct the examination. This was doubtless because of Williamson's fear that he might not be able to view the actions of a judge with impartiality.[48]

Williamson was loyal to his past and to the memories of the revolutionary days. It is a pity that the speech was not preserved in which he opposed William N. Porter's proposal to change the name of Bowie County to Pulaski. Such a suggestion, to Williamson, was sacrilegious. He entered into "much discussion, in which the memory of Bowie as one of the Spartan band who fell at the Alamo was extolled."[49]

As to holding an annual adjourned session of the supreme court in the eastern section of the Republic, Williamson enthusiastically recommended Washington, the county seat of

[46] *Ibid.*, 400.

[47] *Ibid.*, 186.

[48] *Ibid.*, 190.

[49] *Ibid.*, 247.

his home district, as the site. He declared the town to be a virtual repository of wisdom, asserting that the chief justice of the Republic had a library there of twenty-four hundred volumes. "The records will be safe, the locality is central, and the inducement of the libraries great," Williamson contended.

When Congressman Matthias Ward nominated the town of Montgomery, on the grounds that it was even more centrally located, Williamson ridiculed the suggestion by saying that "he would willingly go thirty miles out of the way if it would lead to such advantages as Washington held out." To Van Zandt, who interposed with an argument favoring the retention of the court at Austin, Williamson said Van Zandt's idea was "an insult to the intelligence of the house, after they had determined to alter the present law."[50]

Williamson's notion of the most important legislation introduced during the session was Porter's bill to "reduce into one and amend the several acts concerning executions." He said this affected the people more directly than any other measure, and, as a personal favor, he wished to have its consideration delayed until Tuesday since "the state of his health" would not permit his making "any exertion" until then. The house, after some debate, deferred the measure until the following Wednesday.[51]

During the session Williamson presented the petition of the trustees of Washington College for a grant of land from the Republic, and in general he sought to make himself useful to his constituents in every way compatible with the views of his conscience.[52]

To Williamson's credit it must be recorded that although, having been a ranger, he probably viewed the Indians with the same contempt with which he held the Mexicans, he opposed an amendment to exempt from sale all legally deeded lands which had been granted previous to the treaty or pledge made by the general convention of 1836. In his opposition Williamson said he "would not allude to the rights of

[50]*Ibid.*, 199.

[51]*Ibid.*, 185.

[52]*Ibid.*, 154.

the colonists or those of the Indians, farther than became necessary to make manifest to the house the paramount rights of the republic, in contradistinction to either."

The bill was unjust, he thought, and he declared that "to boast of the glorious privilege of stealing Cherokee lands" constituted "a new species of larceny, as yet unknown and undefined in any of the books my two blue eyes have ever gazed upon."[53] His wish to have a bill deferred on account of his health was an ominous foreshadowing, probably unrealized by anyone at the time. The house adjourned on February 5, 1842, with the speaker's wishes that the members' paths might be "green by land and smooth by sea," ringing in their ears.[54]

As noted, Williamson was returned to a seat in the Seventh Congress, and he began a term in the Eighth Congress as a senator. The returns in the senatorial race were contested by Jesse Grimes, who had been one of his opponents. After Williamson had served in the Senate from December 4, 1844, to January 4, 1845, his seat was declared vacant. He was succeeded by Grimes on January 28.[55]

A study of the available papers on the election throws little light on the question of who the winner actually was. Three candidates were in the race, and, according to Grimes, who based his statement on "the best information" he had been able to obtain, Williamson received 451 votes to 476 votes for Thomas W. Barnett and 498 for himself. However, William H. Ewing, chief justice of Washington County, certified from the various returns made to him that Williamson "was duly and constitutionally elected." Montgomery and Brazos counties had been tardy in reporting the election results, and in Washington County some of the votes were disallowed "on account of the illegality of the officers in their manner of holding the election." Judge Ewing, therefore, unhesitatingly pronounced Williamson the winner and issued to him a certificate of election. A tabulation of the votes on file in the archives at the state capitol shows that

[53]*Daily Bulletin* (Austin, Texas), December 7, 1841.

[54]Smither (ed.), *Journals of the Sixth Congress*, II, 450.

[55]Harriet Smither to D. W. R., January 11, 1945.

Williamson received 513 votes to 506 for Grimes and 461 for Barnett. It was probably upon the basis of this tabulation that Justice Ewing issued the winner's certificate to Williamson. The senate committee which later gave the seat to Grimes may have added to these totals, however, the votes in certain precincts which Justice Ewing had ruled illegal. The decision of Judge Ewing, nevertheless, can hardly be termed biased in Williamson's favor, for the records show that Ewing ruled out several boxes in which Williamson established a big majority. In one box, disregarded because "no election was ordered in the county and because it was returned by a person unqualified to do so," Williamson received seven times as many votes as Barnett and Grimes combined.[56]

In 1844 Williamson was back in the House of Representatives for the ninth and final regular session of the Texas Congress, and during the time he was an ardent advocate of the proposal, generally being urged throughout the Republic, that Texas be added as a state to the United States of the North. During this session, he was a signer of a letter from the Congress of Texas to the Congress of the United States intended to correct erroneous opinions which Texas legislators believed prevalent in the United States concerning the feelings of the people of Texas on the subject of annexation. The letter stated it was the belief of the Texas Congress that at least nine-tenths of the people of Texas "would cheerfully embrace any overtures from the government of the United States, having for their object the political annexation of Texas on a footing in all respects equal with other states of the union."[57]

When not urging the proposal of annexation, Williamson busied himself at Washington during a legislative lull in the fall of 1845 by acting as chairman of a mass meeting called to discuss methods "of securing the Harrisburg Railroad." He appointed a committee to solicit subscriptions for the project.[58]

[56]Files of Contested Election Returns, 1843, Texas State Archives.

[57]*The Tropic* (New Orleans, Louisiana), April 26, 1844.

[58]*Texas State Gazette*, October 15, 1845.

At a public meeting of the citizens of Washington County on May 15, 1846, Williamson was one of the speakers who sustained President Anson Jones's proclamation urging the citizens of Texas to elect delegates to a national convention to petition annexation by the United States.[59] In fact, Williamson was such an ardent advocate of annexation that when a son was born to his wife on January 13, 1845, he gave the child the middle name of Annexus—presumably so that no one might ever mistake his father's attitude on the subject uppermost in the nation's consciousness during the year of the boy's birth.[60]

When the ceremony consummating the long awaited event finally took place, on February 19, 1846, Williamson had been elected a senator to the first state legislature. He represented the district of Milam and Washington, and his presence at the inauguration of the first state government and the official end of the Texas Republic, a solemn affair, has been described as follows:

> There sat Robert M. Williamson ("Three-Legged Willie"), the fearless, whose bold and incisive oratory gave him power of control, and whose big heart drew to him the affections of all who knew him.[61]

As soon as the state was safely launched on its new course, Senator Williamson became a staunch member of the national Democratic party. At a public meeting in Austin on April 27, 1846, he was appointed a member of a committee of ten which drew up resolutions sustaining "the principles of the Democratic party" and urging the people of the state to elect delegates to a state convention of Democrats which had been scheduled to meet in Washington (Texas) in November.[62]

During his term as senator in the second legislature, he introduced a resolution at a Democratic state convention held in Austin on January 10, 1848, which indicated that,

[59]*Northern Standard*, June 3, 1845.

[60]J. D. Williamson to D. W. R., January 27, 1945.

[61]Dudley G. Wooten, *History of Texas*, II, 13.

[62]*Northern Standard*, June 3, 1846.

had he lived, he would have become an ardent Confederate. The resolution reads:

> *Resolved:* That we will, as Texans support for the Presidency and Vice-Presidency of the United States such individuals of the Democratic Party as will maintain the Federal Compromise on the subject of slavery, and maintain the establishment of our boundary line as defined by the laws of the late Republic of Texas.[63]

His service in the second state legislature, adjourning on March 20, 1848, concluded Williamson's work as a lawmaker.

During all the years he had served both as a Texas national congressman and state senator, he was the subject of countless legends inspired by his personal characteristics. To hear him challenge his opponents during a legislative campaign was a dramatic treat, and it was just as well that he could take care of himself before the public, for in the political campaigns of the day no holds were barred. Few entertainments were so exhilarating as a first-class election night frolic. While awaiting the official returns, the victors gave vent to their partisan feelings in vigorous celebrations. In 1842, Williamson's old friend Mosely Baker was barely nosed out by Archibald Wynn in Harris County in a race for a seat in the House of Representatives of the Sixth Congress. Baker described the post-election celebration thus:

> Last night the Wynn party had a great celebration and Barbecue had a quarter of beef in the middle of Main Street—Marching around it with their lamps and music. After some time spent in rejoicing—my friends collected, prepared their lamps and sent Mem Hunt disguised to the lower part of the town with instructions to come galloping into town—with the declaration that I had gotten 26 votes at Page's and Wynns 4. He did so in fine style when we all turned out with our Lamps, marched through town huzzaing for Baker and offering to bet them 2 to 1 on the election —The others stood it for about half an hour but were finally bluffed off and retired perfectly chap fallen leaving their Barbecue, whiskey and Bread in the street.[64]

There is no reason to suppose that election celebrations in Williamson's races were any less vigorous. Certainly the

[63]*Telegraph and Texas Register*, March 2, 1848.

[64]Smither (ed.), *Journals of Sixth Congress*, II, 2.

character of his campaigns filled his followers with enthusiasm. Upon one occasion, Williamson was opposed by a doctor who mistakenly assumed that a pioneer Texas audience approved only of refinement in political candidates. The doctor sought to embarrass Williamson by charging that he had shot two men—a legend which Williamson himself may have originated.

In reply, Williamson convulsed his rustic followers by saying:

"On two occasions under the peculiar force of circumstances I have been forced to kill two men. But, my dear doctor, tell us—how many men have you killed in the practice of medicine?"

On election day Williamson is reported to have received every vote from the community in which he made this speech.[65]

Williamson was so well known by the nickname, "Three-Legged Willie," that many of his staunch followers did not know his real name. Once, upon closing a hard campaign, Williamson journeyed into a coast town on election day. Met by his enthusiastic supporters, he inquired as to how the election was going. He was told that every one had voted for his opponent.

"There's a fellow named R. M. Williamson, running," they explained, "but we don't know him."

"You damned fools!" Williamson shouted. "That's my name!"

After a short consultation, the election officials withdrew the ballots from the box. The election was held over, and Williamson is said to have received every vote.[66]

If Williamson was adroit as a campaigner, he was no less skilled in rough and tumble debating upon the legislative floor. Most famous of the anecdotes concerning his performances in this respect is one setting forth a speech he made in opposition to moving the supreme court from Washington, capital of Texas during a part of Houston's second term as president, to Galveston. Williamson, as congressman

[65]John S. Ford, in Galveston *Daily News*, July 16, 1893.

[66]*Ibid.*

from Washington County, naturally opposed the proposal, which was supported by western congressmen and particularly by J. B. Jones, congressman from Galveston County. Other strong advocates of the measure were Simeon L. Jones of San Patricio County and W. E. Jones of Brazoria County.

In the debate, Williamson promptly rose to the defense of Washington, his home town, thus:

> Mr. Speaker, this bill is fostered by my friends, the three Joneses, and in order to distinguish them in what I have to say, I will allude to them as my friend Big-Foot Jones, from Galveston, assisted by my little friend, the astute, tidy little W. E. Jones, from Brazoria, and my red-headed friend, Hell-roaring Simeon L. Jones, from San Patricio County.
>
> Mr. Speaker, remove the supreme control of the government of Texas to Galveston? Where is Galveston? Sir, it is a sand bank detached from the main continent of America, an isolated spot in the middle of the Atlantic Ocean where the pelican lays her eggs and the sea gull screams, and whose inhabitants but yesterday refused to obey the proclamations of our president.
>
> It was formerly inhabited by Lafitte and his bloody set of associated pirates, but now it is inhabited by the lordliest set of damned rascals my two blue eyes have ever gazed upon. No, Mr. Speaker, I go against the bill, with both of my arms and all three of my legs.

This set the house in a roar of laughter which definitely destroyed any chance the bill might otherwise have had. Someone sitting by Congressman Jones from Galveston asked, "Aren't you going to answer that?"

"What would be the use?" replied Jones, joining in the laughter. "The next time he would be still worse."[67]

The Joneses were particular friends of Williamson, and he loved to twit them. Williamson's grandson, J. D. Williamson of Waco, tells another story concerning "Big Foot" and "Hell-roaring" Jones and their opposition to a Williamson measure:

> A bill offered by Grandfather for the benefit of his constituents was opposed by two members of the Texas Congress by whose efforts the bill was defeated. After defeat of the bill he arose and

[67] *Ibid.* See also issue of March 19, 1899. This anecdote was also related to D. W. R. by Mrs. Hally Bryan Perry.

said, Mr. Speaker, I offered this little bill for the benefit of my constituents believing it would have no opposition, but by the astuteness of Big-Foot Jones and the toot-assness of Hell-Roaring Jones, they knocked my bill into Hell-Smithereens.

Upon being called to order by the Speaker for unparliamentary language, Williamson replied, "Latin, if you please, Mr. Speaker."[68]

Further accounts of Williamson's amusing legislative manipulations have been preserved by John S. Ford, who served with the judge in the Congress shortly before the admission of Texas into the Union. Here are Ford's recollections:

The members of Congress from the eastern portion of the state were mostly firm friends of Gen. Houston; consequently they expected every Houston man to support any measure brought forward. They were anxious to have a bill passed providing for taking the census of Texas. Not long before the day fixed for the adjournment of Congress, there was a night session of the House of Representatives. The "census bill" was called up. It had a good chance to pass. Judge Williamson approached the desk of James H. Raymond, the chief clerk, and asked for the privilege of looking at the bill. He took it and tore it in pieces. The house adjourned soon after. Judge Williamson went home that night.

In a conversation with Judge Williamson soon afterward, when we had been admitted into the Union, he said: "You fellows from eastern Texas got mad with me because I would not support the census bill. I felt certain we did not have 150,000 inhabitants, and we would have had only one member of the House of Representatives. As it is we have two." It was a good idea.

Col. Benjamin Rush Wallace was one of the members from San Augustine. He was a Virginia gentleman of the old school. He had graduated from West Point and was a man of undoubted honor and honesty. It was not long after the commencement of the session until Judge Williamson and he had a wordy contest. The San Augustine gentleman came back and made a splendid effort. Williamson appeared very solemn. His sadness became intense. He could not have looked more despondent if he had learned of the death of all his relatives. The colonel took his seat. The most of us thought, well, sir, you have attacked the colonel once too often. Williamson arose to reply, and in a voice with a woe-begone tone, almost groaned out: "Dead, yes, dead, Mr. Speaker, slain by that mighty instrument which in the hands of Samson killed thousands of Philistines." Dignity was cast overboard. Every man in the

[68]J. D. Williamson to D. W. R., December 18, 1944. Related to Williamson by Dr. J. B. Robertson of Washington County. Robertson was a Confederate General.

house laughed immoderately. It was said, although I do not vouch for the assertion, that the colonel wanted to fight.[69]

Even the recurring illnesses of Williamson became the subjects of legends. During his service in the legislature he was seldom entirely well. Sometimes he was confined to his room for several days. A tale, probably spurious, relating to such an occasion was told by Campbell Wood of San Saba. It seems that during a session of the legislature Williamson was a boarder in a small two-story hotel in Austin. Wood tells his story thus:

> While there, Williamson became seriously ill and a little Frenchman was engaged to nurse him. His condition rapidly grew worse, despite the care and attention he received both from friends and physicians. In a little while he apparently died and as the physicians in attendance pronounced life extinct, carpenters were called in to take the measure of the supposed corpse for a coffin, there being no undertakers in Texas at that early day, and all coffins had to be manufactured as needed.
>
> In due time the coffin was completed and being carried into the room where the Judge's body lay, the two carpenters and the French nurse lifted the supposed corpse into the home-made casket. Then to their astonishment the carpenters discovered that in taking their measurements they had failed to make allowance for the left knee. This being bent, it could not be brought down on a level with the body, and so prevented the fastening down of the lid of the coffin. The sides of the coffin needed to be built higher, and to do that they lifted the body out, placed it again on the bed and carried the coffin back to the shop.
>
> Speaking of the incident afterwards, Judge Williamson said that all this time he was entirely conscious of all that was going on around him, but was utterly powerless to move a muscle or make a sound, though he tried with all his might to do so, fully realizing that unless he quickly succeeded he would surely be buried alive.
>
> In the course of an hour or two the carpenters, having made the necessary alteration, returned with the coffin. Placing it upon two chairs and calling the little Frenchman to their assistance, they took hold of the still recumbent and apparently inanimate body and began to lift it. Aware that now or never was the supreme moment for him, Judge Williamson exerted all his remaining strength of will; his power of speech and movement suddenly returned, and with his hands sweeping the white shroud from his face and shoulders he exclaimed: "What the h—l and d—n are you doing?"

[69]Ford, in Galveston *Daily News*, July 16, 1893.

Such a sudden coming back to life of one they thought as dead as any man well could be was more than the carpenters and nurse could stand. Being close to the door, the carpenters shot out of it and went head foremost down the short flight of stairs. The window his nearest place of exit, the French nurse went though it with a howl of fright, to land on the ground a story below too demoralized to feel the shock of his fall.[70]

It is a pity that Williamson was not in his best form in the race he made for Congress of the United States in 1849. Weary and ailing, the judge entered the campaign late, and "owing to his want of acquaintance on the Rio Grande," where many newcomers to Texas had lately settled, he was narrowly defeated by Volney E. Howard, a Mississippian.[71] Even so, Williamson went down firing both barrels. At Clarksville at a joint-speaking he was the first to appear—by prior arrangement, he declared, "to clear away the cobwebs from the path in which the others are to follow, a task I have frequently before performed."[72]

He then succinctly stated his own platform, announcing himself a Democrat in principle but expressing his disregard of party names. With regard to party platforms he announced he would "support the measures most beneficial to Texas without reference to parties." He said he would rather be called a Texian than by the name of both parties. On the question of slavery he contended for "the right of the southern planter to carry his slaves to California or any other portion of the United States territory south of the compromise line." The Clarksville, Texas, *Northern Standard* added that "on the subject of our boundary and frontier protection," his views were "sound and patriotic."[73]

At least one of Williamson's opponents in this race was a pretty good match for the judge in wit. He was Colonel Hansbrough Bell, who made the race on the issue of his own outstanding honesty.

[70]Document in J. D. Williamson Papers. See also San Antonio *Express*, May 24, 1908.

[71]"Robert M. Williamson," *Texas Almanac for 1861*, p. 88.

[72]*Northern Standard*, July 14, 1849.

[73]*Ibid.*

Referring to Williamson, the colonel said, "Perhaps Bob Williamson thinks himself an honest and an honorable man, but if so, it is that wild harum-scarum kind of honesty that I know not where to place it."

Colonel Bell's peroration must have established a precedent of some sort. He declared:

> But, gentlemen, I take it, an honest man nowadays is hard to find. Aesop sought for one three thousand years ago, with a candle lighted to aid the sunshine, but failed to find one. Jesus Christ when on earth, eighteen hundred years ago, failed to find twelve honest men. To be sure he did not look among honorable office seekers or he might have succeeded better, but as it was, Peter denied him, and Judas Iscariot, God damn him, betrayed him. I, too, fellow citizens think myself honorable and honest; but if I am not I have the brains. . . .[74]

One may be sure that Williamson responded appropriately although his reply has not been preserved. A month later, the campaign was still going strong. In Houston, candidates Volney E. Howard, Timothy Pilsbury, and Williamson addressed a meeting and "took up so much time that General McLeod, also a competitor, deferred the expression of his views to another meeting."[75] Perhaps none in the laughing crowd that night guessed that the old fighter was at the end of his public career.

[74]*Texas Banner*, July 22, 1849.

[75]*Northern Standard*, June 30, 1849.

CHAPTER XII

Retirement

Williamson's last decade, in general, was a period of eclipse. Following his defeat in the race for Congress in 1849, he retired to his farm near Independence. He was a sick man, although no record which would indicate the exact nature of his illness has survived. Increasingly towards the end of his legislative service he had been absent from his seat in the Congress because of poor health.

That he was not able to attain the power which had characterized his oratory in the revolutionary days when there was "fire and vigor in his speech which surpassed description" was plainly evident in the campaign of 1849, when the *Northern Standard* alluded to a speech he delivered, thus:

> We confess we were rather disappointed in Mr. Williamson's speech. We cannot say that he was either confused or embarrassed, but his language, sometimes, was not the more correct nor his meaning always intelligible. There was, on this occasion, neither the fluency nor boldness we had expected.[1]

But despite his sickness, he was unable to accept the role of an idle dweller on a farm. He devoted himself to supervising the education of his children, and he undertook the task of writing a history of the events leading up to the recent revolution from Mexico.[2] Apparently his health was improved in 1851, for he entered the race for lieutenant-governor, but the labors of campaigning proved too much for him. When, during his campaign in 1851, he spoke in Galveston and was twitted about his famous speech in Congress in which he had humorouly claimed the town's inhabitants were a set of damned rascals, he was unable to

[1]*Northern Standard*, July 14, 1849.

[2]*Texas State Gazette*, March 31, 1855.

reply appropriately. According to reports he became confused and "broke down."[3] In campaigning previously he had referred to the Galveston speech "as remarks which had been attributed to him," and by thus bringing up the subject himself he forestalled any possible heckling on the subject by drolly eliciting a roar of laughter from the crowd.[4]

Soon afterwards he found it impossible to continue in the race. In announcing his withdrawal, the newspaper account stated, "Considerations of a private nature render it absolutely necessary that he should withdraw from the contest. He feels under obligations to his friends for their interest in his behalf."[5]

During this period of his life he may have drunk more whiskey than was good for him; but as in other respects with regard to him, the talk about his drinking greatly enlarged upon the facts. Although the legend has persisted that Williamson was consistently a hard drinker, the assertion seems improbable from the record of his accomplishments and from the esteem in which he was generally held. The honors accorded to him in San Felipe at the instance of Stephen F. Austin are indicative that in the early days in Texas, at least, Williamson was not overly addicted to drink. Had his habit been excessive, Austin, a strict judge of human fraility, would not have honored Williamson as he did. Whatever else Williamson was, he was no hypocrite. His implied disapproval of the conduct of Judge John M. Hansford while allegedly inebriated can only mean that Williamson's own habits were generally different.

Here is a story, picked up by Stanley Vestal, which tells of Williamson's inviting Big-Foot Wallace to a convivial bout in San Felipe. Since Wallace did not arrive in Texas until after San Felipe had been destroyed, the story can have no basis in fact, but it is an example of the sort of talk that enhanced Williamson's reputation as an imbiber:

> One day Wallace went down to San Felipe for supplies. There he met up with "Three-Legged Willie" . . . . The Judge was a joker

[3]Unsigned manuscript in J. D. Williamson Papers.

[4]*Northern Standard*, July 14, 1849.

[5]*Texas State Gazette*, June 7, 1851.

and story-teller and a man of education. His eye lighted on Wallace: "Hello, young man," he said. "What brought you to Texas?"

In those days it was generally bad judgment to ask a man on the frontier where he came from, but Wallace had a clear conscience, and saw the twinkle in Three-Legged Willie's eye. So he replied, "Oh, I had more wives than the law allowed me and could think of no better place to come to than Texas."

The Judge laughed. "Come along and have a drink," he suggested.

Wallace shook his head and excused himself as politely as he could. "I don't drink," he said.

At that another man in the crowd marched up and declared, "I'll make him drink."

Wallace turned to face the stranger and drawled, "My friend, you will have to spell *able* first."

Before the trouble could begin, Judge Williamson drew his pistol and covered the trouble-maker. "Let that young fellow alone," he said. "If he does not want to drink today, sometime likely we'll meet him on the road when we are thirsty, and he will have a full bottle."[6]

Williamson's drinking during his active days was probably average. Touching on this, in the notice of his death, the Dallas *Weekly Herald* remarked, "His faults, if any he had, were the outgrowth of the times and of his own genial nature, in regard to which now that the grave has closed upon his mortal form, the voice of his countrymen will be *tacemus de his*. He was emphatically one of the fast men of a fast age."[7] But a more reasonable statement of the matter is one attributed to James M. Willie, a close friend, who said that near the end of his life Williamson drank to alleviate his suffering. Concluding an estimate of Williamson's character, Willie said: "May I supplicate for Robert M. Williamson (who, if he was a great sinner was *also a great sufferer*) the kind charity of all Christians."[8]

Williamson's chief defect was an inability to retain his money. He was generous to a fault—so much so that despite the enormous lands he acquired, towards the end he was sometimes actually in desperate financial straits. Even be-

[6]Stanley Vestal, *Big Foot Wallace*, 32-33.

[7]Dallas *Weekly Herald* (Dallas, Texas), December 21, 1859.

[8]"Robert M. Williamson," *Texas Almanac for 1861*, pp. 85-89. J. D. Williamson infers that James M. Willie was the author of the article.

fore his retirement from the legislature, he had sold most of the enormous land grants he received for his services as Milam's agent. Three sales from these grants, completed before 1842, have been previously related. Others soon followed. In 1843 he sold certificate No. 7—his claim in Robertson County—to Mary Bullock for $300. On May 16, 1846, he sold his claim in Bexar County—secured by certificate No. 5—to Aaron H. Bean for $2,000, and in 1847 he sold a claim in Refugio County to Jacob De Cordova for $275.[9]

The money he received for these sales soon slipped from him. In his typical style he spent lavishly to gratify the slightest whim of any member of his family. In his home were lodged orphans adopted by his wife, whose heart was as big as Williamson's. Judge Charles L. Cleveland is the authority for the statement that "Williamson's law office was a school without pay for every aspiring youth who desired an education or a profession. His pocketbook was the treasury of the needy and helpless." A biographer in the *Texas Almanac* recollected that to "the younger members of the bar Williamson ever extended a helping hand . . . . The writer is but one of hundreds who remember gratefully the kindness extended to them in days long past by Judge Williamson."

Thus although his opportunities for acquiring wealth were golden, so generous and improvident was his nature that like "Mr. Jefferson and Mr. Monroe . . . he was often embarrassed in his pecuniary affairs."

But sick and pressed for funds though the crippled old eagle was, the final years were not altogether grey. Mary Jane was a good wife, and the children were a joy to him. Sitting on his front porch in the summer evenings, Williamson would play his banjo and sing. The negroes about the place sat in the yard, and everyone joined in the choruses. Williamson generally sang light, rollicking songs, but sometimes when his mood was serious, he sang hymns. One of his favorites was "Light House," "which no voice sang so sweetly as his own." After his death, his friends remembered in particular a stanza which Williamson loved:

[9]Record of First Class Certificates, General Land Office.

In life's closing hour when the trembling soul flies,
And death stills the heart's last emotion,
Oh, then may the seraph of mercy arise
Like a star on eternity's ocean.[10]

Even then the fire of battle had not entirely faded from his "two blue eyes." With all thought of re-entering politics clearly out of the question for him, the erstwhile crusader against tyranny could still be roused if he sensed a threat to the liberties he cherished. In the emergence of the Know-Nothings he suspected such a threat. The Democratic party which he had "sustained" during his campaign for Congress had made little headway in Texas. During the Republic the only political alignments suggestive of parties in the state had been "Houston" and "Anti-Houston" followers. After annexation, sporadic semblances of Whig and Democratic parties appeared. In 1854, however, following an original emergence nationally on the Atlantic seaboard, the Know-Nothings organized a party in Texas. They elected a slate of city officers in San Antonio. In 1855 a Know-Nothing candidate was elected mayor of Galveston. Under the pretense of holding a river improvement convention, the new party selected a slate of candidates for state offices in a meeting held at Washington-on-the-Brazos in June. Raising his voice in apparent support of the secret group was Sam Houston, who wrote a letter which appeared in the *Texas Ranger* of Washington on July 24, endorsing Know-Nothing principles. A week later the Democrats held a convention in Austin and selected E. M. Pease as their candidate for governor.[11]

Williamson entered into the heated controversy at the request of friends who were anxious to help Pease. In declining the request of the Washingon editor to campaign over the state against the Know-Nothings, Williamson wrote, "my feeble health compels me to decline the proferred honor," but he penned a long letter scoring the Know-Nothings and General Houston. The *Texas Ranger* had gone to press when the letter came to the editor's desk, but the forms

[10]"Robert M. Williamson," *Texas Almanac for 1861*, pp. 85-89.

[11]Richardson, *Texas, the Lone Star State*, 175.

were remade to make room for it. It appeared in the issue of July 28, the day the letter was dated in Independence, with the following editorial comment:

> The letter should be carefully read by every Republican from one of the best patriots in the land—a man who has done more hard service in the cause of Texas both Military and Civil, without fee or reward, than any other now living. Who was fighting against Mexican Tyranny, before ever Gen. Houston placed his foot on Texas soil.

In the letter Williamson's style lacks the polish of his greater utterances. At times it grows verbose and rambling, but the sick man still had traces of "the glory in his heart" and in one fine paragraph he approximated his former eloquence:

> Have the Protestant churches seen and felt the withering influences of the Pope in this great nation? No, not one. Then the deductions of the general are that this secret order is to take the place of all others, as their only defender from Despots and Tyrants and the Pope, whenever they shall come to this nation. I thank him for this suggestion. You may exclude me from the secrets of this new order, but whenever the above mentioned little fellows show themselves upon American soil, I will not rely upon this order, exclusive and proscriptive as it is, to defend my country—and I speak out for all Masonry, for all Protestantism, for all Catholicism, and for all foreigners, and for all who love and cherish the Democratic-Republican principles of the institutions of this nation, that they will not hazard their liberties in the hands of this new political, exclusive and proscriptive order.[12]

This was his last important public declaration. Soon afterwards came the great darkness. At Independence, on November 17, 1856, his wife, Mary Jane, suddenly died,[13] and Williamson never recovered from the blow. His family rapidly broke up, the children going to live with relatives in Georgia.[14] Completely exhausted and groping desperately for sanity, Williamson stumped through the streets of Independence, "speaking neither to friend nor to foe, mumbling something to himself about having the job of revising Webster's spelling book, which, he said, weighed on his mind like a

[12] *Texas Ranger*, July 28, 1855.

[13] *Texas State Gazette*, December 13, 1856.

[14] Thad B. Rice to D. W. R., June 29, 1946.

mill-stone."[15] He was rescued by his father-in-law, Gustavus Edwards, who brought him to Wharton and established him in a house where he could be cared for by slaves.[16]

There he spent three lonely and miserable years, until on November 17, 1859, with "one old faithful servant" attending him, he became critically ill. For three days he lingered in feverish delirium as into his fading mind came dreams of the great days of the Revolution.

It had been twenty-three years since Travis, that daring and best of friends, fell dead at the Alamo. Yet to the dying old ranger, Travis once again was on the prison ship at Anahuac. To an illusory but still contemptible Bradburn, the dying man shouted: "I say, Sir, he must be delivered up—instantly released!" Then it seemed to Williamson that he was leading his rangers again. His voice rang out, "Hark! to the right boys—quick to the right! Who follows? Now, come on!"

In the last few hours his attending physician could still wake him to get a lucid answer to a question, but when the doctor quit speaking, Williamson lapsed into his dreams.

At length his voice grew weaker, and he spoke in whispers to the phantoms he was now rejoining. They were phantoms of the past, ghosts of the days when he had moved like a flame at Turtle Bayou, at Bastrop, at San Jacinto—they were friendly spirits, dispelling the loneliness of the late years, and they loved him well. But he was tired—so tired he could whisper to them no more. For half an hour, barely breathing, he clung faintly to life, and then suddenly he raised his hand. In a clear voice he said, "Life sinks beneath the horizon." The hand fell limp, and when the doctor leaned over him, Williamson was dead.[17]

Thus on November 20, 1859, ended the life of Robert McAlpin Williamson, the Georgian who would rather have been known as "a Texian" than by any other name. He was buried in Wharton, where his body rested for nearly seventy years, but in 1930 his remains were brought to Austin

[15]Fanny Chambers G. Iglehart in San Antonio *Express*, April 2, 1911.

[16]Thad B. Rice to D. W. R., June 29, 1946.

[17]*Daily Ledger and Texan* (San Antonio, Texas), September 5, 1860.

to be buried in the State Cemetery.[18] There he lies today, surrounded by the state's illustrious dead, not far from the tomb of Stephen F. Austin, who, in the happy days at San Felipe, had cherished him as a younger brother.

Posthumous tributes and honors were not lacking. John S. Ford, Williamson's contemporary in the Texas Congress, said: "He was a man of wonderful powers, an able and finished orator. No man seemed to have more complete control of his audience.... He was one of the prime movers of the Revolution."[19] His friend James Willie is thought to be author of the following tribute: "When fully roused, there was a fire and vigor in his speech that surpassed all description.... The eloquence of Judge Williamson more nearly resembled that of John Randolph than of any other historical character."[20] The historian Henderson Yoakum declared that after a minute search of the records he was of the opinion that Williamson had done as much as, if not more than, any other man in bringing on the revolution.[21]

On San Jacinto day in 1891 a portrait of Williamson was presented to the Senate of the Texas Legislature. In the speech of presentation, George Clark of Waco zealously declared that Williamson was the "Mirabeau of our revolution" and that "Rome, even in the palmiest days of her evolution, never had such a man."[22] In accepting the portrait for the state Lieutenant-Governor George C. Pendleton alluded to Williamson "as the idol of the people . . . an upright and honest judge who unflinchingly administered the law."[23] Upon the occasion of his reburial in Austin, in 1930, a joint session of the legislature honored his memory.

From this study of the records, it seems apparent that Williamson's character was dominated by two outstanding traits—unflinching courage and a sense of humor which humanized him and made him a favorite of fun-loving male

[18] J. D. Williamson to D. W. R., March 1, 1946.

[19] Galveston *Daily News*, July 16, 1893.

[20] "Robert M. Williamson," *Texas Almanac for 1861*, pp. 85-89.

[21] Benjamin R. Sleeper, Three-Legged Willie.

[22] Galveston *Daily News*, March 22, 1891.

[23] *House Journal*, *Twenty-second Legislature*, April 21, 1891, pp. 686 ff.

colonists who delighted in horseplay. He was also honest and independent in his thinking; but these were traits which many of his contemporaries also possessed.

Singular about Williamson was a certain quality of unselfishness which contrasted sharply with the self-seeking tendencies of many of his fellows. With the notable exception of Austin, who envisioned a community in Texas which might become "a home for the unfortunate, a refuge from poverty, an asylum for the sufferers from avarice,"[24] Williamson stands almost alone among the colonists as a sensitive and tenderhearted man.

Hospitality was a pioneer tradition, but Williamson was so generous that he died in poverty. In an age characterized by laws which now seem excessively cruel, this most fearless of judges, beneath a stern exterior, was so soft that he did not favor the imprisonment of women at all. He begged Houston to make a soldier out of a man who, in 1836, had been only lately respited from a sentence of death for grand larceny; and if the records of the court at Nacogdoches were typical, the sentences he imposed as a district judge were as light as the law allowed. In an age in which land speculations offered fortunes to those whose inclinations were acquisitive, Williamson occupied his leisure in fathering orphans and extending never-to-be-forgotten kindnesses to struggling young lawyers. It was not mere courtesy that prompted Austin to instruct his secretary to give Williamson as many blanket certificates—good as passports into Texas and as such worth a league and labor of land—as Williamson might desire.

Although it is true that Williamson was an expansionist, he was no mere follower of a movement then sweeping all North America. What he saw of Mexican administration convinced him that Anglo-Saxon procedures were definitely superior to the practices of the Latins.

It is also true that towards the end of his career Williamson was a conservative. The matter of his conservatism presents a problem for more acute analysis. A descendant of Southern forebears who were men of property and aristocrats, Williamson had a background, essentially con-

[24]Barker, *Life of Stephen F. Austin*, 271.

servative. But to classify him as a mere conservative is to be stupidly inept. Indeed Williamson's conservatism flowered late, for in the colonial days his activities so agitated certain conservatives—the members of the peace party—that he was considered a dangerous radical. In most respects in colonial times he was out of sympathy with the conservative tradition.

It was the conservative Houston who continually retreated and waited until he was sure he could win, and not Travis, who tried to stand off a force of Mexicans greater than his own by odds of twenty-five to one, who wrested the state from the Mexican grasp. In 1832 it was the officials of the ayuntamiento of San Felipe who were pleading frantically with the insurgents to come home and be clapped into jail like nice gentlemen, and not Williamson, who was roaring into Anahuac in company with a pack of fiery Brazorians, who were evidencing conservative instincts. Ten years later, Congressman Williamson, at the time a considerable landholder, might fume that his cousin, President Mirabeau B. Lamar, had "broken in upon the treasury" by sending out the Santa Fe Expedition and by dispatching the Texas navy to ally with Yucatan. The congressman might even petulantly disavow "the glory" he suspected such actions would bring, but by so speaking Williamson was assuming a role inconsistent with the part he played as the speaker of the war party when his address of July 4, 1835, brought upon him the ire of Mexican officialdom and sent the respectable majority of the citizens of San Felipe scurrying to bolt their doors as he rode by.

The metamorphosis he evidenced in his later years was perhaps natural. Lawyers, as a class, tend to be conservative, and Williamson could hardly have escaped being influenced by his associates. Such an evolution has many historical parallels. It was Daniel Webster, for example, whom Whittier lectured in "Ichabod."

But despite Williamson's never-failing kindness, his superior sensitivity, and his intelligence, the man regarded the Mexicans as an inferior race, and he contended for the rights of the Southern planter with regard to slavery. But should some young "Texian" of the hour cry "Ichabod," let him remember that Williamson knew and loved many of the men whom the Mexicans, in terrible demonstrations of savagery, butchered. As a slaveowner, Williamson must have been kind, for his only companion at his death was "one old faithful servant who rather chose to linger by the death bed of a master, whom he loved, than leave him alone with a comparative stranger [the doctor in attendance]." Thus if one cannot say that Williamson was a liberal, there is no justification for classifying him a reactionary. His record of complete personal unselfishness shines singularly bright in an age in which many were as stolid as oxen.

For his country he risked his life upon several fields of battle. His story is essentially one of honorable labor for the cause of Texas independence, and in the crises which befell the Austin colonists before 1836, Williamson's fighting speeches lighted a spark in men's hearts.

Whether, as contemporaries and historians have claimed, he was the man most instrumental in initiating the Texas Revolution is a matter which does not lend itself to proof. In the colonial days many bold spirits were in Texas. It is incontrovertible that Williamson's voice was a mighty factor in nerving his fellows for their roles. The Mexicans feared it enough to order his arrest.

Of all the eulogies which have been written and spoken of him, perhaps none so aptly fits him as his own forthright appraisal of his worth. In one sincere sentence Williamson wrote a characterization of himself which might well serve as his epitaph: "I have lived in Texas near thirty years, and in that time I have rendered all the service in my power, so help me God—and my only regret now is that in the darkest hours I could then do no more for her."[25]

Like Cyrano whose features were marred by his nose, this Williamson with the crippled leg kept his white plume unspotted from the world.

[25] *Texas Ranger*, July 28, 1855.

Bibliography

Primary Sources

Manuscripts

Army Papers, 1835, Archives, State Library, Austin, Texas.

Bexar Archives, 1699-1836, Originals in University of Texas Archives.

Committee Reports, Fifth Congress, Archives, State Library, Austin, Texas.

Comptroller's Military Service Records, Archives, State Library, Austin, Texas.

Consultation Papers, 1835-1836, Archives, State Library, Austin, Texas.

Contested Election Returns, 1843, Archives, State Library, Austin, Texas.

Department of State Papers, Letter Book, No. 2, Archives, State Library, Austin, Texas.

Diary of William Barret Travis, August 30, 1833-June 26, 1834. Copied from original in Starr Collection, University of Texas Archives.

Domestic Correspondence Papers, 1835-1846, Archives, State Library, Austin, Texas.

Nacogdoches Archives, 1731-1836. Originals in State Library, Austin, Texas. Transcripts in ninety volumes in Archives, State Library, Austin, Texas, and University of Texas Archives.

Spanish Archives in General Land Office, Austin, Texas.

J. D. Williamson Papers. A collection of original documents and notes collected from secondary sources accumulated by J. D. Williamson of Waco, Texas, in possession of Duncan W. Robinson.

R. M. Williamson Folder, Biographical File, University of Texas Archives.

Books

Barker, E. C. (ed.), *The Austin Papers*, Vol. I, Part I [August, 1789-December, 1824], in *Annual Report of the American Historical Association for the Year 1919*, Vol. II, Part I. Washington: Government Printing Office, 1924.

Barker, E. C. (ed.), *The Austin Papers*, Vol. I, Part II [January, 1825-December, 1827], in *Annual Report of the American Historical Association for the Year 1919*, Vol. II, Part II. Washington: Government Printing Office, 1924.

Barker, E. C. (ed.), *The Austin Papers*, Vol. II [January, 1823-September, 1834], in *Annual Report of the American Historical Association for the Year 1922*, Vol. II. Washington: Government Printing Office, 1928.

Barker, E. C. (ed.), *The Austin Papers*, Vol. III [October, 1834-January, 1837]. Austin: University of Texas Press, 1927.

Gammel, H. P. N. (ed.), *The Laws of Texas, 1822-1897.* 10 vols. Austin: Gammel Book Company, 1898.

Gray, William F., *From Virginia to Texas, 1835, Diary of Col. Wm. F. Gray.* Houston: Grey, Dillaye & Co., Printers, 1909.

Gulick, C. A., and others (eds.), *The Papers of Mirabeau Buonaparte Lamar.* 6 vols. Austin: Texas State Library and Historical Commission, 1921-1928.

Holley, Mrs. Mary (Austin), *Texas.* Austin: Steck Company, 1935. A facsimile reproduction of the original edition, Lexington, Kentucky, 1836.

Smither, Harriet (ed.), *Journals of the Sixth Congress of the Republic of Texas, 1841-1842.* 3 vols. Austin: Texas Library and Historical Commission, 1940-1945.

Smithwick, Noah, *The Evolution of a State.* Austin: Steck Company, 1935. A facsimile reproduction of the original edition, Austin, Gammel Book Company, c. 1900.

Articles

Barker, E. C. (ed.), "Minutes of the Ayuntamiento of San Felipe de Austin, 1828-1832," *Southwestern Historical Quarterly*, XXI, 1917-1918; XXII, 1918-1919; XXIII, 1919-1920; XXIV, 1921-1922.

Clopper, J. C., "Journal and Book of Memoranda for 1828," *Quarterly of the Texas State Historical Association*, XIII, 1909-1910.

Harris, Mrs. Dilue, "Reminiscences of Mrs. Dilue Harris," *ibid.*, IV, 1900-1901.

Johnson, F. W., "Further Account by Col. F. W. Johnson of the First Breaking out of Hostilities," *Texas Almanac for 1859.* Galveston: Richardson & Co., 1859.

Kleberg, Rosa, "Early Experiences in Texas," *Quarterly of the Texas State Historical Association*, II, 1898-1899.

Labadie, N. D., "Narrative of the Anahuac or Opening Campaign of the Texas Revolution," *Texas Almanac for 1859.* Galveston: Richardson & Co., 1859.

Old Soldier, "First Breaking out of the Texas Revolution at Gonzales," *Texas Almanac for 1861.* Galveston: Richardson & Co., 1860.

Smith, Henry, "Reminiscences of Henry Smith," *Quarterly of the Texas State Historical Association*, XIV, 1910-1911.

Smithwick, Noah, "Early Texas Nomenclature," *ibid.*, II, 1898-1899.

Wood, N. D., "Reminiscences of Texas and Texans Fifty Years Ago," *ibid.*, V, 1901-1902.

SECONDARY SOURCES

Manuscripts

Mixon, Ruby, The Life and Letters of William Barret Travis. MS., Fort Worth, Texas.

Mixon, Ruby, William Barret Travis, His Life and Letters. M.A. Thesis, University of Texas, 1930.

Sleeper, Benjamin R., Three-Legged Willie and the Texas Revolution, a paper read before the Philosophers' Club of Waco, Texas, February 28, 1936. Typescript in R. M. Williamson Folder, Biographical File, University of Texas Archives.

Books

Baker, D. W. C. (ed.), *A Texas Scrap Book.* New York: A. S. Barnes and Company, 1875.

Barker, E. C., *The Life of Stephen F. Austin.* Dallas: Cokesbury Press, 1926.

Barker, E. C. (ed.), *Readings in Texas History.* Dallas: Southwest Press, 1929.

Bartlett, Lanier (ed.), *On the Old West Coast: Being Further Reminiscences of a Ranger, Major Horace Bell.* New York: W. Morrow and Company, 1930.

Brown, John Henry, *History of Texas from 1685 to 1892.* 2 vols. St. Louis: L. E. Daniell, c. 1892-1893.

Brown, John Henry, *Life and Times of Henry Smith.* Dallas: A. D. Aldridge and Company, 1887.

Callcott, Wilfrid Hardy, *Santa Anna.* Norman: University of Oklahoma Press, 1936.

James, Marquis, *The Raven: A Biography of Sam Houston.* Indianapolis: Bobbs-Merrill Company, 1929.

Richardson, Rupert Norval, *Texas, The Lone Star State.* New York: Prentice Hall, Inc., 1943.

Thrall, Homer S., *Pictorial History of Texas.* St. Louis: N. D. Thompson and Company, 1879.

Vestal, Stanley, *Big Foot Wallace.* Boston: Houghton Mifflin Company, 1942.

Wooten, Dudley G., *A Comprehensive History of Texas, 1685-1897.* Dallas: W. G. Scarff, 1898.

Yoakum, Henderson, *History of Texas from Its First Settlement in 1685 to Its Annexation to the United States in 1846.* 2 vols. Austin: Steck Company, 1935. A facsimile copy of the original edition, New York, Redfield, 1856.

Articles

Barker, E. C., "The Government of Stephen F. Austin's Colony, 1828-1831," *Southwestern Historical Quarterly*, XXI, 1917-1918.

Barker, E. C., "Land Speculation as a Cause of the Texas Revolution," *Quarterly of the Texas State Historical Association*, X, 1906-1907.

Barker, E. C., "Notes on Early Texas Newspapers," *Southwestern Historical Quarterly*, XXI, 1917-1918.

Barker, E. C., "The San Jacinto Campaign," *Quarterly of the Texas State Historical Association*, IV, 1900-1901.

Barker, E. C., "The Texan Declaration of Causes for Taking Up Arms against Mexico," *ibid.*, XV, 1911-1912.

Garver, Lois, "Benjamin Rush Milam," *Southwestern Historical Quarterly*, XXXVIII, 1934-1935.

Rowe, Edna, "The Disturbances at Anahuac in 1832," *Quarterly of the Texas State Historical Association*, VI, 1902-1903.

Sinks, Mrs. Julia Lee, "Early Courts of Fayette County," *ibid.*, VII, 1903-1904.

Steen, Ralph W., "Analysis of the Work of the General Council of Texas, 1835-1836," *Southwestern Historical Quarterly*, XLI, 1937-1938.

Townes, John C., "Sketch of the Development of the Texas Judicial System," *Quarterly of the Texas State Historical Association*, II, 1898-1899.

Williams, Amelia, "A Critical Study of the Siege of the Alamo," *Southwestern Historical Quarterly*, XXXVI, 1932-1933; XXXVII, 1933-1934.

"Robert M. Williamson," *Texas Almanac for 1861*. Galveston: Richardson & Co., 1860.

"Williamson Family, of Georgia and Texas," *Southern Historical Research Magazine*, I, April, 1936.

Newspapers

Arkansas Gazette, Little Rock, Arkansas, 1834.

Atlanta *Constitution*, Atlanta, Georgia, 1881.

Bastrop *Advertiser*, Bastrop, Texas, 1884.

Daily Ledger and Texan, San Antonio, Texas, 1860.

Dallas *Weekly Herald*, Dallas, Texas, 1860.

Democratic Statesman, Austin, Texas, 1874.

Galveston *Daily News*, Galveston, Texas, 1878, 1891, 1893, 1906, 1911.

Houston *Post*, Houston, Texas, 1936.

Mexican Citizen, San Felipe de Austin, Texas, 1831.

Northern Standard, Clarksville, Texas, 1845, 1846, 1849, 1856.

San Antonio *Express*, San Antonio, Texas, 1911.

Telegraph and Texas Register, Houston, Texas, 1837, 1839, 1848.

Texas Banner, Huntsville, Texas, 1849.

Texas Gazette, San Felipe de Austin, Texas, 1829, 1830, 1831, 1832.

Texas Ranger, Washington, Texas, 1855.

Texas State Gazette, Austin, Texas, 1845, 1851, 1855.

The Tropic, New Orleans, Louisiana, 1844.

Index